15

THE DUKES OF NORMANDY

THE
DUKES OF NORMANDY
AND THEIR ORIGIN

by

The Rt. Hon. the
EARL of ONSLOW
P.C., G.B.E., F.S.A., F.R.Hist.S.

Author of "Sixty-Three Years," etc.

With 21 Illustrations

HUTCHINSON & CO. (Publishers), LTD.
London   New York   Melbourne   Sydney   Cape Town

Printed in Great Britain
by The Anchor Press, Ltd.,
Tiptree, Essex.

FOREWORD

The history of the Dukes of Normandy and their Scandinavian ancestors cannot fail to interest many of us today. This book is an attempt to record their early origin from their perhaps mythical ancestor, the King of the Fenni, mentioned by Tacitus as one of the least known peoples of Europe, through their reputed ancestors in Northern Norway to the time of Eystein Glumra, the father of Rögnwald, Earl of Moere, the right-hand man of Harold Haarfager, the first King of Norway. Rögnwald was the father of Rolf, or Rollo, the Conqueror of Normandy and ancestor of William the Conqueror and his son, Henry I of England. He was also the ancestor of the Scandinavian Earls of Orkney. Through Henry the First's daughter, the Empress Maud, Rögnwald, or Reginald, is the direct ancestor of his present Majesty, King George VI.

In preparing this book I would like to thank Mr. A. L. Haydon and my private secretary, Mrs. M. N. Brooks, for much valuable help.

ONSLOW

Clandon Park,
Guildford, Surrey.
   April 1945.

EDITOR'S NOTE

The late Earl of Onslow died in June 1945, while this work was in the press; as I was closely associated with him in its preparation it has fallen to me to complete the task of publication. One note that I have to make refers to the spelling of Saxon, Danish and Norman names. After due consideration, Lord Onslow decided to adopt "Brittany, Harold, Cnut, Osmund and Osborne" in place of other forms used by historians.

Acknowledgment must be made here to the authorities at the British Museum for permission to reproduce prints of the Great Seals of Edward the Confessor and William I, and of old coins, charters and missals; and to the Curator of the Reading Museum and Art Gallery for the reproduction of prints of the Bayeux Tapestry.

A. L. HAYDON

CONTENTS

CHAPTER I

THE NORSE FOREBEARS

CHAPTER II

THE CONQUERORS OF NORMANDY

CHAPTER III

ROLLO

CHAPTER IV

ROLLO, PATRICIAN OF NORMANDY

CHAPTER V

WILLIAM LONGSWORD—PART I

CHAPTER VI

WILLIAM LONGSWORD—PART II

CHAPTER VII

RICHARD THE FEARLESS—PART I

CHAPTER VIII

RICHARD THE FEARLESS—PART II

CHAPTER IX

RICHARD THE FEARLESS—PART III

CHAPTER X

RICHARD II—PART I

CHAPTER XI

RICHARD II—PART II

CHAPTER XII

RICHARD III

CHAPTER XIII

ROBERT I—PART I

CHAPTER XIV

ROBERT I—PART II

CHAPTER XV

WILLIAM II, DUKE OF NORMANDY

PAGE

CHAPTER XVI

NORMANDY AND FRANCE

CHAPTER XVII

ANJOU AND FURTHER REBELLIONS IN NORMANDY

CHAPTER XVIII

KING HENRY'S ATTEMPT UPON NORMANDY

CHAPTER XIX

THE RELIGIOUS HOUSES

CHAPTER XX

THE ADMINISTRATION OF NORMANDY

CHAPTER XXI

FINAL DEFEAT OF THE FRENCH

CHAPTER XXII

MAINE

CHAPTER XXIII

ENGLAND

CHAPTER XXIV

THE CROWN OF ENGLAND

CHAPTER XXV

THE EVE OF THE CONQUEST

NOTES ON ILLUSTRATIONS

1. The magnificent Church of the Abbaye-aux-Dames at Caen was founded in 1062 by Matilda, wife of William the Conqueror, as an expiation of the sin she had committed in marrying William within the forbidden degrees of consanguinity. The style of architecture is Norman Romanesque.

2. The Drawing from the "Liber Vitae of the New Minster of Winchester" is a fine specimen of the work of an Anglo-Saxon artist. The scenes represent:

   Top (across) : Angels conducting spirits of benefactors to the Heavenly Jerusalem. The portal is being opened by St. Peter. On the left is the name "ALGARUS", probably Ælfgar, or Æthelgar, Abbot of Newminster (965).

   Middle : Two saints looking on a contest between Peter and Satan for a soul at the Last Judgment.

   Bottom : The Jaws of Hell. Satan thrusting down a man and woman. The gate is being locked by the Archangel Michael.

   The drawing was executed in ink, with occasional colour. Date, 1016-20.

3. The Church of the Abbaye-aux-Hommes at Caen was founded in 1062 by William I. The Conqueror's tomb is now empty, his bones having been scattered at the Revolution.

4. The Church of St. Ouen at Rouen is one of the most beautiful Gothic churches in existence. It was built between 1318 and 1339. The exquisite central tower is 269 feet high and is surmounted by a delicate turreted gallery called "La Couronne de Normandie".

5. This Charter of Edward the Confessor is of a grant of land to one Ordgar, in 1044. (*From the Cotton MSS., British Museum.*)

6. This Charter records a grant from Ealdred, Bishop of Worcester, to Dodda, of land in North-tun. Date, 1058. (*From the Cotton MSS., British Museum.*)

LIST OF ILLUSTRATIONS

CHAPTER I

THE NORSE FOREBEARS

The Norse Sagas—Snorre Sturleson—The Heimskringla—Are Fode—The Skalds—Norway in the 9th century—King Harold—Earl Rögnwald—The Viking ships—Earl Sigurd—Rolf the Ganger—The Earls of Orkney.

It was at one time usual to regard the Norman Conquest as the real starting point of English History. This, of course, is erroneous—the starting point of English History is the Anglo-Saxon, not the Norman, Conquest. But, although our history does not begin in 1066, the Norman Conquest is perhaps the most important single event in the history of the English, except their own arrival in the island. If we agree as to the importance of the Norman Conquest in our development as a nation we cannot fail to be interested in the origin and early connections of our Norman ancestors.

Unluckily, the records are both scanty and, in some cases, unreliable. Curiously enough, the early Norse records, those contained in the Sagas, are in some ways more trustworthy than the French and Norman Chronicles.

For early Norse history we are completely dependent on the Sagas. These were first edited by Snorre Sturleson, an Icelander who was born in 1177; so that the first written history is three hundred years later than the date when the events which we shall attempt to describe occurred. This may seem to place a severe strain on its reliability; but after a careful consideration of the facts we are disposed to think that considerable trust can be placed in Snorre Sturleson's *Story of the Kings of Norway*, as he himself called his book—or the Heimskringla, by which name it is generally now known.*

Now, although the Heimskringla of Sturleson is the earliest written record of the Sagas that has come down to us, he had a predecessor who wrote the first Norse Chronicle and upon whom he largely drew. This man's name was Are Fode (Are, the wise or learned), who wrote a history of the settlement of Iceland and also biographies of the Kings of Norway, Denmark and England. Sturleson, who writes of him almost like a modern historical critic, says: "His narratives are considered by many

---

* So called from this being the first prominent word in the MSS. that catches the eye—it means "the world's circle".

men of knowledge to be the most remarkable of all because he was a man of good understanding and so old that his birth was as far back as the year after Harold Sigurdson's fall.''

This places the date of his birth in 1067, or 110 years before that of Sturleson. Are drew his information from Od Kolson, who had learned his history from Thorgeir Afrudskol, who was dwelling at Nidarnes (now Trondjem) when Earl Haakon was killed—an event that took place in 995. Are, though born in Norway, came to Iceland when seven years old and lived at Haukadal with Hal Thorarinson until he was twenty-one. Hal was born four years before the establishment of Christianity in Iceland, which took place also in 995. Another source whence Are derived his information was from Teit, a son of Isleif, first Bishop of Iceland, and he also owed much to Thurid, daughter of Snorre Gode, who was born in 964, thirty years before the introduction of Christianity into Iceland. In Pagan times the Godes in that island were an hereditary Clan of priests and judges.

Are tells us in a preface to his own work which Sturleson quotes at length that he wrote the stories down as told him by intelligent people; and, although he could not exactly say what truth there might be in them, he had the certainty that old and wise men held them to be true, and he finishes his preface as follows: ''There were Skalds in Harold's (Haarfaager) Court whose poems the people know by heart even at the present day . . . and we test the foundations of our story principally upon the songs which were sung in the presence of the Chiefs themselves or of their sons, and take all to be true that is found in such poems about their feats and battles, for although it is the fashion with Skalds to praise most those in whose presence they are standing yet no one would dare to relate to a Chief what he and all those who heard it knew to be false and imaginary, not a true account of his deeds; because that would be mockery and not true praise.''

Are's criticism seems very apposite and it is interesting, therefore, to examine what sort of men these Skalds were upon whose accounts Are and his informants based their history. The general idea of a Skald, if anyone thinks of him at all, is that he was a sort of Northern troubadour, or minstrel, who wandered about the country giving entertainments. True, the Skalds did a certain amount of this, but they had much more important functions to perform as well.

The literature of Norway composed by the Skalds and handed on orally is very voluminous. Mr. Samuel Laing, the translator of the Heimskringla Saga, enumerates some 170 Sagas composed between the 9th and 13th centuries, most of which were not written down till long after their composition. Some of these works are historical, some mythological, and some are pure fiction, but they are all of them the work of the Skalds. It is clear from this, and also from many other sources, that

Edward the Confessor speaking to two persons (one of them
probably Harold) about Harold's journey to Duke William
in Normandy.

At a feast in Harold's house. A messenger announces that
the ships are ready.

Harold seized by Count Guy of Ponthieu and made prisoner.

Harold (on right) and Count Guy in converse.

the Scandinavians in their own way were a highly civilized race, and it is curious that they should have remained for so long ignorant of, or at least indifferent to, the use of writing. The memory of the Skalds was the Scandinavian substitute for the written word. It was their business to carry in their minds the precedents, laws, usages and customs of the country.

Genealogy was a very necessary subject for Skaldic knowledge owing to the complicated system of land tenure. Feudalism was non-existent in Norway. Land was held on the udal system. Every bonde or noble was udal-born to certain land. The udaller was the free owner of his little plot of land. When he died his children by his wives and concubines had equal rights of inheritance, so that it was to the interest of everybody that a careful record should be maintained of each man's status. In a society where writing was unused such a record could only be kept by means of a class such as the Skalds, who committed facts to memory and handed their knowledge on orally to their successors.

Accuracy of tradition, therefore, was essential. But there is internal evidence of the truth of the Sagas. They are essentially "meaty". They are full of facts and details, some of them rather dull details, especially those that deal with genealogy. Moreover, Sturleson certainly subjected them to criticism before accepting them and, indeed, on occasions he added to them. Thus, in his account of Rolf the Ganger (Rollo), he states that he was the ancestor of William the Conqueror. As the latter lived long after the Skaldic record of Rolf's banishment by King Harold of Norway was composed it is obvious that the additions were made by Sturleson. For these reasons, therefore, we are tempted to place considerable value on the accuracy of the historical Sagas and to believe with their editors, Are Fode and Snorre Sturleson, in their essential truth.

Before, however, we attempt to give an account of the early lives of Rolf and the members of his family we must pause for a moment to give some description of the state of Norway and its history in the early 9th century.

The country is mountainous. The rivers are short and flow from the hills into the fiords, arms of the sea which, like the sea-lochs on the West Coast of Scotland, cut into the land. The fiords are separated one from another in most cases by mountain and forest, and each little community of udallers tended to have a separate existence from its neighbours. The fertile land was but exiguous in extent—just the strips running along the side of the fiord. This geographical condition produced two results. The first was the growth of separate communities, and the second was the necessity of depending largely on the sea for a livelihood. The Norsemen became expert seamen. At first they preyed on their neighbours; later they became pirates and colonists.

At the beginning of the 9th century the most powerful of the kinglets

B

of Norway was Black Halfdan, who ruled over the Vik, where Oslo now stands.   During his reign he conquered a number of petty kings in Southern Norway, and when he died he undoubtedly ruled over considerably more territory than any other Chief. Black Halfdan died in or about 860 and his son, Harold, succeeded him. Harold's mother was a daughter of Sigurd, King of Ringevike, and her brother, Guthorm, became Regent for his nephew, who was but ten years old when his father died.   At first Guthorm had some difficulty in defending his nephew's dominions. But he successfully withstood those who attacked him, and in addition conquered the whole of Southern Norway up to the River Glommen.   The story goes that when King Harold was of marriageable age he sought the hand of Gyda, daughter of King Eric of Hordaland, but she haughtily declined to have anything to do with him until he had subdued the whole of Norway; so Harold swore that he would not cut or comb his hair until he had accomplished this task!

We need not pursue Harold's conquests in detail; it is sufficient to note that in 866 or thereabouts he had become master of the inland country as far as Trondjem. The territory over which he now ruled was so extensive that it was difficult to administer from one centre, so he found it necessary to create Earldoms to govern the various districts. This has been called an attempt to establish feudalism in Norway, but Harold's system differs really considerably from the feudal system. His Earls were Civil and Military Governors, not vassals in the feudal sense of the term.   Nevertheless, his administration was looked upon with grave suspicion by the small udallers, but with some favour by the greater men, who saw therein opportunities for furthering their own ambitions. Hrollaug, King of Naumdal, immediately surrendered to Harold and was invested with his own kingdom of Naumdal as Earl under him.

The summer of 867 was occupied in the conquest of North More and Raumsdal, and now we come to the first historical appearance of the family of Rolf. He was the son of Rögnwald, who submitted to Harold at the same time as Hrollaug of Naumdal and seems very soon to have become his Chief Adviser in the North, for Guthorm apparently remained as Regent in Southern Norway. Rögnwald's descent is carefully traced from legendary to authentic ancestors in the Orkneyinga Saga.   His earliest forebear was said to have been Fornjot, King of Finland and Kvenland. This King's great-great-grandson, Thorri, had two sons, Norr and Gorr, who emigrated Westwards.   Norr took the mainland called Norway and Gorr took the islands.

Gorr's son, Heiti, was father of Sveithi the Sea King. Sveithi's son was named Halfdan the Old and he was the father of Ivar, Earl of the Uplands, whose son was Eystein Glumra, or the Noisy.   According to both the Heimskringla Saga and the Orkneyinga Saga, Eystein Glumra was father of Rögnwald. This genealogy may be mythical in whole or

in part, but there may be a good deal of truth in it. One cannot reject
it as certainly pure invention. From Fornjot to Rögnwald is twelve
generations—say, in those days when life was short, twenty-five years
each. This would bring the date of Fornjot to about A.D. 500. Gorr,
who emigrated to the West, presumably *via* Torneo and the head of the
Gulf of Bothnia, must eventually have reached the Lofoten Islands.
There may be some truth in the story; the family of Rolf were certainly
Northerners.

Rögnwald in 867 was created Earl of North More (or Moere) and
Raumsdal, and in the following year he accompanied Harold from
Trondjem to South More, whence after a hard struggle they succeeded in
driving out King Solve, who became a sea king and for many years a
thorn in the side of King Harold.

Rögnwald now added South More to his Earldom and was left there
to reduce it to order, while Harold returned to Trondjem. The Firda
district still remained unconquered under Vemund, brother of Audbiorn,
whom Harold and Rögnwald had driven out with King Solve. The
Saga tells us that Rögnwald attacked Vemund and burnt him and his
fortress and ninety men—we often hear of these burnings of fortified
places. The Norwegian stone does not lend itself to castle-building,
hence the Norwegian fortresses were all made of wood and easily burnt.

So Rögnwald, son of Eystein Glumra and father of Rolf the Ganger,
became undisputed in his Earldom of More and King Harold's chief
adviser in Northern Norway. Evidently he was a man of considerable
attainment, and in the Sagas he is called Rögnwald the Mighty, or
Rögnwald the Wise. He had several children by concubines—Einar,
the son of a thrall woman, who subsequently became Earl of Orkney
and was called Torf Einar; Ivar, who was killed in King Harold's
expedition to the Hebrides; and Hrollaug, who, according to the Orkneyinga Saga, became one of the pioneers in the colonization of Iceland.
Rögnwald had several other sons as well. Late in life he married Hilda,
daughter of Rolf Nefia, by whom he had two sons, Thorer and Rolf the
Ganger.

It is said that Thorer and Rolf were much younger than Einar, who
was a grown man when Rolf was a child. As Rolf seems to have been
about the same age as King Harold—i.e. was born about 850—Rögnwald
must have been born early in the 9th century. Rolf was the more adven-
turous of the two brothers and probably the younger. He early took to
piracy, for we are told that he plundered much in the East sea—i.e. the
Baltic. He was called the Ganger because he was too heavy a man for
a horse to carry. But this does not mean that he was necessarily a giant.
The Norwegian ponies are doubtless much the same today as they were
in Rolf's time, and any moderately big man would find them inadequate
in the rough country and hilly land of Norway. Rolf is only known as the

Ganger in his native country. In France he seems to have had no difficulty in mounting himself. Thorer was the least enterprising of the
family. He was known as Thorer the Silent. His half-brother, Einar,
scoffed at him for sitting at home and dreaming beside the mead-bowl.
He married King Harold's daughter Alof, otherwise known as Arbot.

Rögnwald seems to have remained in charge of Harold's Northern
dominions for the next two years (869–871), for we do not hear of him
participating in the King's campaigns in the South and East. In the
latter year Harold went North to Trondjem, where he was joined by
Rögnwald.

They had now to face the crisis of the reign. A formidable army
gathered in the South from Hordaland, Telemark, Rogaland and Agder.
Harold and Rögnwald collected their forces and attacked the rebels at
Hafresfiord near Stavanger. Harold won a complete victory and thereby
became supreme Sovereign of Norway. The story says that he immediately claimed from Gyda her promise and sent for her to become his
wife. But, although Gyda had refused him until he had subdued the
whole country, it does not follow that Harold had eschewed marriage.
Indeed, he was a much-married man. The Norsemen were a polygamous
race and were as unfettered as King Solomon in the numbers of their
wives and concubines.

The practice of polygamy went on well into Christian times, and it
was not until the 13th century that a Bishop of Bergen refused the request
of a King of Norway to celebrate a bigamous marriage. "Danish"
marriages were common enough in Normandy; all the Dukes, except the
brothers Richard III and Robert the Magnificent, were the offspring
of such unions, and William the Conqueror was a bastard, as is well
known.

Polygamy among the upper classes in Norway no doubt increased
the number of the Vikings. All children were equally udal-born to the
family estates; but there was not enough land to go round, so the family
fitted out the superfluous sons with longships and sent them off to seek
their fortunes on the seas; for piracy was the only profession for a landless
gentleman.

The Vikings had complete command of the sea. Their warships show
a high development in naval architecture. We know a good deal of
them from the "burial" ships that have been discovered. One of the
most perfect of these is a ship found at Gokstad. She was built towards
the end of the 9th century and might conceivably have been one of
Rolf's fleet. These warships were eighty feet in length and had very
little draught. They had sixteen oars and carried one large square sail.
The crew numbered from forty to fifty, but sometimes there may have
been more. The ships were steered with a tiller and the captain's place
was aft. The vessels were not decked and the crew slept between the

thwarts, wrapped in skin sleeping-bags. They were handy craft and light, so that they could be portaged over rapids. So seaworthy were they that a model of the Gokstad ship was sailed across the Atlantic to America in four weeks, sometimes attaining a speed of ten to eleven knots.

Usually they had the head of a dragon as a figurehead and they were painted in gay colours. With their shallow draught they could sail up any river and could be drawn up on the beach in winter. As there was no navy to rival them they could lie at anchor in rivers like the Seine in complete safety and, being propelled by man-power, they were largely independent of the weather and the wind.

The Battle of Hafresfiord took place in 872, but Harold, though acknowledged King of all Norway, was by no means secure on his throne. The dispossessed Chiefs and kinglets, like Solve of More, had taken to the sea and were constantly raiding the Norwegian coasts. There were nests of pirates in the Orkneys, Shetlands, Hebrides and Faroes, and even as far as the Isle of Man. Iceland was colonized at this time by malcontents from Norway, but the colonists of Iceland were peaceful people. The island never became a base for Viking pirates.

In 873, or perhaps a year or two later, Harold fitted out a considerable fleet and sailed for the West to punish the pirates and to make them respect his kingdom. He first reached Shetland, chased away the Vikings, and annexed the islands to Norway. Next he subdued the Orkneys and thence pursued his conquests in the Hebrides and the Isle of Man.

It is unknown whether Rögnwald accompanied the King on this expedition. Neither the Orkneyinga nor the Heimskringla Sagas say anything about him, so probably he remained to look after affairs in Northern Norway, as Guthorm did at Tunsberg in the South. Ivar, Rögnwald's son, however, served in this expedition and was killed in the Hebrides. To compensate Rögnwald for his son's death, Harold offered to add the Earldoms of Orkney and Shetland to More, but Rögnwald, feeling presumably that he would be unable to govern such a scattered territory properly, offered them to his brother, Sigurd. King Harold agreed to this arrangement, and Sigurd became Earl of Orkney and Shetland, the first of the Earls of his family to reign in Orkney. They continued to rule the islands until, with the death of Earl John in 1231, their line became extinct.

Sigurd, when he had taken over his Earldoms made an alliance with Thorstein the Red, son of Olaf the White, King of Dublin. Between them they made extensive conquests in Scotland and Sigurd added a considerable area as far as the Firth of Dornoch to his dominions.

Earl Sigurd was unlucky, and here we have one of those details which, to my mind, do much to prove the accuracy of the Sagas. On a campaign in Scotland he killed a Scottish Mormaer, or Earl, named Melbrict the Toothy. He was so proud of his feat that he cut off his victim's head and hung it to his saddle like a fox's mask. But Melbrict had his revenge. His teeth scratched Sigurd's leg and the Earl died of blood-poisoning and was buried near Dornoch.

Sigurd was succeeded by his son, Guthorm, who died within a year. The islands were immediately attacked by Vikings and Rögnwald sent his son, Hallad, to deal with them. But Hallad had no stomach for the fight and returned to Norway, where old Rögnwald was thoroughly disgusted with him and told him he was no credit to the family.

Einar had never been a favourite with his father—he was an able man, but ugly and blind of one eye. He went to Rögnwald and said, "I have enjoyed but little honour among you and I have little affection here to lose: now if you will give me force enough I will go West to the islands and promise you what, at any rate, will please you—you will never see me again." Rögnwald replied very ungraciously, but gave him the necessary ships, and Einar sailed for his new Earldom, where he soon established his sovereignty.

But we must turn back a little now to deal with the history of Rolf the Ganger. King Harold came back from his expedition to the West in the year 874, or a little later, and on his return Rögnwald entertained him at a great feast in honour of his victories. For many years Harold's hair had been uncombed and uncut, and he was called Lufa, or Mophead. Now Rögnwald cut his hair with great ceremony and renamed him Haarfaager.

We have heard very little hitherto of Rolf—all we know is that he had an island somewhere to the North of the mouth of the Namsen whence he fitted out his Viking forays. His sphere of activity was the Baltic. Returning from one of his expeditions and reaching the coast of the Vik—i.e., the bay on which Oslo now stands—Rolf's fleet became short of food. This must have been subsequent to 875, an important fact as we shall see hereafter, for the Norman chronicles date Rollo's arrival in the Seine in 876—an impossibility if the arrangement of the Sagas by Sturleson is chronologically accurate.

Rolf, with supreme impudence, landed a party and raided the cattle of Harold's subjects. Unfortunately for Rolf, King Harold happened to be at Vik and he flew into a towering and somewhat excusable rage. With the assistance of Rolf's father, Rögnwald, Harold had for years been successfully endeavouring to put down these Viking depredations, and here was Rögnwald's own son committing this robbery, so to speak, on the King's threshold. The King at once summoned a Thing and proclaimed Rolf an outlaw throughout Norway. His mother, Hilda, hastened from More to Vik and tried to beg Rolf off; he seems to have been her favourite son—the "name child", she calls him, of her father, Rolf Nefia. But not all Hilda's eloquence nor all his regard for Rögnwald could move the King and he insisted on Rolf's banishment from Norway. The history of the world might have been different had it not been for that day's cattle-lifting!

So Rolf sailed away and eventually reached the Hebrides. What he did there we do not know, for neither the Sagas nor the chronicles tell us anything about it; but he must have stayed some time in the Hebrides for the Landmannabok of Iceland tells us that he had a daughter born there who subsequently married a Scottish chieftain.

King Harold had many wives, many concubines and many children. His sons now were beginning to grow up and to become a nuisance. In 890 two of them, Halfdan Haleg and Gudrod Liome, angry with their father for refusing to give them a share in the kingdom, and doubtless jealous of Rögnwald, fitted out an expedition to attack More. They surrounded Rögnwald's fortress and burnt it and with it himself and his men. Rögnwald must have been an oldish man when he died, for we have seen that he was probably born early in the century.

Halfdan took Rögnwald's ships and sailed westwards, doubtless intending to surprise Einar and make himself Earl of Orkney. Gudrod, meanwhile, set himself up as Earl of More. But he had reckoned without his father. The latter collected a large force, compelled Gudrod to surrender and banished him. The King then made his son-in-law, Thorer, Earl of More in the place of his father, Rögnwald.

Halfdan Haleg took Earl Einar by surprise and forced him to escape to Scotland; but here he soon raised a force and returned to Orkney, defeated Halfdan and took him prisoner.

The obligation of the blood feud rendered it necessary for Einar to take a terrible vengeance on Halfdan for Rögnwald's death. He made "a spreadeagle of him" i.e., he cut his ribs from his backbone and tore out his lungs. Einar seems to have been rather proud that he—the despised son—should have been the avenger of his father's murder, for he composed a poem—he was well known as a Skald—in which he made some rather disagreeable remarks about his brothers.

Rather reluctantly King Harold was forced by his family to take up the blood feud against Einar. He sailed for Orkney and again Einar took refuge in Caithness. Harold was not bloodthirsty, but he was thrifty and contented himself by inflicting a fine of sixty gold marks on the islands. Einar paid the fine on condition of the islanders surrendering their udal rights to him.

Einar ruled his Earldom well. He taught his people to burn peat as there was no wood in the Orkneys—hence he was called Torf Einar. He died in 910, leaving three sons, Arnkell, Erlend and Thorfinn. Eric Bloodaxe, King Harold's son, took refuge in the Orkneys when driven from Norway with his wife, Queen Ranghilda, and later Arnkell and Erlend were killed fighting for King Eric.

Thorfinn, who married the daughter of a Scottish Earl named Duncan, reigned as Earl till 963. He had five sons, who succeeded one another to their father's Earldom. The three elder brothers married successively Ranghilda, daughter of Eric Bloodaxe, but she murdered all three of her husbands! Eventually Thorfinn's youngest and last surviving son succeeded. His name was Lodre and he died in 980, being succeeded by his son, the famous Earl Sigurd II. Sigurd became a Christian in 995 and added a considerable territory to his inheritance. At his death he ruled not only over Orkney and Shetland, but also over the Hebrides and Man, Sutherland, Ross, Moray and Argyll on the mainland. He was killed at the battle of Clontarf.

In 1014 the Viking power in Ireland was giving way before the onslaught of the Irish under King Brian Boru. The Irish Vikings called for aid from the powerful Earl of Orkney. Sigurd responded and collected a substantial force from his dominions in Orkney, Shetland, Scotland and the Hebrides. He also received reinforcements from the Norse settlements in Cumberland and Wales. The Norse army under Sigurd and Broder met the Irish under Brian Boru at Clontarf, where it was annihilated and the dominions of the Norsemen in Ireland destroyed.

Sigurd's activities caused a certain amount of discontent among his subjects and he was obliged to surrender his rights over the udallers, which they had handed over to Torf Einar in exchange for their liability for the blood money due for the killing of Halfdan, King Harold's son.

Sigurd's second wife was a daughter of Malcolm II, King of Scotland. After some quarrelling over the succession with his sons by a former wife, Thorfinn, the son by the second wife succeeded to the Earldom. This Thorfinn died in 1064. The line of Torf Einar flourished in the Orkneys for nearly another two centuries, but the only remarkable Earl of the family was Magnus, Erlend's son, afterwards known as St. Magnus. He was murdered by his brother, Haakon, in 1115, and in 1231 the line of Einar died out on the male side.

I have delayed over the history of the Earls of Orkney, firstly because they were, like the Dukes of Normandy, direct descendants of Rögnwald of More, and, secondly, because it is interesting to note that while one branch of the family ruled in England and Normandy, another ruled in the Orkneys and in Scotland. There is, however, no record that the cousins ever had any relations with one another.

CHAPTER II

THE CONQUERORS OF NORMANDY

The Norman Chronicles—Dudo of St. Quentin—His unreliability and sources of information —State of Western Europe in the later 9th century—Disintegration of Charlemagne's Empire—Louis the Pious—The Emperor Lothar and his sons—Charles the Bald— Treaty of Verdun—Charles the Bald becomes King of territory between Channel and Pyrenees—Viking invasions of France—Louis the Stammerer succeeds Charles the Bald—Louis dies, leaving infant son—Odo of Paris chosen King—Carolingian line restored by Charles the Simple.

A MUCH more difficult task awaits us now. We have traced, or endeavoured to trace, the origin of Rollo (as we must now call him) and we have pursued the fortunes of the other members of his family so far as the records enable us to do; our duty now is to follow up his personal biography and trace the steps whereby he established himself as the ruler of Normandy.

Unluckily, the Norman chronicler is not so reliable a historian as the Sagaman. Dudo of St. Quentin is practically the only contemporary authority for the period; we get scarcely any help from any other writer. The historians who follow Dudo have taken his account as accurate from the time of William of Jumièges to that of Sir Francis Palgrave, though it is significant that the former is perhaps more cautious in his endorsement than the latter. But of recent years there has been much searching examination and criticism of Dudo. Some authorities, such as Howarth, reject him altogether; others, such as M. Lair, are apt to give him considerable acceptance; others, again, accept or reject him in varying degrees; so it is hard to know how to treat him.

Dudo was not a Norman. He was a Frank born in the Vermandois and employed in the first instance by Albert, Count of Vermandois, who sent him on a mission to Richard I, Duke of Normandy, to ask his assistance against Hugh Capet who had raided the Vermandois. Dudo seems to have been well received at the Norman Court and to have struck up a friendship with the Duke, who presented him with two livings near Caux. This must have been in or about the year 986. He was then a young man and Lair places the date of his birth about 960. During the ten years preceding the death of Richard I (986–996) Dudo, though remaining a Canon of St. Quentin, frequently visited Richard at Rouen and also the Norman monasteries, expecially Fécamp. This is important to note because it proves that Dudo had many opportunities of learning from

Duke Richard and his companions first-hand particulars of the history of Normandy and of the ducal family. Two years before his death, Richard I asked Dudo to undertake the History which he entitles *De moribus et actis primorum Normannorum ducum.* The sources whence Dudo, who now became Dean of St. Quentin, drew his material are obscure, but he must have obtained much information from Richard, and a great deal more, as he says himself, from Richard's brother, Raoul d'Ivri.

Raoul d'Ivri was the son of Sprota, Richard's mother, by a marriage contracted with a rich miller named Sperling of Vaudreuil. Richard I was born in 933 and succeeded his father in 943. Sprota did not marry Sperling until a year or two after William Longsword's death, so that Raoul d'Ivri could not have been born until shortly before 950—that is to say, some twenty-five years after the death of Rollo. Although, therefore, D'Ivri was a good deal younger than his brother, the Duke, he was old enough to have known men who were contemporary with Rollo in his old age. So far as Richard I is concerned, he was, in his childhood and early youth, well acquainted with such men as Botho, who, Dudo says, was his tutor, and Bernard the Dane, both of whom were contemporaries of Rollo.

The fact that Dudo owed so much of his information to Richard I and his brother makes it fairly probable that, at any rate, in so far as family history is concerned, he is mainly accurate. Indeed, he does not mince matters about the morals of his heroes; he tells us that not only William Longsword, but also Richard, were the sons of concubines. Surely, if Sir Henry Howarth is right in thinking that Dudo's object was to paint the Norman princes in the best colour and to make them out to be civilized persons and not pagan pirates, he would have laid less stress on these inconvenient details?

For his history Dudo seems to have browsed freely in the chronicles of the various monastic annals—those perhaps of St. Bertin, of Fulda, of Rheims (where he could have had access to the works of Flodoard and Richer), of St. Vaast and of Fécamp. Certainly he made use in his compilation of some of these sources. But Dudo was no doubt a bad historian and a worse geographer. He had no critical spirit; he was flamboyant in style, an intentional sycophant and flatterer, and an open propagandist, but not a deliberate liar. Such an author is hardly a satisfactory source on which to base serious history or biography; but we have no other, for Rollo is not mentioned by any other chronicler until 921, when we learn from Richer *Dum habe gerebantur Rotbertus Celticae Galliae dux piratas acrites impetebat. Irruperant enim duce Rollone filio Catilli* (he here attributes his paternity presumably to Ketil, Earl of the Hebrides; but quite incorrectly).

And now, before we try to draw such facts as we can in regard to Rollo from Dudo, we must endeavour to give some kind of description of the state of affairs obtaining in Western Europe at the time that the Vikings were establishing themselves in Neustria.

Charlemagne died at Aix-la-Chapelle on January 28, 814, and no sooner was the breath out of his body than his revived Empire of the West began to disintegrate. He was succeeded by his only surviving son, Louis the Pious, an excellent and highly moral man, but a very inferior ruler. Much of the trouble which arose in those days on the death of a sovereign was due to the custom of the Franks, and of other Teutonic nations as well, for the inheritance to be divided amongst the sons. There was no rule of primogeniture. Charlemagne accepted the division of his Empire as a matter of course, and made elaborate arrangements to provide for it. During his lifetime, Louis (his successor) became King of Aquitaine, Charles King of Austrasia, and Pipin King of Italy. Both Pipin and Charles predeceased their father. Charles was childless, but Pipin left a son, Bernard, who succeeded him as King of Italy, but died in 817, leaving issue who became the Counts of Vermandois, of whom we shall hear much later. Their Carolingian descent is not without importance.

Louis the Pious associated his eldest son, Lothar, with himself as co-Emperor. His nephew, Bernard, was King of Italy already. His other two sons, Pipin and Louis the German, became respectively Kings of Aquitaine and Bavaria. In 817, Bernard revolted against his uncle and tried to make himself independent. The revolt was suppressed, Bernard dethroned, and Lothar, the eldest son and co-Emperor, became King of Italy.

Unfortunately, as it transpired, the Empress Ermengarde, Louis the Pious' first wife, died in 818 and he married in the following year, Judith, daughter of Welf, Count of Altdorf on the Lake of Lucerne. By Judith he had one son, Charles, afterwards known as Charles the Bald. It was the old story—a middle-aged man (Louis was forty-five in 823), a young second wife ambitious for her own son, and a grown-up family by a first wife. Had Louis not been so foolish as to divide up the whole of his dominions between Ermengarde's children, things might have been easier. for now Louis and Judith were determined on carving out a kingdom for young Charles, and obviously they could only do so at the expense of Louis' three elder sons.

In 829, Louis deprived his son, Louis the German, of what now corresponds more or less to Suabia and Switzerland and created a kingdom for young Charles, then aged six. Revolt immediately broke out; Lothar and Pipin, doubtless fearing an encroachment on their own domains, took sides with their brother, Louis the German. They gathered their forces at Paris, surprised their father and his wife and imprisoned them.

A lucky chance restored Louis the Pious to his throne, but the three sons revolted again. Louis was again taken prisoner and deposed in 833. The brothers, however, soon quarrelled afresh and Louis was restored, but the mischief was done.   The three brothers had no confidence in each other, and they were suspicious of their father and hostile to their young half-brother.   And not without reason, for Louis, unwilling to learn by experience, showed himself still anxious to increase young Charles' share.   Partition after partition took place—there were at least ten of such arrangements during Louis the Pious' reign.   Alamannia and Neustria were added to Charles' kingdom and, when Pipin died in 838, he also gained Aquitaine, although Pipin left issue.

Louis the Pious maintained a precarious hold on the Empire, but his dominions were a welter of discord.   His sons were fighting against their father and with each other.   Confusion was hopeless.   Naturally, when they saw the Empire of the Carolingians in such a plight, the barbarians took advantage of it.   The Northmen, who had proved a nuisance to Charlemagne but had been held in check by him, seized the golden opportunity.   In 833 they appeared on the Scheldt and at the same time the Slavs began to give trouble on the Eastern frontier and the Saracens in the Mediterranean.

Such was the state of affairs in 840 when Louis the Pious died.   Bad as things were during Louis' lifetime they became immediately worse on his death.   Lothar now became sole emperor.   He held the two capitals, Aix-la-Chapelle and Rome, and he tried to impose his authority on his brothers, Louis the German and Charles the Bald.   The two united against the Emperor Lothar.   Circumstances seemed to favour them. There had always been jealousy and distrust between the Germans of Bavaria and the Franks of the Rhine.   Similarly, the Latin population of Aquitaine felt jealousy and distrust of the Rhinelanders.   Louis the German profited by this during his father's lifetime and established himself securely in his Bavarian dominion.   Charles the Bald, though there was a rival claimant in Pipin's son to the throne of Aquitaine, likewise profited by the jealousy that existed and began to make himself formidable in the countries between the Loire, the Seine and the Rhone.

In 841 Louis the German and Charles the Bald in alliance met their brother, the Emperor Lothar, at Fontenoy.   A great battle ensued in which Lothar was defeated but not destroyed.   The result of the battle, however, showed that the Empire as established by Charlemagne was at an end.   In 843 a Treaty was signed at Verdun between the three brothers.   The Emperor Lothar retained Frisia (now Belgium and Holland), Aix-la-Chapelle, Burgundy, Provence, Lombardy and Rome. Louis the German took the German lands from Hamburg in the North, Thuringia, Suabia, Bavaria and Switzerland, and Charles the Bald became ruler of the territory from the English Channel to the Pyrenees. Roughly speaking, Charles the Bald's kingdom corresponded with modern France; Louis the German's with modern Germany, and they had in each country the nucleus of a common language.   Charles the

Bald's subjects spoke *Romane*—not Latin nor yet French, but the *lingua Romana*; Louis the German's subjects spoke German. But the Emperor Lothar's subjects had no national unity or national language. Austrasian Franks, Romane-speaking Burgundians and Italian Lombards had no bonds of cohesion.

Now, the Treaty of Verdun has been described as the beginning of modern Europe, and it is, therefore, of great importance; but it had little effect at the time. The unedifying and senseless quarrels went on. No man was loyal to another; every man tried to get a little more for himself and to filch something from his neighbour. In fact, all Europe from the Elbe to the Atlantic and from the Channel to the Tiber wallowed in a welter of Civil War. Naturally, the barbarians took courage. This discord was their opportunity. In 841 Osker the Northman entered the Seine and plundered Rouen; in 843 the Vikings burnt Nantes, in 845 they plundered Paris and levied blackmail in the form of Danegeld, and in the same year another band destroyed Hamburg. Every year saw the Frisian Coast ravaged and plundered.

Although Charles the Bald had secured himself for a time in Aquitaine his nephew began to make trouble there, and Charles thought more of defeating Pipin than of defending his realm against the pirates; moreover, Pipin, the nephew, allied himself to the Northmen and used their help against his uncle. And so the tedious tale of strife goes on, brother fighting against brother, uncle against nephew—law and order disappear and the coasts are ravaged by pagan pirates with practical impunity.

The Emperor Lothar died in 855 and immediately war broke out over the inheritance between his three sons, the Emperor Louis II, Lothar and Charles, in which their greedy uncles, Charles the Bald and Louis the German, took part. Fortunately, all Lothar's three sons died without issue before 875, when, on the death of Louis II, the last survivor, his uncle, Charles the Bald, succeeded in making himself Emperor for two years. Charles the Bald died in 877. Louis the German died in 876, leaving three sons who, having spent their earlier years in revolting against their father, passed their later ones in quarrelling over his inheritance. They were Carloman, King of Bavaria and Carinthia, Louis the Saxon, King of the East Franks, and Charles the Fat, who became King of Alamannia and Italy and Emperor in 881. The last-named was a weak, lethargic creature and was deposed in 887.

We are, however, more concerned with the fortunes of the West Franks. When Charles the Bald died in 877 the usual division took place. His elder son, Charles, became King of Aquitaine, and the younger, Louis the Stammerer, King of the West Franks. The latter died in 879 and his relative, Charles the Fat, seized the opportunity to try and deprive Louis the Stammerer's children of their inheritance. The usual strife took place. Charles the Fat was successful but, as we have seen, he was disposed of in 887.

Louis the Stammerer left an infant son born in 879, but a child of eight (as he was in 887) was hardly fitted to be king in such turbulent times as the concluding years of the 9th century. Even the most devoted adherents to the Carolingian tradition—and, curiously enough, there were in spite of everything still such to be found—felt this. Odo, Count of Paris, was chosen King and he reigned until 899, when he died, and the young Charles, called Charles the Simple, was called to the throne.

CHAPTER III

ROLLO

Date of his departure from Norway—Leaves Hebrides—Adventures in England and Frisia—Arrives in France—Siege of Paris—Rollo in Normandy—Marries Popa—Untrustworthy records between 900 and 911—Rollo besieges Chartres—Recognized as leader of Vikings in France—Charles the Simple recognizes Rollo's sovereignty in Normandy—Brittany—Treaty of St. Claire sur Epte—Rollo and his Vikings become Christians—Gisela.

WE have endeavoured to show the utter disruption of the Carolingian Empire in order to explain the position in Western Europe when Rollo came there to carve out a realm for the Normans. And now we must revert to such records as have come down to us and try to find out how he did it. Practically we have no help beyond Dudo, and all we can do is to endeavour to winnow the truth from the falsehood in his writings.

We left Rollo, or Rolf, banished from Norway by Harold Haarfaager and an emigrant to the Hebrides, then ruled by the powerful Earl Ketil. According to Snorre Sturleson, this event could not have taken place before 874 or 875, at the earliest. Laing puts Rolf's departure from Norway as occurring in 890, but that would seem to be too late if he took part in any of the earlier campaigns described by Dudo.

The Norman chronicler begins his story by saying that Rollo came from Dacia, that he and his brother, Gurm, quarrelled with the King of Dacia, that Gurm was killed and Rollo banished, that he went to Scanza (most probably Scania) and thence to England. This is not much in accord with Snorre Sturleson's account, but it does not clash violently with it since Rollo did go to Scania on a piratical cruise and was banished by Harold and then came to the British Islands.

Snorre Sturleson tells us that from the Hebrides, Rollo went to Valland—which was a generic term for Western France—to the country of the Welsh, so perhaps more particularly to Brittany. The date of Rollo's departure from the Hebrides is uncertain. Dudo tells us that after his English and Frisian adventures he sailed up the Seine in 876. This, clearly, is too early a date and even M. Lair, a stout upholder of the accuracy of Dudo, cannot accept it. He inclines to the view that the date is a mistake of the copyists and that 876 really should be 886. The suggestion is ingenious and not only possible but probable: it only means an X less for DCCCLXXVI instead of DCCCLXXXVI.

If M. Lair is correct, a good deal of Dudo's tale is rendered more

likely, but it would not explain the fact that, while Rollo is described by
Dudo as the leader and prime mover in all these various campaigns,
no other single writer mentions his name at all, though they speak of many
other Viking leaders. We know that Dudo was a propagandist and he
attributed to his hero all the glory and fame that he could. But we also
believe that Dudo was not a deliberate liar; even Sir Henry Howarth, his
most destructive critic, admits this, so that it seems more than likely that
while Rollo was never the leader in these early campaigns he was a subordinate commander. Indeed, there is a passage in Dudo that suggests
this. He tells us that when the Northmen were asked who their leader
was they replied that they were all equal and that they had no leader.
This is a correct statement, for we know from other sources that the Viking
fleets and armies consisted of a number of contingents the leaders of which
were equal in rank, but, being practical people, they naturally agreed
upon a commander-in-chief, and a proper hierarchy of officers.

That Rollo was not a commander-in-chief is certain; that he was a
subordinate leader in some, if not all, of the campaigns mentioned by
Dudo is probable. Between the time that he was banished from Norway
and when he is first mentioned by Richer he must have been doing something. Rollo can only have been doing one thing and that is following
the trade of pirate. It was the only trade he knew. He must have been
in France for some time to become the recognized leader of the Seine
pirates. It is impossible to suppose that he arrived from the Hebrides on
the banks of the Epte in 911 and was immediately handed the Neustrian
domain by Charles the Simple. Rollo, like everyone else, had to prove
his worth and serve his time as a subordinate, and much of that time must
have been served in France, so that it is not really unlikely that he took
part in the campaigns described by Dudo, but certainly not as leader or
commander-in-chief.

If M. Lair is correct that 876 should be 886, the dates accord fairly
easily. Rollo stayed some time in the Hebrides, long enough at least to
have a love affair and to beget a daughter, as we learn from the Icelandic
Landmannabok. From the Hebrides—and if M. Lair is correct it would
be about 879 or 880—Dudo tells us, Rollo journeyed to England. Here,
so the chronicler says, he entered into friendly relations with the "most
Christian King Alstemus".

Now, there was, of course, no King of England named Alstemus. Some
have thought that Alstemus is a corruption of Alfred, but there seems to
be no ground for this. The more likely interpretation is the following.
The Danish leader Guthrum was first the most formidable rival and
latterly on good terms with King Alfred. In 880, Guthrum accepted
Christianity and was baptised under the name of Athelstane. It is quite
probable that Rollo, sailing from the Hebrides, came into contact with
Guthrum Athelstane.

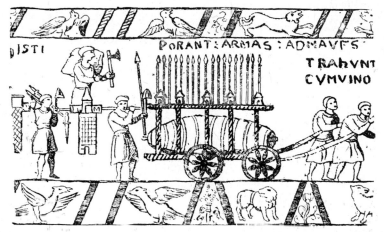

Workmen dragging a cart loaded with a barrel of wine and
lances to the sea.

Fight between Normans and English with swords and
javelins.

Church of the Abbaye-aux-Dames, Caen.
(see No. 1. *Notes on Illustrations.*)

From England, Rollo is said by Dudo to have undertaken an expedition to the country of the Walgri—*i.e.* Walcheren. Now, the monastic annals tell us that between the years 881 and 884 there were numerous Viking raids on Flanders. If M. Lair's conjecture as to the dates is correct, nothing would be more easy than for Rollo to have taken part in them. Dudo tells us that the leaders opposing the Vikings were Ragner Longi Collis, Count of Hainault and Radbrod, Duke of the Frisians. Both these people are historical characters and appear in contemporary annals.

Now from Flanders Dudo takes Rollo to Rouen, giving the date 876, but if the date is really 886 we get some confirmation from the annals of St. Vedast. According to these the Northmen defeated in that year a French force under Ragnald, Count of Maine. Rollo is not mentioned, but he may perhaps have held a subordinate command in the Viking army.

We have noted that when Charles the Fat died in 887 the natural heir, the posthumous son of Louis the Stammerer, was but eight years old and obviously unsuited to become King. Odo, Count of Paris, was, it will be remembered, elected King of the Franks. This choice was doubtless largely due to Odo's stout and successful defence of Paris against the Northmen in 886 or 887.

We are told by Dudo that Rollo was the leader of the army which besieged Paris. This, of course, is untrue. We have a trustworthy account of the siege from Hincmar and also from the Monk Abbo, who was actually in Paris at the time. Neither says anything of Rollo. The Viking leader was Sigfrid, and not Rollo, who may, though, have taken part in the siege.

Odo, Count of Paris and in 888 King, repulsed the Northmen and the siege of Paris was raised, but the enemy was only checked, not destroyed. Although the Vikings were defeated at Montfaucon, they took and burnt Méaux, but though they attacked Paris again and again it was successfully defended by King Odo. A third attempt in 890 was equally unfortunate for the Northmen.

We now come to more trustworthy information about Rollo. In 890 the Vikings, disgusted at their failure to take Paris, marched under Sigfrid, who was still their leader, into the Cotentin and sacked and burnt St. Lo. This we learn from the annals of St. Vedast. According to Dudo, Rollo on this occasion besieged and captured Bayeux. Bayeux is not specifically mentioned in the St. Vedast annals, but it could hardly have escaped the enemy in view of its geographical situation.

But the interest and importance of Dudo's story lies not on the military, but on the personal side. Dudo tells us that among the defenders of Bayeux was Count Berenger de Senlis. This individual was killed in the fighting, and his daughter, Popa, taken prisoner. Popa was allotted to

Rollo, as was Briseis to Achilles, and he proceeded to contract with her a Danish marriage. The result of this marriage was a son, afterwards William Longsword, Rollo's successor.

Attempts have been made to deny the whole story; but we venture to urge that it is true for the following reason. Dudo was the friend of ten years' standing of Richard I, the grandson of Rollo and Popa. Raoul d'Ivri, Richard's uterine brother, was Dudo's main source of information, especially as regards personal details. Is it really conceivable that Dudo (who even Howarth says was no liar) would have invented the whole of the story? And, if he did do so, what possible reason could he have had?

But there is even better proof. We are constantly reminded of the strong tie between the rulers of Normandy and their De Senlis relatives. It was to Bernard de Senlis that Osmund de Centeville took young Richard I when they escaped from imprisonment at Lâon. Throughout Dudo's history the connection between the De Senlis family and the ducal house is emphasized. Surely it is impossible to believe that Richard I or his brother would have allowed Dudo to take this attitude had the relationship not been a real one? Common sense seems to tell us that the story of Rollo and Popa is true, and we therefore can perhaps safely draw the conclusion that in 890 Rollo had been some time in France. That being the case, it is a certainty that he had been fighting and, if so, why not in the campaign described by Dudo?

Encouraged by at last finding something in Dudo's book which we may reasonably regard as reliable, in the story of Rollo's life, we might have hoped for more facts in future. But we are doomed to disappointment. It is true that Dudo tells us of the siege of Evreux by Rollo's army, and we get some confirmation of this from the Rouen Chronicle, which records the taking of Evreux in 892. But henceforward the story becomes more and more vague and untrustworthy, till in 900 it dwindles away altogether.

Let us turn now from Dudo and follow William of Jumièges. The latter copied and abridged Dudo, but he was careful not to take personsal responsibility for the other's history. In a letter to William the Conqueror he says that for his account of Normandy until the time of Richard II he has relied solely on Dudo, but that the material for the rest of his book has been drawn from many different sources, including his own experiences. So that we may conclude that William of Jumièges was none too certain of the accuracy of all that he read in the Dean of St. Quentin's work. Perhaps, therefore, that which he left out in his abridged version is that which he concluded to be least probable.

William of Jumièges tells us that after the siege of Evreux, at which Rollo was not present, the latter again took part in a siege of Paris. This vague statement seems quite unsubstantiated. Rollo is portrayed as attacking the walls of Paris with all the artillery of the day, such as battering-rams and catapults throwing large stones, and successfully levying Danegeld. Doubtless desultory warfare continued between Vikings and Franks, but no organized siege took place at this date.

After this we get into very deep water indeed, and William of Jumièges cuts his narrative down to a minimum. Rollo's old friend, Alstemus, is said to have sent to ask for his aid in England and Rollo undertook an expedition to help him. But if the date of the Rouen Chronicle is correct, and Evreux was taken in 892, this Alstemus could not be Guthrum Athelstane, for he died in 890. Rollo may have paid a flying visit to England; but the fighting between the English and the Danes was inland in Mercia, where the Danes gained the victory in the battle of Holme. One small matter gives slight confirmation of the story that Rollo left France at this time. About this date, Rollo's son, William, was born. A MS. has been found at Clermont of which a copy has subsequently been discovered at Florence, where it is said that William Longsword was not born in France; but the reading may very easily be corrupt,* and the probability is that William was born in Normandy.

To continue William of Jumièges' narrative, Rollo, after having returned from England, sent his generals all over Central France, to the Seine, to the Loire, to the Gironde and to Burgundy. We must assume from this very short statement that neither William nor Dudo had any notion where Rollo was at this time. After the repeated failures of the Vikings to take Paris it is quite true that their forces split up into various marauding expeditions to the places William of Jumièges quotes, but as William carefully avoids saying which expedition Rollo accompanied and carefully states that he sent his *men* on the various campaigns, it seems pretty clear that all touch with Rollo's actual exploits is missing.

But now complete darkness descends upon the scene. After the year 900 and until 911 practically no records exist. The confusion, disturbance and civil wars existing during these years in Germany and France, coupled with the ravages of the Vikings, the Magyars, the Slavs and the Saracens, seem to have dried up all sources of information and we know literally nothing of what passed in N.W. Europe during that decade. But here again we get a little negative help. If Dudo could find nothing to attribute to Rollo—anyway, he did not invent. He is just silent, and we hear no more of Rollo till we find him attacking Chartres in 911; at least, this is the date that seems the most probable, and it appears to receive confirmation from Frodoard.

But it must be admitted that the year is otherwise given in other chroniclers, who attribute it to dates varying between 891 and 911. The latter year, however, seems the most probable one and has been accepted as such by most of the authorities, including M. Lair and Sir F. Palgrave.

---

* For *Hic in Orbe Transmarino Natus Pantre* read *HAC in Urbe*, etc.

M. Licquet even, who is with the exception of Sir H. Howarth the strongest critic of Dudo, accepts the siege of Chartres as authentic, and admits that Rollo by this time had become the Chief Viking leader in North France.

It is generally accepted, therefore, that the Treaty of St. Claire sur Epte, whereby Charles the Simple recognized Rollo's sovereignty over Normandy, was concluded in 911. Frodoard seems to support this, though the passage in the text is vague. If we assume that this date is correct, we may confidently state that the dark decade during which the chronicles are silent as to Rollo's deeds was spent by him in consolidating his power in Rouen and its district, otherwise it would be ridiculous to suppose that the Frankish King would have confirmed the detested pirate in the possession of territory which belonged to his crown.

Charles has been called the Simple, but why is not apparent. He seems to have been a good deal less of a fool than many of the other Carolingians. Indeed, he showed, in times of almost incredible difficulty, qualities which, had he lived in more quiet days, might have gained for him the reputation of a considerable ruler. He seems to have recognized the fact that he could not subdue the Northmen.

When Henry VII was told that all Ireland could not rule the Earl of Thomond, he said that the Earl of Thomond must rule all Ireland. Similarly, Charles the Simple agreed that Rollo should rule all Normandy; and, as will be seen later, his decision was a wise one in his own interest.

Unfortunately, there is no text of the Treaty of St. Claire sur Epte and we have to rely on varying accounts for its provisions. It is quite impossible to say with any precision what were the exact limits of the territory conceded to Rollo. The most authoritative statement comes from Frodoard, who says that Rollo received certain maritime districts, together with the city of Rouen. Dudo tells us that he received the land from the Epte to the frontier of Brittany, but we must be very careful as to how we accept Dudo in this case of all others, for the following reason.

Dudo was a political writer and a propagandist. One object of Norman foreign policy at the time when he wrote was to establish Norman suzerainty over Brittany, and he claims that Charles the Simple gave Rollo feudal rights over the country. Naturally, such rights would have been of less importance were Normandy and Brittany not to possess a common frontier, so he interprets the cession of the maritime districts mentioned by Frodoard in the widest possible manner. But we learn from Frodoard that Normandy only acquired the Bessin in 924, so that the probability is that the original cession included Rouen and the land on the Seine comprised in the dioceses of Evreux, Lisieux, Rouen and Séez.

Dudo's claim that Rollo was granted the overlordship of Brittany, therefore, is hardly admissible, though his object in making it is clear. A claim, however weak, was, in those days, a useful pretext. We have an example in the case of Scotland. In the Anglo-Saxon Chronicle of the year 920 there is a statement to the effect that Edward the Elder received a Mission from Donald of Strathclyde and Constantine III of Scotland, saying that the whole nation of the Scots was prepared to take the West Saxon King for "their father and lord". This vague statement was used many years later to claim legal feudal lordship over Scotland!

Charles the Simple may possibly have agreed to something in the Treaty encouraging Rollo to direct his attention towards the West; it would not be surprising had he done so. He had no more authority over Brittany than he had over the moon, and he would no doubt have been glad to see Rollo embroiled with an enemy so far away from his own dominions—especially as in doing so Rollo might perhaps find himself in conflict with the other nest of pirates on the Loire.

Next we come to the personal clauses. Rollo and his men were to become Christians. This condition they seemed to have no difficulty in accepting, and we hear that this polygamous old pagan pirate and his crew arrayed themselves in white robes of innocence and were solemnly received into the Christian Church. The sight must have tickled the sense of humour of the spectators.

As a reward for his conversion it is said that he received the hand of the King's daughter, Gisela, in marriage. This union is very problematical and not a matter of importance, for poor Gisela, if she really ever existed, soon passes from the scene. Charles the Simple at this time was but thirty-two years old, so Gisela must have been quite young. As it is a personal detail and the truth of the story must have been known to Duke Richard I and D'Ivri, there is probably something in it. Perhaps Gisela was a child and betrothed to Rollo, and died soon after. By Rollo himself, who no doubt had had wives in every port from the Baltic to the Seine, the matter would have been regarded as of the most trivial importance.

The Treaty was endorsed by Duke Robert of Paris, who stood godfather to Rollo and gave him his name, and other prelates and princes, and, Dudo adds specially, by Beranger and Alan of Brittany. This last statement, however, is improbable for the reasons already given.

CHAPTER IV

ROLLO, PATRICIAN OF NORMANDY

Rollo's homage—Danes come to Normandy—Rollo's administration—Rollo as a lawgiver—"*Clameur de Haro*"—Peace from 911 to 920—Charles the Simple annexes Lotharingia—Rollo's foreign policy—His steady support of Charles—War between Charles and Robert of Paris—Vermandois and Burgundy support Robert—"Diffidation"—Regnald of Northumbria comes to the Loire with Vikings—Relations between Loire Vikings and Rollo—Robert of Paris proclaimed King—Rollo and Regnald support Charles—Robert of Paris killed at Soissons—Raoul of Burgundy chosen King—Herbert of Vermandois seizes Charles and imprisons him—Raoul buys off Rollo—Regnald killed—Rollo's failing health and abdication—His death.

ROLLO was now confirmed in his sovereignty, but he was not styled Duke, but Patrician. The title of Duke of Normandy was not regularly assumed until the reign of Richard I. The preliminaries having been concluded, Rollo had to do homage to King Charles. The story is told circumstantially; it is confirmed by a statement in the Chronicles of Tour and it bears certainly the stamp of truth. Moreover, it is just the sort of thing that one might expect from a pirate chief.

In an earlier passage in his book Dudo lays stress on the fact that Rollo owned no man as his lord. This is, of course, true; Rollo was a udal-born man, there was no feudal system whence he came, and he had never done homage to anyone; indeed, he probably did not know what homage meant at that time. But to Dudo, a Frenchman of the 11th century, such ignorance would have seemed striking.

Rollo was told that he must do homage by kneeling down and kissing the King's feet. This he firmly and roughly refused to do. He said he had never knelt before to any man and he was not going to begin at his time of life! So he told one of his men to do it; this man, instead of bending down over Charles's foot, seized it and lifted it to his lips, thereby causing the poor King to tumble over backwards, a circumstance which created great merriment among the people.

Rollo, the pirate, now becomes Patrician of Normandy and we must examine how he turned his sword into a ploughshare. We may certainly take it that Rouen and the banks of the river had long been settled by Normans and that they had either brought women from Norway, from Denmark and from England or, probably in most cases, had intermarried with the local population. A number of Danes emigrated from England to Normandy after the Treaty of St. Claire sur Epte, and doubtless this increase of the Scandinavian population was of considerable help to Rollo in repopulating the devastated regions. For the cause of this emigration we must turn for a moment to events in England.

When King Alfred the Great died in 899 he left a compact and powerful kingdom to his son, Edward the Elder. But Alfred was only King of Wessex. He had no sovreignty over the Danish Kingdom and the English Dukedom of Mercia was practically independent. But Wessex and Mercia were in close alliance and, indeed, by an arrangement concluded between Aethelred of Mercia and Alfred in 880, a vague suzerainty had been granted to Wessex over Mercia.

Aethelred of Mercia married Alfred's eldest daughter, Aethelflaeda in 885, and after the great King's death Edward the Elder worked in the closest co-operation with his brother-in-law and, when the latter died, with his sister, who was known as the Lady of the Mercians.

Aethelflaeda was probably the greatest Englishwoman before Queen Elizabeth. For eight years, from 912–920, she led the Mercians and, indeed, one may say her brother, Edward the Elder, and the men of Wessex as well. But before her husband Aethelred's death she had been the leading spirit in the warfare between the English and the Danes, and it is largely due to her energy that the Danish dominions disintegrated so rapidly during the reign of Edward the Elder. But there were other causes as well. One was the total lack of cohesion among the Danes. They were split up into little Earldoms and no Earl would help another. Moreover, the settled Danes began to care more for peace than plunder and sought for settled rule. But this applied rather to the Christians than to the heathen. The latter had much of the old Adam left in them, and when they heard of the new Daneland established in Normandy many of them hastened to join Rollo. Every encouragement to do so was given by Edward and Aethelflaeda. Thus Thurketyl, Earl of Bedford, with Edward the Elder's assistance, "fared overseas with such men as would follow him".

A number, therefore, of the Normans were of Anglo-Danish extraction; but the Norman aristocracy was Norwegian, for we read in William the Conqueror's confirmation of the laws of King Edward that the Norman nobility who accompanied him to England derived their descent from Norwegian ancestors. The Scandinavians in Normandy were in a minority and were outnumbered by the indigenous population who spoke the *lingua Romana*, which was soon to become French. It is to this that we must attribute the rapid Gallicization of the Normans. In the Rouen district, for example, Norse ceased to be spoken not long after Rollo's death. William Longsword was more of a Frenchman than a Norseman, and he had to send his son, Richard, to Bayeux to learn Norse.

Dudo, of course, waxes eloquent over the virtues of Rollo as a sovereign in peace time, but we must take what he says with a considerable grain of salt. Rollo was no fool, though. He may have been a pirate by trade and inclination, but he was very well aware that the settled colonizing Viking wanted peace, land, the means to cultivate it, and opportunity for trade.

Rollo retained, so far as we can see, the existing administrative system —in so far as any existed at all after the ravages of the last few years. Possibly the old Frankish division of "pagi" and "centenae" still survived. In any case, Rollo made no startling innovations in land tenure. He did not introduce the udal system, for instance. He no doubt made large grants of land to his followers in allodial tenure. Dim ideas of feudalism existed. Rollo had done homage for Normandy to Charles the Simple, but the feudal system was as yet in embryo, though after Rollo's time it developed rapidly. But feudalism, as M. Lavisse points out in his *Histoire de France*, developed differently in Normandy from elsewhere. Normandy became distinguished from other French fiefs by the absence of the hierarchy of feudalism—Rollo and his successors set their faces against the creation of powerful barons. The Norman nobility never acquired that independence of their Duke that characterized the nobility of other great fiefs. Henry II discovered this when he became Duke of Aquitaine and found his Southern barons far more independent and powerful and consequently much greater nuisances than their equals in Normandy.

Thus the chief characteristic of Norman Government was autocracy. Rollo kept the government in his own hands and his successors did not let it go from theirs. But, although the Norman sovereigns were autocrats, Rollo seems to have brought with him from his native land the idea of the Thing: an idea certainly foreign to Western Europe. In Norway we find the Thing operating as a recognized instrument of government. Doubtless in an illiterate country it was necessary to collect all the people together to proclaim laws and decisions. Traces of this method of publishing the law exist in the Isle of Man at the present day. But the Things were Councils as well, and we see among Norman institutions that such Councils were not discouraged in the early days.

We now come to Rollo's activities as a lawgiver. He certainly was not a legislator in the sense that he invented laws. Nor was Napoleon: but he was the originator of the Code Napoleon. Rollo was something of the same kind of lawgiver as Napoleon. In this he differed not at all from other Viking colonists. When they settled in any country from Russia to Iceland they brought their laws and customs with them; but they adapted them to their surroundings, and for this we must give credit to Rollo and his companions. Gradually thus grew up the great customary Code of Normandy: and although this Code is mainly French in character and contains very little of Scandinavian origin, as the founder of the State and its first ruler we must allow to Rollo the honour of being a lawgiver.

Rollo followed the example of most, if not all, rulers of his time in making grants to the Church. These grants in the Middle Ages were not made solely, if indeed mainly, for the benefit of the souls of erring donors. The abbeys were a necessity of civilization, not only for religious but for secular purposes. Learning, art and education were in the hands of the monks. The practice of medicine was shared by them with the Jews. They were the solicitors, conveyancers, clerks and registrars of the country. They administered charity, fostered agriculture, encouraged forestry and land drainage, and in general were the only leaders of education, learning and culture. The abbeys were the only places where travellers could find a lodging outside the towns; in short, prosperous monasteries and abbeys were a necessity in every country pretending to civilization.

Rollo's Christianity, however, sat lightly on him, and, although he had marched barefoot and in a white robe at his baptism, he did not hesitate to profit largely by the sale of Norman relics to the English. When about to die, it is true, he gave largely to the Church for the good of his soul; but either he still hankered after Valhalla or he wished to make assurance doubly sure (or his enemies maligned him), for it was said by Adhemar of Aquitaine that on his deathbed he ordered the sacrifice of a number of Christian slaves to Odin and Thor!

Dudo paints Normandy under Rollo as enjoying a golden age, and so, comparatively speaking, must have been the case. For years the unhappy country had been ravaged and devastated. There is scarcely a church in Normandy which dates before the 10th century. Rollo and his people were the principal offenders before the days of their colonization. As an illustration of the new prosperity, the story went that one day, after hunting, luncheon was spread by the servants under a tree by a lake. The conversation turned on the prosperous condition of the country under Rollo's rule and the absence of thieves and robbers. To test the matter, Rollo hung his golden armlet on the tree and three years later returned to find it untouched. The lake was then named Roumare— the mere of Rollo. Tales such as these, however, are common enough in countries which have been harried by war and to which peace has brought prosperity.

Other stories testify in the same direction. Even at the present day there exists in the Channel Islands, the last portion of Normandy to belong to the British Crown, though they did not form part of Rollo's dominions, the right to raise the *"clameur de Haro!"*. This right enables anyone who is injured or fears injury to himself or his property to raise the cry of Haro (Ha Rou) and invoke justice in the sovereign's name. It is then the duty of all good men to go to his assistance. It is said this custom dates from Rollo's day. Those who failed to go to the injured person were liable to fine; but if a man raised the "*clameur de Haro*" without proper cause he was equally liable to punishment.

Yet a third tale gives evidence of Rollo's desire to protect the agriculturist. One may well believe that this was one of the most urgent needs in the devastated land of which he had now become the ruler. This particular story has an additional interest, as it shows traces of a law of Scandinavian origin.

In the hard climate of Norway it was of the utmost importance that the udallers should be able to raise the maximum crop from the small area of fertile land that lent itself to the purpose. If a man's own thralls were insufficient to gather in his harvest he could claim the help of his neighbours; similarly, it was the custom that the crops and agricultural implements should be left in the open and the severest penalties were imposed on thieves. Obviously the reason for this was that all hands should be free to use the short period of the year open to agricultural operations, without being hindered and wasting their time by carrying their goods to places where they could be placed in safety from thieves and pilferers.

Rollo enacted a similar provision—or it is said that he did so. Agricultural implements, ploughs, harrows, etc., and cattle had to be left in the open field by night as well as by day; if they were stolen compensation was payable by the Government, which undertook the safeguarding of property of this kind. The story goes that in the village of Longpaon a farmer's wife, in order that he might claim compensation, hid her husband's plough. Rollo found out the fraud and hanged both the man and his wife; the wife for engineering the fraud, the farmer for not keeping her in better order!

These stories may be legendary, but they prove that in the popular tradition Rollo worked hard and successfully to introduce good government into his new territory.

Luckily for Normandy and for Rollo's administration, Northern France enjoyed comparative peace from 911 to 920. The years of peace were equally welcome to Charles the Simple. But the restless vassals of the Crown could not keep quiet. The trouble began over Charles's Prime Minister, Hagano. He was, it was said, of low birth, impudent, vulgar and overbearing—a beggar on horseback, in fact. Probably this was not the real reason why he was unpopular; it is more likely that he incurred dislike because he was a very able and energetic man and refused to betray his King.

Another cause for apprehension was the acquisition by Charles the Simple of Lotharingia. This event took place in 912. The most prominent man among the Lotharingian nobility was Rainier, Count of Hainault. Rainier took the lead among the Lotharingians and persuaded them to accept Charles the Simple as their King. This acquisition of territory came as a boon to Charles, following as it did on the Treaty of St. Clair sur Epte which had pacified Normandy and gained for him a strong and useful ally in Rollo. Rollo's foreign policy was straightforward and clear. Having made his bargain with Charles the Simple, he stuck to it through thick and thin. His new compatriots might, and no doubt did, hate him as a pirate, a pagan and an outcast, but the heathen Viking gave a lesson in straightforwardness to the so-called civilized Franks.

The revolution against Charles the Simple started in Paris. It will be remembered that when the crisis caused by the death of Charles the Fat took place in 887 his heir, Charles the Simple, son of Louis the Stammerer, was but eight years old. He was too young to be made King in such difficult times, and by common consent Odo, Count of Paris, was elected King of the West Franks. Eleven years later Odo died. His brother, Robert, refused the Crown and accepted Charles the Simple as the heir of Charlemagne, doing homage to him as Duke of France, his duchy comprising Paris, Orleans, Tours, Chartres, Beauvais and Le Mans; but in 920 he rebelled. His allies were his two sons-in-law: Raoul, Count of Burgundy, who had married his daughter, Emma; and Herbert, Count of Vermandois, married to his other daughter, Hermengarda. Soon the conspirators were joined by Gilbert, son of Count Rainier of Hainault, whom Charles the Simple on his father's death had created Duke of Lorraine. They had the tacit support of Henry the Fowler, who in 918 had succeeded Conrad of Franconia as King of Germany. Henry the Fowler was Duke of the Saxons before his accession to the throne. His object was to recover Lotharingia from the King of the West Franks.

The first move made by Robert of Paris and his fellow conspirators (except the Count of Vermandois, who did not show his hand yet) was to demand from Charles the Simple the dismissal of his Prime Minister, Hagano. Charles naturally refused, whereupon the conspirators "defied" him. "Diffidation" in feudal custom was a right very rarely exercised, but according to the old Teutonic law it certainly existed. It consisted in the vassals by solemn declaration throwing off their allegiance to their "Senior". Doubtless they hoped that others might follow their example; but in this they were disappointed. Rollo remained true to his engagements and, worse still for the conspirators, the other Lotharingian Magnates did not copy the action of the Duke of Lorraine.

Then a further and unseen complication ensued. In 920 Edward the Elder forced Regnald, King of Northumbria, to submit to him. This Regnald was an Irish Viking from Waterford, who left Ireland to seek his fortune in Cumberland. He got his military reputation by his successful attacks upon the lands of Ealdred, reeve of Bamborough, and of Constantine III, King of Scots. The Danes of Northumbria, quarrelling as usual among themselves, invited Regnald to be their King and he accepted. When, however, the Northumbrian resistance to Edward the Elder collapsed in 920, Regnald became disgusted and, handing his kingdom over to his brother, Sihtric, set forth for France to seek his fortune afresh. He did not go to Normandy to join Rollo, as so many other restless Anglo-Danes had done; but, perhaps hoping to carve out a second independent Norman principality for himself, he joined the Northmen of the Loire.

We suspect that when Charles the Simple appeared to have given Rollo some encouragement to cast his eyes towards Brittany he hoped that trouble might arise between the Normans of the Seine and those of the Loire. Very likely this was the case, and it is unlikely that Charles expected that Rollo would remain so faithful an ally as he subsequently proved to be. Instead of quarrelling with the Loire Normans, Rollo not only remained on good terms with them but negotiated some kind of supremacy over them.

Regnald, joined by the Normans of the Loire, now proceeded to ravage the country north of Nantes and to penetrate into Brittany. This diversion acted powerfully in favour of Charles the Simple. Robert of Paris led an army to attack Regnald, but he thought discretion the better part of valour and refrained from doing so. Still, something had to be done to get rid of Regnald, especially as he had the tacit, though not the active, support of Rollo, who had definitely refused to have anything to do with the conspirators and remained faithful to Charles the Simple. Robert, therefore, chose the easy way of giving the invaders something that did not belong to him—he granted to Regnald and his Vikings Brittany, Nantes and the Marshlands.

Hitherto luck had favoured Charles the Simple, but unfortunately for him an adroit move of the army commanded by Hugh of Paris, afterwards known as Hugh the Great, cut his communication with Rollo. Charles the Simple, threatened by Hugh's army on the one side and by the Burgundians on the other, had to do the best he could by himself. Moreover, Herbert of Vermandois, one of the conspirators, who had hitherto pretended to be on Charles's side, now joined the rebels openly. The King was defeated at Rheims and by a *coup de main* the Duke of Paris seized Lâon and with it King Charles's treasure.

The conspirators now proceeded to follow up the "diffidation", and proclaimed the Duke of Paris king. Things looked very bad for Charles the Simple, but he faced the situation with courage and Rollo came to his aid. In 923 Rollo was ready with an army to assist the King and he was supported by Regnald's army as well. The conspirators met Charles the Simple's forces at Soissons and defeated them; but Charles's luck still held, for the Duke of Paris was killed in the fighting.

A new king had to be chosen, and this took time. Hugh of Paris refused, and eventually the Crown was offered to Raoul of Burgundy, who accepted. For the moment the contest languished. Then Herbert of Vermandois changed sides again and declared in favour of Charles the Simple; but it was only a ruse; Herbert invited Charles to meet him, seized him and imprisoned him.

The war now became a contest between the Normans under Rollo and Regnald and the Franks under King Raoul. It was the old story over again. The Northmen advanced into the enemy's country, burning, wasting and ravaging. Raoul had got what he wanted, and now tried to obtain peace. The irrepressible Regnald had penetrated Burgundy, and this was very much to the distaste of Raoul. The latter's first move was to buy off Rollo. Raoul had to accede to all his terms with the enemy, Regnald, at the gate. Rollo's terms were heavy. The Bessin was to be ceded to Normandy and a large indemnity in the shape of Danegeld paid.

But the luck turned before the money was paid, for Regnald was defeated and killed by Raoul. As the indemnity was not forthcoming, Rollo renewed the war, he took Amiens, ravaged the Artois and invaded Flanders; but he suffered a severe blow in the fall of Eu, and it looked as though the tide had turned against him. But fortune served him at the end. News came that an invading army of Magyars had crossed the Rhine and were about to attack Burgundy. Raoul at once gave way; the money was paid, the cession of the Bessin ratified, and peace proclaimed between France and Normandy. So Rollo won a complete triumph. But he was getting very old and failing—he must have been at least eighty years of age—and it was time that a younger man should assume responsibility.

Rollo at the request of his councillors (again we find the procedure of the Thing) nominated his son by Popa, William Longsword, as his successor at the close of the year 925. From this time we hear no more of Rollo; he had definitely gone into retirement. It is believed that he lived another five years or so, but in 927 William Longsword did homage for Normandy.

So the founder of the Duchy of Normandy died and was buried in the sacristy of Notre-Dame at Rouen. When, in the days of Archbishop Maurilius, the cathedral was restored, his coffin was moved to the Chapel of Saint Romanus, where he remains undisturbed to this day. A recumbent statue lies above the tomb, dating perhaps from the time of St. Louis.

CHAPTER V

WILLIAM LONGSWORD—PART I

France at Rollo's death—Feudalism, its virtues and defects—William Longsword's birth and
education—His French tastes—Botho and Bernard the Dane—William follows his
father's foreign policy—Herbert of Vermandois seizes Rheims—Charles the Simple
nominally restored—Herbert of Vermandois brings Charles to Normandy—Herbert's
bad faith—Charles the Simple murdered—Breton war—Annexation of Avranchin,
Cotentin and Channel Islands to Normandy—Sprota—Riulph's rebellion—Birth of
Richard the Fearless—William does homage to King Raoul—He marries Liutgarda de
Vermandois.

WILLIAM LONGSWORD's position was not affected by his father's death,
since the latter had abdicated some years before. Before, however,
dealing at length with his reign it may not be inappropriate to examine
the condition of affairs in Western Europe as they were at Rollo's death.
They differed very widely from those that Rollo found nearly fifty years
before when he sailed up the Seine to seek his fortune. Then Charlemagne's inheritance was being torn to pieces by his greedy and in-
competent descendants. Like vultures round a carcase they tore and
wrenched at the unfortunate Empire and pecked and scratched at each
other in the process. Occasionally barbarians—Northmen, Saracens or
Magyars—rushed in like hyenas and carried off a few bones. The end
of this disgraceful and deplorable state of affairs was very nearly complete
chaos, and Europe was only saved by one thing, the development of the
feudal system.

It is true that feudalism was not unknown in the days of Charlemagne;
the idea was there, but it was in embryo. With the disruption of the
Empire it was every man for himself; and the lesser rulers, the Dukes and
the Counts and the Barons, developed unexpected powers of resistance
to the dangers wrought by disruption. The Kings had failed to maintain
internal order or to defend the realm from external enemies; the Dukes
and Counts succeeded in driving back the enemy from without, but
before long the feudal system brought with it worse disasters perhaps than
it had avoided, and after the fall of the Carolingians and the division
of the realm of Charlemagne Europe became wholly decentralized and
its history nothing but a tedious record of petty wars and disreputable
local squabbles.

The success of the feudal system was largely due to the development
of military science during the later 9th and early 10th centuries. The

armies of Charlemagne and his successors in the Empire consisted mainly of large bodies of slow-moving, heavily armed infantry. The barbarians, whose object was not conquest but loot, easily evaded them. When, however, the land became split up into small states, each petty potentate built his stronghold. Castle-building developed. Stone fortresses had been hitherto but rarely constructed. Now not only the Duke and the Count but their Barons and vassals built their castles, so that all over the country there arose a chain of fortified bases whence small armed forces could descend upon an invader.

The development of cavalry helped the defence. Heavily armed cavalry soldiers were like the feudal castles. Their defences were too strong for the light-armed invader to harm and, being mounted men, they had the speed of him. The growth of feudalism provided an efficient and effective military police, but from the political point of view it was an unmixed disaster. Bitter feuds, petty jealousies, narrow particularism and complete degradation of the lower classes were the later results, but these were perhaps a lesser evil than the one that feudalism kept at bay.

The lesson that was learnt from the Carolingian quarrel was the chaos which the division of the realm among a King's sons must bring about. Men saw that at any rate this must be abolished and the system of primogeniture soon took root in the small states that grew up during the period. The hereditary states were of French recent establishment. Flanders dates from 862, Poitou from 867, Burgundy from 877, Auvergne from 886, Gascony from 872, Anjou from 870, and Paris, which developed out of the Marquisate of Neustria, from 866.

William Longsword was born probably at Rouen; the story of his birth overseas which is mentioned in the Clermont MSS. is discounted by Lair. He was carefully educated. It is a marked feature in the family of Rollo that particular care was given to the education of its members, and the founder of the family paid no less attention to this matter than did his descendants.

Our account of William Longsword's youth and, indeed, of the whole of his reign is largely derived from Dudo, though it is possible to check Dudo's account to a certain extent from the French Chronicles. One may rely, however, more on Dudo's story for essential truth, seeing that he must have received a great deal of his information from Duke Richard I and more still from his brother, Raoul d'Ivri: Dudo lived close to the times and was too intimately acquainted with eye-witnesses to fall into serious error and inaccuracy from ignorance. If he was inaccurate he was so deliberately and for propaganda purposes.

According to Dudo, as one might naturally expect, William had every virtue both mental and physical; in fact, he was the Prince Charming of his age, but whether even Dudo's account of his subsequent history bears this out we shall see. Stress is laid upon his French tastes, his friendship with the De Senlis family, and his preference for the Christian and Gallicized Normans. But in spite of all this, and in spite of his French mother, William was educated under the supervision of the Viking Botho. He seems to have been much with his father, who certainly spoke no language but Norse; and in later life his Chief Councillor was another Viking, Bernard the Dane. This man, though a Dane, not a Norseman, was trusted by Rollo and had become a Christian. But, in spite of this latter fact, Bernard regarded Scandinavia as his home and so spoke of it, and although a Christian he was on the best of terms with his heathen compatriots.

After his accession William for some time avoided becoming embroiled in the quarrels of his neighbours. He adhered to his father's foreign policy and insisted upon his allegiance to Charles the Simple. That unfortunate individual was in the clutches of Count Herbert of Vermandois. The latter was a Carolingian himself; he was the descendant of Bernard, King of Italy, who was dethroned by Louis the Pious in 817. The county of Vermandois could not be considered of equal importance to the other great Northern fiefs, Paris, Flanders or Burgundy, for instance; but Herbert of Vermandois was consumed with ambition for aggrandizement. His descent may have given him secret hopes of an eventual succession to the crown, though in regard to this the Chronicles are silent; but there is no doubt that he was deeply jealous of the other parties to the conspiracy, his father-in-law, Robert of Paris, and his brother-in-law, Raoul of Burgundy, who had been chosen to be King when Charles the Simple was dethroned.

Herbert of Vermandois' first encroachment was upon the property of the Church. According to Frodoard, Count Herbert caused Seulph, Archbishop of Rheims, to be poisoned. He had a good deal of influence at Rheims and on the death of the Archbishop immediately betook himself thither. Raoul of Burgundy could not afford to quarrel with his brother-in-law, who held Charles the Simple in prison and was prepared to produce him as a rival. Herbert's first step was to procure the election of his son, Hugh, then aged five (!), to be Archbishop. This was followed by a grant of the temporalities of the See to Herbert to administer until his son came of age, and, at the same time, as compensation for his trouble, the Count of Vermandois appropriated the Barony of Coucy for himself. The account of these iniquitous transactions is given in detail by Frodoard, who was a Canon of Rheims at the time and imprisoned for not assisting Herbert in his machinations.

The Count's next attempt was upon Lâon, the capital of the King. It will be remembered that this important position had been captured from Charles the Simple in 922 and it was now in the possession of King Raoul. Necessary though it was for Raoul to keep on good terms with Herbert of Vermandois, he would not concede this new demand. Herbert then

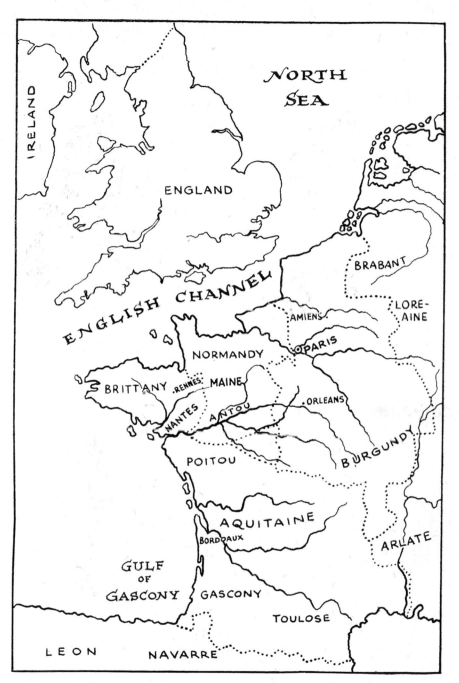

Sketch Map of Normandy, 11th century.

Edward the Confessor's First Seal and Counterpart.

Second Seal and Counterpart.
(From Wyon's *Great Seals of England*.)

tried force and attempted to take Lâon by surprise, but in this he failed. So now he played his trump card. He wrote to the Pope, John X, asking him to excommunicate the ruffians who had deposed their lawful sovereign. He solicited and obtained the support of Henry the Fowler, who had no liking for new and upstart kings such as Raoul. All that remained was to gain the support of William Longsword, and this did not seem to be difficult since both he and his father had always remained true to Charles the Simple and had refused to have anything to do with Raoul.

But William Longsword did not prove so easy to deal with. When the Danegeld due to Rollo under the 923 agreement was not paid, important hostages were required by the Norman Government. One of these was Count Herbert's son Odo, whom his father wished to make Count of Lâon. So William held a strong card.

Herbert now produced Charles and proclaimed his restoration publicly at St. Quentin. Raoul's difficulties had still further increased. A Saracen army was reported from the Alps advancing towards Burgundy. Raoul had to go hastily homewards to defend his own territory, leaving his wife, Emma, in command at Lâon. The whole country was in a panic at the news of a possible Saracen invasion, but William Longsword did not allow himself to be disturbed. He made no haste to come to terms with Vermandois. The latter enlisted the services of William's uncle, Bernard de Senlis, who was a kinsman of the Vermandois' family, to influence him. Perhaps he promised him the Seigneurie of Coucy, recently stolen from the See of Rheims, as an inducement, for it was conferred on him some years later.

William Longsword consented to meet Herbert, but forced him to come to Normandy and to bring Charles the Simple with him. They all three met at Eu, where William did solemn homage to Charles for his lands. But he would not release Odo de Vermandois unless his father, Herbert, and other men of his father's would also do homage to Charles. So a deadlock threatened to supervene. The danger in the South was serious. If Burgundy were overrun by the Saracens, Paris might come next. Normandy and Vermandois, being further situated from the Saracen menace, were unmoved; but it was imperative to the two Southern powers, Paris and Burgundy, that the quarrel should be settled. Hugh of Paris offered to mediate. He persuaded Raoul to surrender Lâon to Count Herbert, and the latter and his allies complied with William's demand and did homage to Charles the Simple.

Vermandois had now acquired Lâon, and the price he paid must have seemed to him trifling. It is extraordinary to see all through medieval history the value which people seemed to attach to oaths or promises. Never were the most solemn engagements regarded as binding. No one had the slightest compunction in throwing them over at the first

moment that it suited his convenience. In fact, a medieval prince
bound by every tie of honour thought far less of disregarding his obligations than a modern politician thinks of crossing the floor of the House of
Commons. William Longsword, who seems to have placed such faith in
Herbert of Vermandois' bond, was himself, perhaps, in later years the
most ready and frequent to disregard his obligations and to change sides.

Taking Charles with him, Herbert met Raoul at Rheims. There the
brothers-in-law no doubt concluded a bargain, and the unfortunate
Charles was hurried back to prison. He died a year later, starved to death,
it is said, in a dungeon at Peronne.

Hitherto William Longsword's reign had been untroubled by external
war, but in 930 trouble broke out in Brittany. The Bretons had always
resisted the shadowy claim to supremacy of the Normans, and they would
have paid even less attention to their pretensions had it not been for the
threat to their frontiers offered by the Loire Northmen with whom both
Rollo and William Longsword had always been careful to cultivate friendly
relations.

In 930, however, probably learning that the Saracens' threat on the
South-East frontier had drawn away the forces of Burgundy and Paris,
the Northmen of the Loire started a marauding expedition on their own
account and proceeded to ravage the surrounding country. For once
Raoul acted resolutely. He had a considerable number of men under
arms, crossed France from Burgundy by forced marches, and inflicted a
severe and crushing defeat on the Northmen at Limoges.

The Breton Counts now repudiated Norman supremacy. William
acted without delay. Though the Loire Normans had been recently so
severely defeated at Limoges they were numerous and powerful in
Brittany. They joined William's army and overran the whole country,
scattering the unfortunate Bretons like sheep. William returned rather
too quickly to Normandy, for the Bretons soon rallied and took the
offensive, threatening Bayeux. William, however, drove them back, and
this time ravaged Brittany from end to end, completely subduing the
whole country.

Juhel Beranger, Count of Rennes, made haste to submit and William
wisely forgave him. He did homage and acknowledged the Norman
supremacy in every detail. William confirmed him in his county of
Rennes, but he would have nothing to do with the other Breton leader,
Alan Barbe Torte, who was forced to cross the sea and take refuge in
England with King Athelstane.

William Longsword acquired considerable reputation in these two
campaigns. He annexed the Cotentin, the Channel Islands and the
Avranchin, fixing the Norman-Breton frontier along the river Coesnon.
In this newly annexed territory he conferred a Countship upon one
Riulph, who shortly afterwards showed his gratitude by revolting against

his Sovereign. Not only did William gain reputation and territory in these campaigns, but he won a lady as well. Sprota, a Breton girl, attracted his attention. He fell in love with her. Reckless in some things, William was careful in his relations with women. Although he had the reputation of being exceedingly devout, his caution was greater than his Christianity. He did not marry Sprota in orthodox fashion, but, like his father, contracted with her a Danish marriage. In plain words, Sprota became his mistress.

William now settled down at Fécamp. The ancient monastery there had been completely destroyed by the Vikings, and while building his new house William discovered its remains. He restored the chapel, and later his successors added to it and built the celebrated Abbey of Fécamp.

William settled at Fécamp in 933, and no doubt hoped for a peaceful life, but he was not destined to enjoy it. He had always shown his predilection for the French, his mother's people, and he seemed to wish to be considered a Frenchman. There were two parties among the Normans, the Gallicized and Christian Normans who spoke French and who dwelt in the neighbourhood of Rouen, and the heathen Normans whose headquarters lay at Bayeux. Bayeux, therefore, was the centre of the Norse-speaking population. Possibly this was due to the fact that from ancient times a Saxon colony had existed at Bayeux, the Saxon tongue prevailed there, and the immigrant Norwegians and Danes gravitated naturally to the place where their language was understood.

So two rival parties grew up in the Northern State, the Christian French and the heathen Norsemen. William Longsword with his French sympathies favoured the former, and so incurred the enmity of the latter. Probably William was right. The Normans had settled in France, they had left Scandinavia for ever, and it was to their interest to amalgamate with the citizens of their new country. The French had no cause to love the Northmen, and for the latter to maintain themselves as a kind of *imperium in imperio* in France was not a wise proceeding. The malcontents found a leader in Count Riulph, who had recently distinguished himself in the Breton War. It is not clear exactly whence this Riulph came. One would have imagined that he was one of the heathen Normans, but he was the uncle of the Fleming Balzo, Bauce or Baldwin, as he is variously called, who, as is proved by a royal Charter, was connected by blood both with the family of Charles the Simple and with Arnulf of Flanders whose Chamberlain he was. In view of Balzo's subsequent connection with the murder of William Longsword this relationship to him of Riulph is of importance.

Riulph's object seems to have been personal ambition. He tried to separate the Norse-speaking from the French-speaking Normans, and probably if he had won the victory he would have tried to set up an independent heathen Norman state. His proposals were impudent. He asked for the whole of Normandy westward of the river Risle (two-thirds of the whole country)! If William would agree to this, Riulph would render him feudal service; if he refused, he would throw off his allegiance altogether. William Longsword was a curious mixture in character. He had plenty of physical courage, but at times he seemed to be smitten with utterly craven panic and to lose his head completely. He did so now. Riulph and his army were a long way off yet. Rouen was well fortified. William's troops were numerous and loyal. He was supported by Bernard the Dane, by Botho, and by another Viking follower of Rollo named Oslac, but he thought of nothing but flight. At first he tried to buy off the rebels—the old expedient of Danegeld—but this offer was refused. Still William did nothing to stop Riulph's advance, but remained panic-stricken behind the walls of Rouen. Sprota, who was shortly expecting the arrival of an infant, was very properly sent to Fécamp, out of danger for the present.

Riulph marched on unhindered, and soon appeared before Rouen. William became incoherent. He offered them all they asked for and more. He would evacuate Rouen. He would abandon Normandy altogether and run away to take refuge with his uncle, Bernard de Senlis.

Bernard the Dane, Botho and Oslac were aghast and disgusted at this exhibition. Bernard told him plainly and frankly that he and his friends would see him across the Epte out of Normandy, and then they would pack up their belongings, return to Scandinavia and shake the dust of Normandy from their feet for ever. Botho added his reproaches to those of Bernard and Oslac, and their sarcasm had its effect. William became ashamed, pulled himself together and showed as much courage as he had hitherto shown cowardice. He took over the command, led the troops himself and without any great difficulty completely routed the enemy. Riulph was captured and put to death in good old Viking fashion; but his son, Anketil, escaped.

Just after the victory news came from Fécamp of the birth of a son to Sprota. He was named Richard, and he became in the future Richard I—known as Richard the Fearless. He was the first recognized Duke of Normandy, for William Longsword, like Rollo, still only bore the title of Patrician.

The defeat of the heathen party among the Normans encouraged William in his French proclivities. Charles the Simple was dead and Raoul of Burgundy had no rival as King of France. Moreover, Hugh the Great, of Paris, was an inconvenient neighbour. He might cast envious eyes on the Norman territory, and if William remained estranged from the King the latter might not be very ready to help him. It had been Rollo's sound foreign policy to be on terms with the King. William had followed that policy and had remained true to Charles the Simple. But Charles the Simple was now dead and buried and Raoul was undisputed

King. The same sound policy induced William to come to terms with him. He offered Raoul his homage, and Raoul gladly accepted it, and in return recognized all William's recent conquests and annexations.

William Longsword was now at the zenith of his popularity—at least, with his Christian subjects. He was able to turn his attention to internal affairs. Rollo has been reproached for having been niggardly in his support of the Church. This appears to be an unjust accusation. He seems to have been as well aware as anyone of the need of encouraging the Church as the only civilizing influence of the day. He made considerable grants of land to ecclesiastical foundations; but he had scarcely time to found abbeys and monasteries and erect huge buildings. William in more settled days was able to do so. He had already laid the foundation of an abbey at Fécamp; now he did the same at Mortemer. His vanity must have been much tickled at this time by a visit he received from Hugh the Great, of Paris, and Herbert of Vermandois. Moreover, Ebles, Count of Poitou, asked for the hand of his sister, Gerloc, Popa's only other child. William's vanity thus received a further fillip, for although some might still sneer at him as the *Dux Piratarum* he was connected now with two of the great French Houses, Vermandois and Poitou.

Since a further opportunity of aggrandizing himself had come forward, Herbert of Vermandois, always scheming for his own advantage, saw that a closer alliance with the powerful Norman sovereign must redound to his advantage, and proposed a marriage between William and his daughter, Liutgarda. As a Danish marriage was no marriage at all from the legal point of view, Sprota was no difficulty, and she was conveniently relegated to the background; but it seems that William, in spite of his new marriage, continued to live with her as his mistress until his death. These complications do not appear to have increased William's domestic happiness, however greatly his marriage may have ministered to his vanity. Richard, Sprota's son, by the custom of the Normans was still recognized as William's heir, for Liutgarda had no child. Naturally, the wife hated the mistress and even more the bastard brat to whom the succession would go if she continued to be barren. So William had to hide his son away.

In providing for the child he showed the forethought that was a characteristic in his family in seeing that he was thoroughly well educated. He sent him to Bayeux under the care of his own old tutor, Botho, with injunctions that the boy was to be well instructed in the Norse language. The consequence was that Richard grew up bilingual and, in after life, showed a marked taste for forgathering with his less polished heathen or moderately Christian subjects. This circumstance had no inconsiderable effect in uniting the two parties in Normandy in later years.

CHAPTER VI

WILLIAM LONGSWORD—PART II

Restoration of Louis d'Outremer under guardianship of Hugh of Paris—William's Foreign Policy—Otto of Germany—King Louis—Founding of Jumièges—Settlement of Danes in the Cotentin—Sweyn Forkbeard—William seeks to abdicate—Council of Attigny— Arnulf of Flanders—Murder of William—Burial at Rouen—Death of Herbert of Vermandois.

DURING the few years of peace and quiet, William's power and popularity grew rapidly. He was a capable administrator, and as he had no rivals his position grew strong. He was accepted by his subjects as an autocrat, the supreme authority both in Church and State. So long as he governed well his most influential subjects, like Bernard the Dane, had no desire to interfere with him, ready enough as they had been to do so when he showed signs of backsliding.

The best trait in William's somewhat complex character was his love of justice and, as ruler of Normandy, so far as lay in his power, he saw that justice between man and man was done. He was not cruel, though he did Viking's justice on the rebel Riulph; and posterity, overlooking his many faults, has praised him as the just and merciful sovereign who deserved well of his people.

But trouble was again brewing abroad. Raoul died in January 936. The question of the kingship rose afresh. Little as the great feudatories respected their King they seemed all of one accord in thinking that they could not do without one. None of them wished to see a colleague elevated to the throne, so their minds, not unnaturally, turned towards the heir of Charles the Simple.

Charles had married Eadgifu, or Ogiva, a daughter of Edward the Elder and niece of Aethelflaeda, Lady of the Mercians. There was one son, Louis (d'Outremer). When Charles the Simple was dethroned, Ogiva and her son were allowed to take refuge in England with her brother Athelstane, and young Louis was brought up at his uncle's Court till he was about fifteen years of age.

Dudo tells us that William Longsword took the lead in the negotiations with Athelstane which led to the restoration of the Carolingian line. He did nothing of the sort. In the first place, William was not particularly interested as to who might be selected as King. He was sufficiently powerful to be able to regard this matter with comparative indifference.

Secondly, he possessed little, if any, influence with Athelstane. The Normans were unpopular in England. They were regarded as pirates across the Channel, just as they were in France. But there seems no doubt that William gave his support to Louis' candidature and informed Athelstane accordingly. A conference was held at Sens, and it was decided by general agreement to invite Louis to return. It was Hugh of Paris, and not William, who took the leading part in the negotiations. Athelstane made stipulations for his nephew's safety, but eventually agreement was reached and Louis arrived in France in June 936 and was duly crowned at Lâon.

Coincident with the restoration of Louis another refugee at Athelstane's Court was allowed to return. It will be remembered that after the second campaign of Brittany, William pardoned Juhel Beranger, but refused to come to terms with Alan Barbe Torte, who fled to England. Athelstane now entered into negotiations with William Longsword and obtained his agreement to Alan's return, on condition that the last-named did homage for Vannes. Alan, supported by an English fleet, landed at Dol, raised Brittany, drove out the pagan Danes and Normans, seized, rebuilt and fortified Nantes, and established himself in that city as his headquarters. William must have been privy to this since he did nothing to interfere with it, and Alan later became one of his supporters.

As soon as Louis d'Outremer had been crowned, the great feudatories began to intrigue against him. Although Louis was more than fifteen years old and, therefore, of legal age according to Carolingian rule, Hugh of Paris claimed the right of guardianship over him. Louis, however, objected to this and proceeded to assert himself. After waiting for a year he quietly, in 937, declared the protectorate of Hugh of Paris at an end. Hugh appealed to Herbert of Vermandois, who joined him against the King. But what was much more astonishing was that William Longsword, apparently for no rhyme or reason, declared against King Louis.

Hitherto William's foreign policy had been that of his father. He had adhered to the *de jure* King, first to Charles the Simple so long as he lived and even after he had ceased to reign; then to King Raoul when Raoul became undisputedly King; and after Raoul's death he had been one of those to support the recall of Louis and to do him homage. For the rest he had kept himself aloof from the squabbles and conspiracies of the others.

From 937 onwards till his death in 943, William was continually changing sides; apparently without cause, unless, indeed, the following circumstances may have, on occasion, influenced him.

Arnulf, Count of Flanders, and William Longsword were brothers-in-law; both had married daughters of Herbert of Vermandois. For some reason or another—perhaps because Balzo, the nephew of the rebel Riulph, had been favoured by Arnulf, but probably for other causes also

—Arnulf of Flanders and William Longsword hated one another. Arnulf at present was the only one of the Northern French feudatory powers who remained loyal to King Louis. To find a pretext for attacking Arnulf may have been William's reason for deserting the King. He invaded Flanders and laid waste the country from the sea to St. Omer and Therouanne with all the thoroughness of his Viking ancestors. His ravages were so terrible that he was excommunicated, but in spite of this, spurred on by his hatred of Arnulf, he renewed his work of destruction.

Besides the personal element, political considerations were involved. Between Normandy and Flanders lay the small county of Ponthieu, which contained the important and prosperous city of Montreuil. Both Flanders and Normandy had their eyes on Ponthieu. In 938 the Seigneur of Ponthieu was Herlwin of Montreuil, who was the vassal of Hugh of Paris. Arnulf, regarding Herlwin as an enemy, attacked and seized Montreuil, but William Longsword recaptured it and reinstated Herlwin on terms. This gave Normandy the important fortress of Montreuil, together with the command of the Channel ports—a matter of great importance and detriment to Flanders.

But events in Germany now had their repercussion on the situation. Henry the Fowler died in 936 and Otto, his son, succeeded him. As usual among the Franks, there were disputes as to the succession, and it took Otto some time before he had made good his claims over those of his brother.

It will be remembered that Charles the Simple had received the allegiance of Rainier, Count of Hainault, and with him that of the nobles of Lotharingia, making that domain an appanage of the Western Kingdom. On the fall of Charles the Simple, Henry the Fowler reasserted his authority over Lotharingia. The people of that country, always more attached to the West than to the East, took advantage of the confusion in Germany consequent upon the death of Henry the Fowler to make overtures to King Louis. Naturally, the latter accepted their offers with sincere gratitude and the four principal magnates of Lotharingia did homage to him. The result was the speedy arrival of Otto across the Rhine. He was met by Hugh of Paris, Herbert of Vermandois, William Longsword and Arnulf of Flanders, who had changed sides and joined the rebels. They all four did homage to Otto. The defection of these powers to Otto might have been of the greatest importance. Technically, the whole of Flanders and Northern France from the Rhine to the Atlantic had passed from the Western to the Eastern King. Otto seemed about to re-establish the Empire of Charlemagne; it proved, however, to be no more than a paper transaction.

William Longsword began to have qualms: what exactly they were can only be conjectured. It has been suggested that he thought that the transference of his allegiance from Louis to Otto might vitiate his title to Normandy. In a state of affairs where force reigned as supreme, as it did in those days, the question of law hardly came into account. It seems more likely that William felt that he could not remain in the same camp as Arnulf of Flanders. So he changed sides again and returned to his allegiance to Louis. Hardly, however, had he left Lâon, where he had been entertained by the King, whom he overwhelmed with professions of loyalty, than he entered into negotiations with his father-in-law, Herbert of Vermandois, and joined with him and Hugh of Paris in a successful attack on Rheims. Thence they went to Lâon, where, however, they failed. Queen Gerberge was in command of Lâon. She was well supplied with troops and supplies and held out easily against a lengthy siege.

Otto now came to the help of the rebels and a meeting was held at Attigny. The leaders were there and an important conference took place. But William Longsword was conspicuous by his absence. He was fading away again. Little as the value of William's promises had proved in the past, King Louis had to make the best of circumstances. The adhesion, even the neutrality of Normandy, was of great importance to him. The King's cause was looking up. Lâon had successfully resisted attack. Queen Gerberge had given birth to a son. Louis' blandishments had their effect on William, for the latter changed sides again. Louis did his best to retain his precarious friendship. He loaded him with flattery and invited him to be godfather to his infant son, Lothaire. Shortly after the christening ceremony, King Louis visited William Longsword at Rouen. Considering that he was dealing with so unstable a person, it was a plucky thing to do. But the visit was a success. William was always proud of his hospitality, and he was anxious to show himself off to the best advantage. He received Louis as his sovereign. He entertained him magnificently, and invited his brother-in-law, Gerloc's husband, the Count of Poitou, and his old enemy and new friend, Alan of Brittany, to meet the King.

For a year or more (941–942) William remained in his own realm, and it was during this interval that he founded the Abbey of Jumièges, perhaps his best title to fame. He made a good selection for his first Abbot. He owed the choice to his sister, Gerloc, or Adela, as she had been renamed since her marriage. Gerloc chose Martin, a monk of the Monastery of St. Cyprian's at Poitiers. Martin was a learned man for his age—he even knew some Greek. Accompanied by twelve monks, also of St. Cyprian's, Martin arrived at Jumièges and took over William's foundation.

It would be wearisome to record, and tedious to read, the tale of William Longsword's numerous vacillations and tergiversations. Not that he was alone in his treacheries, for to turn the coat was common to all in those days. Hugh of Paris changed sides for one end, to further his own clearly defined aim of aggrandizing the Duchy of France; Herbert of Vermandois doubtless loved lying and treachery for their own sake, but at least there was method in his madness. He did not turn his coat unless there was something to be got by it. William Longsword, on the other hand, seems to have turned his coat simply for the pleasure of doing so. One searches in vain for an adequate motive. Hatred of Arnulf of Flanders may have influenced him on some occasions; a desire to occupy Montreuil on another; a doubt as to the legality of his position on a third—but none of these reasons is a really satisfactory explanation of his conduct.

One cannot help feeling that one must attribute his actions to a fundamental defect of character or even to want of mental balance. For it was not only in his diplomacy that he was vacillating, treacherous and unstable. He was subject to sudden craven panic, as on the occasion of Riulph's rebellion, and of as sudden change to the contrary, as happened on the same occasion. One wonders perhaps why Bernard the Dane and his other advisers did not interfere when he changed sides, as they did when he ran away from Riulph. Perhaps they did not think it worth while. In their hearts they knew that the French regarded them as sea vermin, and they had no more flattering opinion of the French. Fighting was the proper occupation for a gentleman, and so long as William did no harm to himself or his interests the old Vikings cared nothing as to which party he fought for or against.

Now to his change of front in war and diplomacy we come to his change of front in internal politics. William, as we have seen, had hitherto been anxious to identify himself with the French and with the Gallicized Normans of Rouen. He inclined to his French cousins of Senlis; he was proud to ally himself and his family with Vermandois and Poitiers. Suddenly he changed. Perhaps he realized that for all his lavish hospitality, his good manners and French speech, he was still only regarded as a pirate captain. His wife, the Vermandois princess, may have told him some home truths. He must have realized that his tergiversations had made him distrusted and disliked. He made a complete *volte face* in Normandy. He threw over the French party there and turned to the Scandinavians, but they received him coldly. He had ignored and humiliated the Danes of Bayeux, and the Bessin, but now he turned to them. The Cotentin, his latest conquest, was desolate and depopulated by years of raids and warfare. So he turned to Denmark for settlers.

Harold Bluetooth was King of Denmark. In 936 he had succeeded to the throne vacant by the death of Gorm the Old, who had reigned for eighty-one years. Harold had ambitions for extending his dominions. William invited him to Normandy. According to Dudo and William of Jumièges, Harold, driven from Denmark by the rebellion of his son, Sweyn Forkbeard, arrived at Cherbourg with sixty ships, landed there and took possession of the country. This account is certainly incorrect. Sweyn Forkbeard's rebellion did not take place till many years later. Whether Harold himself on this occasion came to Normandy is doubtful. Sir F. Palgrave accepts the story and, indeed, one must give some credence to it, for Dudo certainly received it either from Richard I or from his brother, Raoul d'Ivri. Richard was a boy of eight at the time, and actually being educated at Bayeux; so he must have remembered the incident; moreover, a few years later Harold Bluetooth in all probability did come to Normandy and met Richard.

Dudo's first acquaintance with Richard was in 960—not more than forty years after Harold's supposed visit to Cherbourg—so there must have been people at Rouen who could have given Dudo accurate information. That he should have been ignorant of Danish history and have ante-dated Sweyn Forkbeard's rebellion is quite understandable; but that he should have said that Harold Bluetooth came to Normandy in 941 when he did not do so is perhaps less so. But Harold may not have come to Normandy on this occasion. There may have been another of the same name who led the expedition, and Dudo with his usual inaccuracy perhaps jumped to the conclusion that this was Harold Bluetooth. Dudo says that Harold settled in the Cotentin; this is certainly untrue, as Danish records can prove. If he did come at all, it was on a short visit only, and he soon returned home. But, whether Harold came with them or not, a number of heathen Danes arrived and settled down. Worse still, they were followed by others until the whole peninsula was peopled by them.

William Longsword's action was bitterly condemned, and he became frightened at what he had done. He decided to abdicate and become a Monk of Jumièges, but Martin, the newly installed Abbot, flatly refused to receive him. He told William plainly that for him to abandon his task of ruling Normandy in order to retire into a monastery would be a wicked desertion of the duty imposed upon him by Heaven, and if he should persist in his design and force himself upon Jumièges he (the Abbot) would resign his charge and leave the country. William swore he would not abandon his design and would abdicate in favour of Richard. Martin was quite obdurate and eventually succeeded in calming him. As a sop to quiet him he gave him the habit of a monk, which William locked up in a box and kept in his bedroom, calling it his most precious treasure.

Clearly William was losing mental stability and he fell seriously ill on his return to Rouen. Bad news and fear of death seem to have steadied and put some sense into him. He sent for Bernard the Dane and Botho, and they, and five others whose names are not mentioned, were made a Council of Regency and guardians of young Richard in the event of his father's death. A solemn ceremony was held at Bayeux and the seven councillors took an oath of allegiance to Richard. In addition, a general assembly reminiscent of a Scandinavian Thing was called, and universal adhesion to the scheme was obtained. This took place on May 29, 942.

Meanwhile, events were moving outside Normandy. Negotiations had taken place between Louis and Otto for some kind of arrangement. The records are hazy and scanty. It is said that William approached Otto on Louis' behalf to arrange a meeting. A meeting, in fact, took place on the banks of the Oise in September, 942. King Louis, accompanied by William Longsword as his principal supporter, together with the Count of Poitou and Alan of Brittany, took up his position on the southern bank of the river. King Otto, Herbert of Vermandois, Hugh, Duke of Paris, and the Duke of Lorraine, ranged themselves on the other side. A general truce was agreed upon and the two Kings, who were brothers-in-law, shook hands.

Peace having been made, it was arranged that a council should be held at Attigny. To this council the two Kings, now apparently the best of friends, came. Hugh of Paris, Arnulf of Flanders, Herbert de Vermandois and William Longsword were all summoned. Either some mistake occurred or William thought he was intentionally insulted, for the others all arrived before him and the council began without him. When he actually did arrive he seems to have behaved himself as intemperately as one might expect from one of ill-balanced mind. He broke into a towering rage and insulted and abused both Kings and Princes. What followed is not clear, but one must assume that William's behaviour on the top of all his other shortcomings sealed his fate.

It is said that Otto, whose German methods were more forcible than those to which the rest were accustomed, wanted to hang him immediately. Arnulf of Flanders, however, offered a better plan for which he was prepared to undertake the responsibility. Hugh of Paris and King Louis, though they afterwards indignantly denied it, were almost certainly in the plot, though Dudo, supported by Richer, attributes it to Hugh of Paris and Arnulf of Flanders alone. Further, it is stated that it was an act of private vengeance of Balzo, the nephew, and Anketyl, the son of that Count Riulph whom William had put to death at the time of the rebellion of 931. Doubtless this may have helped the conspirators, for desire for vengeance on the part of fanatical enemies is always useful in the technique of political murder. We have seen it in such occurrences today, a thousand years afterwards.

But the true reason is obvious: William Longsword had made himself impossible to deal with: he was a pagan, a barbarian, a Viking, and an importer of pagans, barbarians and Vikings. The chance had come—*"Delenda est Normannia"*.

With William out of the way there remained only a bastard of ten years old, and such an one was scarcely likely to hold Normandy together.

This is not told us in any of the annals, but the actions of the conspirators immediately afterwards leave no doubt in our minds. But they reckoned without Bernard the Dane.

As an outcome of the general scheme of pacification Arnulf sent an invitation to William to meet him on the Somme on the Island of Picquigny. William's advisers, especially Herlwin of Montreuil, suspected a trap and counselled him not to go. William persisted, however, and he took every precaution against treachery. A considerable force under Alan of Brittany, now in high favour, guarded William and encamped on the banks of the river. The latter was accompanied to the island by twelve fully armed men. But Arnulf of Flanders was advised by Theobald of Blois—Tricky Theobald, as he was nicknamed. This individual had an unenviable reputation and seems to have been called in when any particularly unpleasant piece of rascality was attempted. Tricky Theobald, it is interesting to note, married Liutgarda, William Longsword's widow, not long after his death.

Theobald was certainly a competent assassin. While William was attended by twelve heavily armed men, Arnulf arrived wrapped up in furs, quite unarmed and, because he pretended to be suffering from gout, was supported by four servants also apparently unarmed. Arnulf and William sat down and began to discuss business. Arnulf told him a long tale of woe. He feared King Louis; he wanted to ally himself to William; he would do homage to William for Flanders, and after his death Flanders should pass to Normandy. William swallowed it all. The date was December 17 and Arnulf's story took a long time to tell. It was dusk before he had done. Then, well satisfied with one another, they prepared to go home. William's men embarked on a barge; a small boat with three men to row it remained for William himself. The barge started and William's boat was following, when Arnulf called to him that there was something he had forgotten to say. William paused: the four men who posed as Arnulf's servants then drew daggers from under their clothes and stabbed him. Their leader was Balzo.

The Normans could do nothing. By the time the guard got back, Arnulf and his assassins had escaped and were safe among their own troops on the other bank. Alan of Brittany's men could do nothing: they had no boats and could not cross the river. So, having rescued the unfortunate William's dead body, they returned to Rouen.

On the corpse was found the key to unlock the box containing William's "treasure", and doubtless some disappointment was incurred when it was found to contain but the habiliments of a monk of Jumièges.

William Longsword was buried at Rouen with great state. During the year 943 another death took place that must have given as much satisfaction to King Louis as the decease of William. Herbert of Vermandois died in the same year. Not only was Herbert one of King Louis' most able, unscrupulous and treacherous enemies, but there was a personal feud between them, since Herbert was the murderer of Louis' father, Charles the Simple. The story goes that Louis seized Herbert and condemned him to death at Lâon, that he was summarily hanged and that Louis himself was the executioner. Another version has it that Herbert died raving mad in his bed, protesting that he was but one of twelve responsible for the death of Charles.

It is, however, immaterial how he died. By whatever end he came, it was undoubtedly deserved, and the world was the cleaner for his death. His dominions and the power he had built up failed to survive him. Albert, the second son, gained Vermandois; Odo, the eldest, had Amiens; Robert (and, after his death, Herbert) became Count of Troyes; while Hugh, the youngest, was left to quarrel with Artaud over the Archbishopric of Rheims. Probably King Louis would have tried to put a spoke in the wheel of the sons over the division of their father's possessions, but Hugh of Paris took up their cause and was rewarded by the cession of Coucy, Thury and Creil, which had been filched from the Archbishopric of Rheims by old Count Herbert. Coucy was already in the possession of Bernard de Senlis and Hugh added thereto Creil and Thury.

CHAPTER VII

RICHARD THE FEARLESS—PART I

Bernard the Dane, regent—Heathen and Christian Normans—Overtures of Christians to King Louis—Investiture of Richard—Discontent of Evrecin Normans—Heathen rebellion under Thormod and Sihtric—Suppressed by King Louis, who enters Rouen—Richard, King Louis's ward, at Lâon—Herlwin de Montreuil—King Louis and Arnulf of Flanders—Osmund de Centeville—Arrest of Richard and Osmund—Escape from Lâon to Bernard de Senlis—Quarrel between King Louis and Hugh of Paris—Their reconciliation and plot to divide Normandy.

THE early history of the reign of Richard I, William Longsword's son and successor, is veiled in considerable obscurity. Not that information is unavailable from the various chronicles: on the Norman side from Dudo and later from William of Jumièges, and on the French side from Frodoard and Richer, the two chroniclers of Rheims. But the authorities differ in many points. In all of them the functions of the historian are subordinated to those of the propagandist, and although we may perhaps feel that Dudo's sources—Richard I himself and his brother D'Ivri—should have been able to supply accurate details, yet we may be sure that Dudo was careful to work those details up to support the Norman case.

Similarly, Frodoard and Richer could no doubt have commanded accurate information, but they also were concerned to present the French view. Both sides, therefore, overstate their own case and understate that of their opponents; both sides omit much that is inconvenient and exaggerate what may appear to them important from their own point of view.

Bernard the Dane was obviously the man to whom all in Normandy looked. It was to him and to Botho and Oslac that William Longsword had confided his son in the case of his own death. After the burial of William, Bernard staged an impressive ceremony. It was at Bayeux, the centre of the Heathen Norman party, that Richard had been accepted as his father's heir on May 29, 942. It was at Rouen, the centre of the Christian Normans, that the recognition of Richard as Sovereign of Normandy took place. It was not Bernard or Oslac who played the leading part, but Juhel Beranger and Alan Barbe Torte, the leaders of the Bretons. The result of this proceeding was that Bernard succeeded in getting Richard solemnly recognized in both the Christian and the heathen parts of his dominions; also, by making Juhel and Alan take the lead, he had manœuvred that the Bretons should be committed to Richard.

It will be remembered that during the latter part of his life William Longsword had given offence to the Normans of Rouen by the sudden change of his patronage from his Christian to his heathen subjects. Bernard may have thought that allegiance to Richard was surer in Bayeux, his place of education, than in Rouen. The scheme met with every success; the boy was welcomed enthusiastically and the first difficulty was surmounted. But the dangers from over the frontiers were obvious. William had been popular in Rouen; that popularity may have waned when he suddenly favoured the heathen party; but the Christian Normans were well aware that they were foreigners in an enemy country and that they would have to face difficulties ahead. They might have passed young Richard over and chosen another leader—Bernard the Dane, for instance. It would not have been out of accord with Scandinavian custom to do so. But Bernard was unswerving in his loyalty to Richard; moreover, the legal force of primogeniture had gained in strength of recent years, and though the ideas of feudal law may not have been very acceptable to the heathen party, they were more familiar to the Christians.

Apart from William Longsword's personal popularity, he had been a successful general in the field; during his time Normandy had certainly been respected. Now danger threatened from Flanders and from other quarters as well. Public opinion seems to have been divided as to where to look for help. Presumably the Normans and Danes of Bayeux and the Cotentin were less apprehensive than the Christians of Rouen; they were farther from either France or Flanders and they had their ships to rely on. The Bretons feared that if trouble arose they might be attacked by the Danes of the Cotentin, aided by the Northmen of the Loire whom Alan Barbe Torte had subdued on his return from England. Though they showed no sign of disloyalty to Richard, the heathen party displayed no love for the Christians.

Unfortunately, the latter were divided against themselves. Some looked towards King Louis, others towards Hugh of Paris. Bernard's task, therefore, was one of infinite difficulty. He had to keep the confidence of the heathen Danes, the Christians who were divided into two parties, and the Bretons. He was too wise a man to have the slightest faith in any of the French powers; he knew perfectly well that the object of all was the same. The King, the Duke of Paris and the Count of Flanders wanted to send the Normans bag and baggage back to Scandinavia and to divide Normandy between them. All Bernard could rely on was their greed, their distrust of one another and their inability to act loyally together. Arnulf was the actual murderer of William Longsword, and it can be almost certainly assumed that the King and Hugh of Paris were also implicated as accessories before the fact.

King Louis moved first. He offered less military danger to Normandy

William I's First Seal and Counterpart.

Second Seal and Counterpart.
(From Wyon's *Great Seals of England.*)

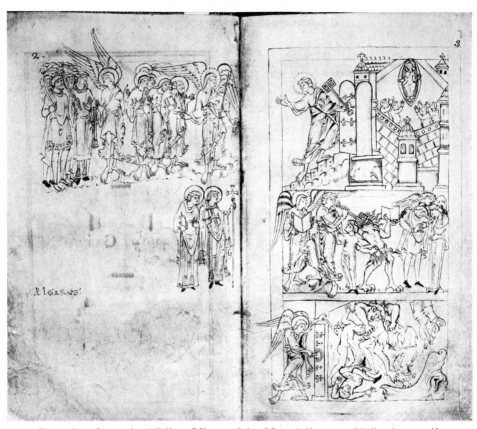

Drawing from the "Liber Vitae of the New Minster of Winchester."
(see No. 2. *Notes on Illustrations.*)

than Hugh of Paris; for the latter held the upper waters of the Seine, and the Evrecin and other Norman territory lay along his frontiers. Moreover, by his recent acquisition of part of the dominions of Herbert of Vermandois he had become the Seigneur of Richard's great-uncle, Bernard de Senlis, at Coucy, Crell and Thury. King Louis claimed his constitutional rights over Normandy. The Duke (we may perhaps anticipate matters and call Richard the Duke now) was his vassal: he was a minor and Louis claimed his feudal rights, though these in law were not yet by any means so well and clearly defined as they became later.

But he had other help. The Christian Rouennais feared their heathen cousins in the north, and they made overtures to Louis. King Louis was nothing loth. The Royalist party in Normandy made perhaps a more favourable proposal than he had expected, and the King had cause to congratulate himself. They asked him to grant investiture to Richard. The King immediately assented, for this was recognition of his legal suzerainty over Normandy, and it also constituted him the child's legal guardian. By this action Richard became the Ward of King Louis. A body of Norman nobles attended the King at Lâon for the ceremony of investiture. King Louis received Richard kindly and the Normans civilly, but in investing him with Normandy he succeeded in putting in a caveat as to his birth. Frodoard says: "*Rex Ludovicus filio Wilhelmi nato de concubina Britanna terram Normannorum dedit.*" In addition, he persuaded the Norman nobles, Richard's vassals, to do homage personally to himself.

Both sides seem to have been thoroughly pleased with themselves. The King flattered himself that not only had he obtained the recognition of his suzerainty over Normandy, but that he had secured the direct fealty of the Norman nobles. The latter thought they had secured the help and support of the King against the Bayeux heathen. One may ask what was Bernard the Dane doing all this time? Why did he let Richard go to Lâon? Why did he permit the Norman nobles to swear direct fealty to Louis? One can only conjecture that he could not help himself, that had he resisted he would merely have been driven out himself, for it seems clear that for the moment the French party dominated Rouen.

But King Louis was just a trifle too clever. The surrender had a very different effect from that which he anticipated. A number of Normans were indignant at the homage done to the King and proceeded to negotiate with Hugh of Paris. The leaders of this party were those who were situated in the Evrecin. The reason is obvious. The Evrecin was a frontier open to Hugh. The party which favoured the Capets was no more mindful of their unfortunate sovereign than were the partisans of King Louis, for they swore direct fealty to Hugh as the others had to the King.

The situation thus was that among the Christian Normans there were

E

two parties both of whom had ignored their own sovereign and had sworn direct fealty either to King Louis or to Hugh Capet. The heathen party of Bayeux were not slow to take advantage. A man of the name of Thormod raised the heathen against the Christian Normans. An opportunity of this kind was not unnaturally a welcome one to the overseas Vikings from Scandinavia and Ireland. The story of this movement is very obscure. Dudo and William of Jumiegès are discreetly vague. Indeed, we must rely entirely on Frodoard and Richer for information.

By some means or another Thormod, now reinforced by a Scandinavian fleet under Sihtric, got possession of young Richard : they proclaimed that he had abandoned Christianity and become a pagan, and advanced southwards to overrun Normandy. This proceeding was as distasteful to Hugh of Paris as to King Louis. Putting aside their mutual hatred for the moment, Paris and Lâon combined against the Northmen. The result was satisfactory to them. Hugh succeeded in driving back the enemy, but the honours of the campaign went to King Louis. He defeated the army of Thormod and Sihtric, killing the former, so it is said, with his own hands. Joined by Hugh of Paris, the allies turned the defeat into a rout, and the King entered Rouen in triumph.

In Rouen, King Louis, who was an accomplished liar, conciliated the Normans by the cheap expedient of professing loudly his abhorrence of the murder of William Longsword and promising his assistance in procuring Arnulf of Flanders' punishment. Doubtless his tongue was firmly fixed in his cheek, and an affecting scene occurred in which he kissed young Richard affectionately and shed crocodile tears over his murdered father. But again King Louis was rather too clever. He got Richard into his own clutches and refused to give him up. Osmund de Centeville, who had succeeded Botho as the boy's personal tutor, asked that Richard should be allowed to return to his own house. King Louis made some excuse. Osmund was suspicious. Next day he came again and said Richard wanted to go home to have a hot bath, but again Louis refused. Osmund was now certain of what was in the wind and took care that Louis' conduct should be known throughout Rouen.

On a third refusal an insurrection broke out in the city. Louis seemingly had not realized the popularity of the boy among the Normans of all parties—they all rallied round their young sovereign. Louis presumably had thought himself so safe that he had dispensed with his troops. In any case, he seems to have found himself at the mercy of the insurgent citizens. Bernard the Dane was at the moment also unpopular, but he knew his people and soon regained their confidence by putting himself at the head of the demand for the surrender of Richard by Louis. The latter had to give in, and with a plentiful supply of soft words, tears and promises Richard was released. Bernard the Dane, Raoul Torta, Oslac and other Norman leaders were summoned to a conference. They demanded that Louis should concede Normandy to the Duke to be held by hereditary right; that he should defend the Normans against their enemies, and that if he did this the Duke would stand by the King against his own enemies. Louis gracefully gave way to everything they asked, and then proceeded to hold court at Rouen and to entertain the Normans lavishly.

The new agreement between the King and the Duke, King Louis said, should be ratified. Not only should the King do so himself, but his French vassals should as well. A solemn ceremony was arranged. Numerous French Counts, Barons and Ecclesiastics arrived at Rouen, doubtless all accompanied by their own troops. The Norman nobles came as well. Richard renewed the homage he had done at Compiègne, and the King and his vassals all took oaths to play their part towards Richard. It seems that Louis had some difficulty in persuading his vassals to follow his example with enthusiasm. Their chronicles suggest that they were restrained by conscience, but it is much more likely that they were by no means sure as to what King Louis was up to. Louis had his plans ready cut and dried; but obviously secrecy was essential and he could not divulge them even to his own vassals.

The King remained at Rouen after the ceremony, as did the French Counts and Barons and their troops. Louis could make himself very agreeable when he liked, and he set out to gain the approval of the Normans. Meanwhile, two other factors began to take effect. In the north, the strength of the heathen Norman party began to recover; and in the south, Hugh of Paris was establishing himself more and more securely in the Evrecin. The Christian Rouen party began to get uneasy. Against the men of Bayeux and against the Duke of Paris they could look to no ally but King Louis, and that individual had been steadily gaining their confidence. He paid a visit to Evreux and persuaded the men of that town to acknowledge young Richard. This was doubtless distasteful to Hugh, but he could not object as he had never actually claimed the Evrecin.

Louis then laid himself out to be civil to Ivo de Bellèsme. Ivo owned the extensive territory of Bellèsme in the Hiesmois, but he also possessed the domain of Creil, held from Bernard de Senlis. Louis appointed Ivo Master of his Arbalasters, thus giving him an important command in his own service. In this way the King completely gulled the Normans; and he did not, we can be sure, again make the mistake of not having his own people's troops to support him should the citizens of Rouen have the bad taste to disagree with him. He had been now some time at Rouen; he had made himself popular there after his first *faux pas*; he had travelled about Normandy full of good words; he had visited the Evrecin and put a spoke in Hugh Capet's wheel there; and he had not unsuccessfully conciliated Ivo de Bellèsme and other important people. He now said he must be getting home to Lâon, and suggested that he should take young Richard with him to be educated with his own children. The boy would, so he said, be brought up as his own son, and Queen Gerberge would be a mother to him, etc., etc., etc.

Also, if they wished him to take vengeance on Arnulf of Flanders, as he himself was dying to do, he must set to work to prepare his forces. He intended, he said, to capture the Flemish strongholds—Arras, Saint Omer and others—and effectually punish the murderer, Arnulf. Richard should have his first taste of war in avenging his father. Apparently Louis either took in the Normans, Bernard the Dane included, entirely, or they did not dare quarrel with him. Anyway, they agreed completely and the unfortunate Richard was sent off to Lâon with the King. Only one stipulation was made, and that was that Osmund de Centeville should accompany him. Ivo de Bellèsme, being an officer in the King's service, went to Lâon too.

So successful had been King Louis's diplomacy that he had been able to introduce into the Norman Government one whom he no doubt knew would be useful to his purpose. Herlwin de Montreuil owed his fief of Montreuil to William Longsword. He was the enemy of Arnulf of Flanders, who had been thwarted in his attempt to seize Montreuil by the assistance afforded by Normandy to Herlwin—who was, as a matter of fact, the vassal of Paris; but when difficulties arose between him and Flanders, the Duke of Paris showed no desire to help him.

Herlwin, therefore, had relied on William Longsword and on Normandy to keep him in his possessions. But things were very different now from what they were in the days of William Longsword. Normandy was not the power she had been. The Civil War had weakened her. So Herlwin was obliged to rely on the friendship of King Louis, and Louis persuaded the Normans to accept him as Governor of Rouen.

Hugh of Paris seems to have been puzzled by the King's actions. He felt the need of extreme caution. Accordingly, he gracefully slipped out of Evreux and awaited his opportunity, doubtful as to his next move.

As to Louis, he had been much occupied with Norman affairs and other business was clamouring for his attention. The King paid a visit to Paris and stayed there with Hugh. Accompanied by Queen Gerberge, he went to Aquitaine, but he did nothing to implement his promise to the Normans to attack Flanders, since he had never had the least intention of doing anything of the kind.

When Louis was away in Aquitaine, Hugh of Paris started to intrigue with the Normans. He had ingratiated himself with them by disappearing from the Evrecin, and he now began to gain over individual adherents in Normandy both among Christians and pagans. But he went very warily.

Whilst Louis and Gerberge were touring Aquitaine, Richard of

Normandy was no doubt enjoying himself at Lâon. It was no part of King Louis' game to undeceive the Normans as to his feelings towards their Duke. As soon as Louis had leisure to attend to them he began to carry out his plans. Richard was the only survivor of the family of Rollo; if he were out of the way Louis could—or thought he could—eliminate the race of pirates and reoccupy Normandy. He had already made tentative proposals to Hugh of Paris during the recent visit he had paid him; now he turned to Arnulf of Flanders.

This evil old man was getting nervous. He must have been well aware of Louis' promises of vengeance against him made to the Normans. He knew that Herlwin de Montreuil, his bitter enemy, was Louis' trusted representative at Rouen, and he was well aware that there was no love lost between Flanders and Lâon. So he determined to appeal to the King's cupidity. He suggested that they should combine and get rid of young Richard and destroy the Norman power. He was preaching to the converted. It was exactly what Louis intended to do as soon as he had the time. He turned a cautious but favourable ear to Arnulf of Flanders' blandishments, and as a first step made sure that Richard should not escape by putting him and Osmund de Centeville under arrest.

At first De Centeville does not seem to have suspected what was really in Louis' mind, nor was the confinement so rigorous as to prevent its evasion. One fine day Osmund and Richard rode out without leave on a hawking expedition. When they returned, King Louis, who must have really feared that they had made their escape, gave himself away. He lost his temper completely, and forgot that he was a gentleman carefully brought up at the civilized Court of his uncle, Athelstane. He swore and cursed in the most undignified manner; threatened Osmund with blinding; told Richard that he would hamstring him or confine him in a dungeon; and indulged in an outburst on the subject of Sprota, whom he called every bad name he could lay his tongue to. Queen Gerberge supplemented this elegant harangue by similar abuse. In the end Richard and Osmund were placed in close imprisonment, and Louis yelled out at them that he did not care who knew how he was treating them.

Osmund de Centeville was a very astute man and he immediately appreciated Louis' intentions and set out to defeat him. Richard's relative, Bernard de Senlis, was living at Coucy, not very far from Lâon. Osmund's first step was to let him know what had happened and to ask him to communicate with Bernard the Dane. But it does not seem that it was necessary to take much trouble to publish the news, since Louis had done that already by his outburst. All Normandy had heard of the King's bad faith. But there was little that the Normans could do. Herlwin was Governor of Rouen and he had a French garrison to help, him, and, anyway, Herlwin was too frightened of Arnulf of Flanders to offend Louis. Moreover, the Normans did not dare to attempt force, for that would no doubt have meant the murder of Richard. The only chance was that Osmund de Centeville would be able to devise some means of escape.

Richard was a healthy, normal sort of boy, and the close confinement told on him. He began to look pale and ill. Osmund made the most of it. There was not really much the matter with Richard, but Osmund pretended that he was at the point of death. Louis and Gerberge were overjoyed; they hoped that the young pirate would soon be removed without their having to go to the trouble of murdering him, so that their scheme for making one of their own children Duke of Normandy should materialize.

Osmund gave out that Richard was dying—almost at his last gasp. Louis and Gerberge gave a huge dinner-party, apparently to celebrate the good news. Then, while everyone was taken up either with eating and drinking or with cooking and serving, Osmund hid the boy in a truss of hay and carried him to the stables as if he were going to fodder his horse. Seizing a favourable opportunity he made off, still carrying the bundle of hay in front of his saddle, and mercifully succeeded in getting out of the town. Once safely outside the two rode for Coucy. Bernard de Senlis was not there, however, so Osmund, leaving Richard, who was no doubt very tired, at Coucy, rode on to Senlis, where he found Bernard.

Bernard was delighted to hear that Richard had escaped from Lâon, but he was at a loss to know what to do. He was a powerful nobleman, but he could not stand up against the great states that surrounded him. Normandy could not help. Rouen was in the grip of King Louis. Obviously, Flanders was out of the question, so that the only power he could appeal to who might be of use was Paris. But Hugh of Paris would only move in his own interest. Doubtless he would have had no objection to having Richard in his hands; but to rescue the poor boy from Louis at Lâon and to hand him over to Hugh at Paris was but to transfer him from the frying-pan to the fire. However, Hugh was the only chance, and on the day after Osmund arrived at Senlis, Bernard rode off as fast as he could for Paris. It was clear that the sooner he got into touch with Hugh the better, before Hugh's intelligence department was able to inform him of the real state of affairs regarding Richard's escape from Lâon.

De Senlis began cautiously. He told Hugh what the latter must have been perfectly well aware of, since it was common knowledge in Normandy —that Richard had been imprisoned by Louis. Hugh was loud in his protestations against the King's iniquities. Having let the other run on for a bit and commit himself, Bernard proceeded to tell him that Richard had escaped and was at Coucy. Hugh had declared that he would leave no stone unturned to secure Richard's restoration to his Duchy, so he could hardly proceed to make war on Bernard to secure the unfortunate boy and treat him in the same way as he had just been denouncing Louis for doing: he accepted Bernard's proposal, therefore, and lent him troops to secure Richard and take him from Coucy to Senlis.

This was something. No doubt Hugh could have made it very unpleasant for Bernard, had he been thoroughly intent on securing Richard's person. But this would not altogether have suited his game. He was busy intriguing in Normandy and endeavouring to entice people to his side. To have attacked De Senlis and seize Richard would have upset his plans in that direction, for their Duke was popular with every Norman. So long as the boy was with De Senlis he was safe from King Louis and from Arnulf, so that the best thing to do was to leave him where he was and to secure Bernard de Senlis against attack. Hugh knew very well that Louis would stick at nothing to recapture the boy.

As no doubt Hugh expected, he received a message from Louis asking him to make De Senlis restore the Duke. This was, naturally, Louis' first step, since Bernard de Senlis was Hugh's vassal. Hugh's answer was unexpected. Not only did he utterly refuse to put pressure on De Senlis, but he threatened to "defy" the King—indeed, he may actually have done so. This threat made it clear that Hugh of Paris definitely declared that he intended to defend the Duke of Normandy against the King. As a safeguard for Bernard de Senlis it was better than all the oaths taken on all the most sacred relics.

Louis was badly frightened. He saw that there was nothing to be done with Hugh of Paris, so he turned to Arnulf of Flanders. Arnulf was practical; he told Louis that the only thing to do was to buy Hugh. He pointed out that the price would be high; but, after all, that was the King's fault for letting Richard escape. Louis followed Arnulf's advice and found Hugh quite ready to deal. The King offered a division of Normandy of which Hugh should have the lion's share. Overboard went all Hugh's oaths and promises, and even his "defiance"—greed conquered everything.

It was lucky for Richard that he had what were probably the only two honest men in France for his supporters. Honest they were in their attachment to the young Duke, but in their methods of diplomacy they were as unscrupulous as the rest. It can, however, be said that they were more astute. It is curious to think that a tarry-handed old shellback like Bernard the Dane should have completely outwitted the sharpest rascals in France. He was greatly helped by Bernard de Senlis. In itself it must have been support of a most valuable kind to Bernard the Dane to know that there was one man, at least, whom he could really trust.

Bernard had had a great part to play since the death of William Longsword. He knew the weakness of his position. He was an old man, some say eighty years of age. As one of the original settlers in

Normandy, and as a companion of Rollo, he no doubt enjoyed much prestige with the Normans, and this was in his favour. But he was in the hands of King Louis, who found it quite easy to set him aside and put Herlwin de Montreuil in his place as Governor of Rouen. Bernard, however, recognized that, if he were got rid of, Richard would have no one left to look after his interests, and he therefore pursued the policy of the Vicar of Bray and determined that even if he lost power he would not lose place. He also kept very carefully in touch with all parties among the Normans.

The compact between Hugh of Paris and King Louis for the division of Normandy was a mere agreement between two thieves to divide the proceeds of a robbery. Louis hated Hugh for many reasons—one being that he was one of the conspirators in the murder of Charles the Simple. For his part, Hugh thoroughly distrusted Louis, and probably hated him also, as people are apt to hate those whom they have injured. Moreover, Hugh's ambitions had grown. Twice married and childless, his third wife, Hedwig, daughter of Henry the Fowler and so sister of the Emperor Otto and Queen Gerberge, had presented him with a son.

Hitherto the Dukes of Paris had been content with the substance rather than the shadow. Hugh might have been king after the death of Raoul of Burgundy, but he knew that by accepting the Crown he would draw upon himself the jealousy and hostility of all the other French powers—who naturally would set up the Carolingian heir against him. But now with a son to succeed, and with the evident decline of the Carolingian line in spite of the efforts of King Louis and Queen Gerberge, his thoughts seem to have begun to turn to the kingship he had refused —not for himself, perhaps, but as a possibility for his son.

In any case, two such astute men as De Senlis and Bernard the Dane were abundantly aware that the alliance between Louis and Hugh was of the most precarious character and that the slightest suspicion on either side would probably break it, since each knew perfectly well that the other intended to cheat him if he could. Bernard de Senlis knew well that, in spite of the unholy alliance between Hugh and King Louis, the former much preferred that Richard should remain at Senlis than return to Lâon. Possibly he would have preferred to obtain custody over Richard himself; but De Senlis was a powerful man, his castles were strong, and Hugh could not, even in the most fortunate circumstances, get hold of the Norman Duke without undertaking operations on a con- siderable scale. He had, therefore, no objection to leaving Richard where he was, at any rate, safe for the moment.

CHAPTER VIII

RICHARD THE FEARLESS—PART II

Tricky Theobald of Chartres—Harold Bluetooth supports Richard—Invasion of Normandy by the King—Paris and Flanders—Louis enters Rouen—Feeling against the French in Normandy—Hugh of Paris turns against the King—Normans and Danes defeat and capture Louis—The King surrenders his claims on Normandy—Richard becomes an independent Duke—Raoul Torta dismissed—The Court at Rouen—Gunnor—"Commendation"—Betrothal to Emma of Paris.

BERNARD THE DANE, in careful co-operation with De Senlis, agreed that he should pose as the adherent in Normandy of King Louis—a part that was not difficult for him to play, since he had all along been careful to keep in with the King. Bernard de Senlis, on the other hand, declared himself openly against the King. This arrangement had two advantages. As Bernard the Dane had declared for King Louis, De Senlis (no doubt, Hugh of Paris thought) was unlikely to send Richard to Normandy, and as De Senlis had declared against the King there was no chance of his sending the young Duke to Lâon. There was no doubt that Hugh wished to keep a sharp eye on Richard, and this made it easy for Bernard de Senlis to keep a sharp eye on Hugh; for it was the plan of the Dane and De Senlis to watch both Hugh and King Louis most carefully and to do anything in their power to sow discord between them. The essence of their policy was secrecy; they were to appear as completely separate, even to go to war with each other should this prove necessary to keep up the deception.

We had occasion to mention Thibaut le Tricheur, Count of Blois, in connection with the murder of William Longsword. This Tricky Theobald was without doubt the worst ruffian in France. He married the widow of the man he had assisted to murder—Liutgarda, a jealous, spiteful cat of a woman whose chief characteristic was hatred of Richard as being her husband's bastard. Anything she could do to hurt Richard she would undertake. Thibaut, in spite of—or, rather, probably because of—his villainies, was one of the most powerful men in France. He had secured Blois, Chartres, Beauvais, Meaux and Tours and was greedy for more. He was, therefore, a danger, and Bernard de Senlis found it necessary to come to terms with him. Tricky ruffian and astute though the man was, De Senlis managed to get the better of him. His main object was to neutralize Thibaut, and he therefore proposed to assist

73

Richard by attacking the King in conjunction with Thibaut. Thibaut's object was to gratify his wife's spite against Richard and his own greed by picking up anything that might be going by betraying De Senlis. The latter was perfectly aware of this, and it just suited him, for his aim was to keep Thibaut in doubt and inactive.

Meanwhile, Bernard the Dane was working very quietly and secretly on another line altogether. Although he had become, or pretended to become, a Christian, he had always considered himself to be a Dane and had never lost touch with Scandinavia. Bernard had had a foot firmly planted in the Bayeux and Cotentin settlement of heathen Northmen. It will be remembered that towards the end of his life William Longsword had actively encouraged a considerable Danish immigration into the territory acquired from Brittany. Certainly many Danes came thither, and it is quite possible that Harold Bluetooth, King of Denmark, actually visited Normandy, though the story of his settlement at Cherbourg is apocryphal.

William of Jumièges, following and explaining Dudo, says that Bernard the Dane sent to Harold, King of the Danes, who was still living at Cherbourg, asking him to raise a force from Bayeux and Coutances to invade Normandy by land, and himself (i.e. Harold) to attack by sea.

This Harold, or Herold, or Hagrold, as he is variously called, is not mentioned as King of Denmark either by Richer or Frodoard. They describe him as Hagrold, who commanded at Bayeux: "*Hagroldus dux qui Bajocis procerat.*"

Now, it is not really very important whether Harold Bluetooth actually came himself to France. We may, however, be practically certain that the influx of Danes into Normandy, both at the invitation of William Longsword in 942 and now in 944 at the invitation of Bernard the Dane, was undertaken and carried out with the lively support and direction of the King of Denmark. The probabilities are that Harold Bluetooth did visit Normandy. There was every reason why he should. That Saxo Grammaticus, author of the earliest Danish history, does not mention it is not peculiar. Saxo only devotes a few lines to Harold's reign of forty-nine years (936–985), which were years crowded with incident of all kinds. Harold may not have been long in the country, but it must be remembered that complete command of the sea was in the hands of the Scandinavians—a voyage from Denmark to Cherbourg would have been quite a simple matter, therefore, for King Harold. Nor is there any reason to doubt Frodoard and Richer, for the officer commanding at Bayeux named Hagrold may quite easily have been someone other than the King, for the name was common enough.

But the main point is that Bernard the Dane secured powerful help from his Scandinavian compatriots, and that with that help he defeated Richard's enemies and reinstated him on his throne. Fortune favoured

Bernard's schemes. Civil war had broken out in Brittany; Juhel Beranger and Alan Barbe Torte had fallen out, and the quarrel offered a golden opportunity for profitable intervention on the part of the Danes. They seized upon it and, making use of the Breton dissensions, they succeeded in overrunning the country. More Danes came in to Cherbourg and probably with the secret connivance—or, at any rate, encouragement— of Bernard, occupied strong places in Normandy.

King Louis and Arnulf of Flanders were considerably alarmed at the Viking invasion. France had been free from this nuisance now for some time and its recrudescence gave them no small cause for disturbance. Hugh of Paris shared their concern. All three powers invaded Normandy. Arnulf took Arques. Hugh occupied the Evrecin. Louis entered Normandy from the east. Burgundy sent troops. From the Evrecin Hugh advanced on Bayeux.

Bernard the Dane's nerve never failed him. He saw that he must divide his enemies, and so kept the Danes in the background as a fresh Danish incursion would only serve to unite the French. But his task was difficult, and all depended on the influence he could exert with his own countrymen. The Normans were seriously alarmed. They were assailed on all sides and their Duke was, if not a captive, at any rate in hands that might not be able to guard him.

To the astonishment of the Normans, Bernard offered complete submission to Louis. There were bitter comments, but Bernard had a hold on his people, and as the French troops immediately ceased their depredations, at any rate, something was gained. Everything was done to deceive King Louis. He entered Rouen amidst cheers and rejoicings. He was flattered and bowed down to on every side. Richard seemed completely abandoned. Louis was King in his own country. Now he began to repent of his bargain to divide Normandy with Hugh. There was no reason to keep it. Richard was discarded by the Normans themselves; Louis was accepted by them as Sovereign of Normandy and the Normans urged on him the disaster that would occur were Normandy to be divided.

Louis naturally agreed with them. The last thing he wanted to do was to divide what was now his own with his most dangerous enemy. Bernard thought that now the critical time had come and that he could proceed to drive a wedge between Louis and Hugh. He gave a great dinner-party. Louis was flattered and made up to more than ever before. Moreover, he was filled with good wine. Bernard, who doubtless could drink enough to float one of his own Viking warships without turning a hair, went and sat down by the King after dinner. Flattery, subserviency, discreet allusion to Hugh's untrustworthiness and disloyalty to Louis—all were used to stimulate the King's greed and hatred towards his rival.

William of Jumièges tells us that Bernard deplored to the King the damage that Hugh was doing to his (the King's) domain of Normandy by his operations round Bayeux, and that he persuaded Louis to send orders to Hugh to desist from hostilities against the Normans. Now, Hugh of Paris was not given to obeying anyone's orders, and the last person in the world from whom he would take orders would be King Louis. What one would suppose really happened was that Louis— rather drunk, perhaps—took the decision that doubtless had been in his mind for long and let Hugh know that he would no longer support him and that their bargain was at an end. Hugh up in the north was in danger. Louis and the Normans might cut his communications with Paris; so he hurriedly raised the siege of Bayeux and made off to his own dominions.

The first part of Bernard's scheme was successful. Louis and Hugh had quarrelled and Louis was living in a fool's paradise at Rouen. Now was the turn of Bernard de Senlis. As soon as Hugh had returned to Paris, De Senlis visited him there and urged him to revenge himself on Louis by espousing the cause of Richard. However, Hugh was too careful to commit himself for the moment. Bernard the Dane kept the game going and nothing was left undone to persuade Louis that he was complete master of Normandy; the deluded King even began to dream of restoring the Empire of Charlemagne! He was now so secure, he thought, that he could turn his attention to civil administration, and he appointed Raoul Torta as his minister.

This man is rather an enigma. He was the son of the Bishop of Pani, a Frenchman and not a Norman, but he was associated with Bernard the Dane and Oslac in the days of William Longsword. Opinion generally has it that he was the creature of the King. This is supported by William of Jumièges, who has no words bad enough for him, though chiefly because he used the stone destined for rebuilding Jumièges Abbey for the fortifications of Rouen. Also, he imposed heavy levies on the Normans. Chancellors of the Exchequer are never popular, but it seems not too much to suppose that Raoul Torta was really in the councils of Bernard, who very possibly was not unwilling that the unpopular necessity of raising money should fall upon Raoul's shoulders rather than on his own.

As a matter of fact, it must have been in any case an improvement that money should be raised even by Louis by means other than exaction and robbery. Moreover, if the Government wanted money, good government must be introduced and ravages cease. If Bernard's scheme was to go through and Richard restored, money would be needed and a full Treasury would obviously be necessary. Still more important was the refortification of Rouen. Hitherto Louis had been mainly concerned to knock the fortifications down, now he was building them up. So that it is not at all unlikely that Raoul Torta was working with Bernard.

Rather unfortunately, perhaps, for Bernard's schemes, the Normans were beginning to settle down under the new regime and to accept Louis—for, after all, peace and quiet were worth something—but Raoul's exactions, though eventually they were to enure to their benefit, stirred up their animosity to the King. Moreover, the French were beginning to act foolishly. Thinking that Normandy was completely subdued, they began to clamour for their loot. Openly they demanded a general redistribution of the land, the dispossession of the Normans and their substitution by Frenchmen. This was bad enough, but what was much worse was a rumour that not only were the French going to seize the land of the Normans, but also their women. Now, nothing enrages men more than a suggestion of this kind. It arouses the primitive instinct inherent both in men and animals. Bernard the Dane must have needed all his address to maintain his hold on his people.

Luckily for him, or perhaps he himself gave every encouragement to the rumour, it was said that his lands were the first to be disposed of. Further, though Bernard was approaching, or perhaps had approached, four-score years, he had recently married a young and pretty wife. Such marriages are apt to give rise to ribald jokes, and doubtless this happened in the present case. Bernard's lady was allotted by gossip to a Frenchman. Feeling against the French ran high, and a general insurrection was imminent. It must have been a very anxious time for Bernard, for premature action might ruin his plans. He succeeded in keeping the Rouennais quiet, and he was also successful in holding back the impatient Danes of the north. The fact that they were so well in hand lends colour to the belief that Harold Bluetooth controlled the situation. Had a powerful influence not been at work it is difficult to believe that the Vikings would have kept quiet for so long. But it would seem that Harold himself could not have yet been on the spot. Had the King of Denmark with an invading army actually been at Cherbourg, King Louis would scarcely have been so certain of his position.

Bernard the Dane's plan was simple. By the aid of De Senlis he persuaded Hugh of Paris and his friends to make a sudden attack on Louis's own dominions. Without any warning they seized Compiègne and Montigny at Easter, 945. Louis was taken by surprise. He rushed off to defend his possessions. This was the signal for the Danes to move. Swarms arrived from Brittany. A fleet anchored in Barfleur, perhaps the fleet that brought Harold Bluetooth from Denmark. It seems probable that he was now on the scene.

Louis came back with all speed from Compiègne. He did not appreciate that he had all Normandy to deal with as well as the Vikings. But he had a formidable army with him, and the Normans and their Viking allies began to hesitate. Probably with the intention of discovering the strength of their respective forces, a conference was agreed to. They met on the banks of the Dive on July 12, 945. It is impossible to say exactly what happened; some say that a personal quarrel arose between Herlwin de Montreuil, who held an important command in Louis' army, and one of the Danes, and that this precipitated the fray. Anyway, a general action broke out. The Normans went over to the enemy. The Danes completely routed the French. King Louis had to ride for his life and was taken prisoner.

There are two accounts of his capture. According to Frodoard, Louis took refuge at Rouen, where he was made captive by the citizens. Dudo tells us that he took refuge on an island in the Seine, where he was taken by a Norman knight and brought to Rouen. It is immaterial which story is true, if either. The important point is that King Louis was a prisoner in the hands of Bernard the Dane. Having caught their fox, the hounds began to quarrel as to who should break him up. The Danes wanted to hold him for ransom: Bernard as a security for Richard's restoration, Hugh of Paris for his own selfish purposes.

The claim to Louis as a prisoner was soon renounced by the Danes, and the contest remained between Hugh of Paris and Bernard the Dane. Queen Gerberge and her children were safe in Lâon. So long as King Louis' heirs were at large his death would not benefit Hugh. So the latter concocted a scheme to get hold of the children. The Normans who actually held Louis in prison were prompted by Hugh to offer Louis' release on condition that all his children should be surrendered as hostages for their further demands.

King Louis was all his life much under female influence; not that of rapacious mistresses, but of two women who were devoted to him and had only his welfare at heart. In his youth he owed everything to his mother; later to Queen Gerberge, a woman of high ability and great strength of character.

Gerberge utterly refused this demand as regards the elder boy, Lothaire; Carloman, the younger boy—an infant—was offered, together with other hostages. This was accepted, but when they arrived at Rouen the Normans coolly repudiated the agreement, seized the hostages as security for their own demands, and handed Louis over to Hugh of Paris. Poor Queen Gerberge was in despair. She appealed to her brother, Otto, for help; she appealed to Edmund of England, King Athelstane's half-brother, whom he had succeeded in 940. Not much resulted from the latter. Otto was more accommodating, and he promised his sister that he would invade France as soon as possible; and it seemed as though he would make good his word. Hugh did not want to undertake a German war, nor would he have had much support from the other French princes had he tried. He came to terms. Louis might have his liberty in exchange for Lâon.

There was no alternative, Louis had to give way, while Gerberge surrendered Lâon and went to live at Compiègne. But he had still to settle with the Normans. Nothing would content them but the complete surrender by the King of all rights over Normandy. This was formally conceded, and Richard became independent Duke of Normandy, though a shadowy acknowledgment of the King's precedence was conceded. The ceremony took place on the banks of the Epte, where Rollo had first received Normandy, and immediately afterwards the Duke made his triumphal entry into Rouen.

Richard came from the banks of the Epte to Rouen, and entered it in triumph as an independent Duke. In 945, when this took place, he cannot have been more than thirteen or, at the most, fourteen, yet he seems to have been regarded as of full age and to have entered into his full powers without the tutelage of a Council of Regency. Boys grew up early in those days, and Richard had experienced many vicissitudes in his childhood. William Longsword had done his duty by his son in regard to his education. Added to this, he was well-grown, good-looking and well-mannered. His people were proud of him—he was popular with both Christians and heathens ; he was bilingual, too, so he had every-thing in his favour. Moreover, instead of resenting the influence of his loyal friends such as Bernard the Dane, Osmund de Centeville and Ivo de Bellèsme, he relied on them and trusted them for so long as they lived.

But one of his advisers suffered. Raoul Torta, the unpopular finance minister, was made a scapegoat. It will be remembered that this man had been trusted by William Longsword and was one of those who administered the Government in Richard's childhood. He was re-appointed by King Louis, and has been accused of being the instrument of extortion for that King. This seems to be untrue. Bernard the Dane trusted him and maintained him in office after the restoration. But he was very unpopular; although Richard found a fairly well plenished Treasury and a fortified capital, his people grumbled over the rigour of Torta's levies, and the monks of Jumièges complained that the stone for their abbey had been seized to fortify Rouen. Raoul had to go. The usual accusations were made against him and, although for a time Richard hesitated, in the end the unpopular minister was forced to leave the country. He went to Paris and took refuge there with the Bishop of Paris and never returned to Normandy.

Probably Richard was just as pleased as anyone else to see the last of the prudent finance minister. He was certainly not slow to make use of the funds which Raoul Torta's care had accumulated. Richard was a wealthy man, for the ducal domain was a wide one. Rollo had seen to this, and in the added territory acquired in the following reign William Longsword had not forgone his share.

A boy suddenly placed at the head of a powerful State, with generous feelings and a taste for extravagance and display, is certain to spend money, and Richard was no exception. The Court of Rouen became famous for its splendour and gaiety. But in spite of outward prosperity, Normandy was by no means secure yet. King Louis at Compiègne nurtured every hope of revenge for the indignities that had been put upon him. Arnulf of Flanders, whose plans had again come to naught, was on the look-out for an opportunity for aggrandizing himself and Flanders at the expense of Normandy. Tricky Theobald and his spiteful, ill-natured wife had got nothing from their intrigues, and Liutgarda, to her intense disgust, saw Sprota's bastard the Duke of Normandy. Brittany was always an uncertain quantity—indeed, nearly all her neighbours would have regarded the destruction of Normandy with satisfaction.

Normandy was in reality surrounded by enemies or potential enemies on every side but one, and Richard could only look to Paris for any hope of support. We have had occasion to appraise the value of Hugh of Paris's word. He kept his engagements no longer than suited him. But the powerful Norman State was becoming as necessary to Paris as Paris was becoming necessary to Normandy. Hugh of Paris, no doubt, would have liked to add Normandy to his dominions. He probably had that in his mind during his tortuous intrigues with King Louis. But, perhaps unexpectedly, events had turned out very differently from what he had hoped. Normandy was now a strong State. The accession of strength which it had gained by the policy initiated by William Longsword and vigorously encouraged by Bernard the Dane of increasing Scandinavian colonization in the Bessin and Cotentin had considerably altered the situation. Moreover, although King Louis' power was much diminished it was not extinguished. In a contest between the Carolingians and the Capets for the kingdoms, a contest the certainty of which was becoming evident, it might well be that Normandy would hold the balance. So Hugh began to extend cautious feelers towards Richard and his advisers.

Richard was, perhaps, only a boy in age at this time, but he was a precocious boy and might be considered a young man already. He was no better than it was absolutely necessary that a young man should be, and he was the leader of a gay and extravagant society where no doubt ladies played no small part. Like most young people of his age, he was an admirer of the opposite sex. He was told that the superintendent of his forests at Secheville near Arques was so fortunate as to be married to a beautiful lady whose name was Sainfrida. Richard paid a visit to Secheville and met the lady, whose charms proved to be all that he had heard they were. He had the impudence to suggest to her husband that he should be allowed to make her better acquaintance.

The poor man was much perturbed and went in trouble to his wife. The lady had no mind to become the mistress of the Duke, but her morals were not so rigid as to prevent her from making capital out of the

Church of the Abbaye-aux-Hommes, Caen.
(see No. 3. *Notes on Illustrations.*)

Towers of the Abbaye-aux-Hommes, Caen.

situation for her family. Sainfrida had three sisters, Gunnor, Adelina and Veva, and a brother named Herfast. Gunnor was a very pretty girl and by no means particular. Sainfrida told her husband to pretend to fall in with the Duke's proposals and give Richard facilities to pay her a visit. But when Richard arrived, Gunnor took Sainfrida's place. The Duke did not discover the trick until the following day; but so delighted was he with Gunnor that not only did he forgive Sainfrida, but thanked her for having saved him from mortal sin! The result was that Gunnor became his wife by Danish custom and eventually the mother of a numerous family, the eldest of which was Richard II of Normandy. Generally speaking, Richard, though he had occasional backslidings, remained tolerably faithful to Gunnor as his father and grandfather had been to Sprota and Popa.

It is said, and her name bears it out, that the lady was of pure Danish blood and of good family. Needless to say that her brother and sisters profited handsomely by the connection.

Gunnor came to Rouen and presided over Richard's festive Court; but she was a Dane and her marriage a Danish one, so that the circumstance was no hindrance to Bernard the Dane's diplomacy. The old man's idea was to cement the links with Paris by a marriage between Richard and Hugh of Paris's only daughter, Emma. Hugh was quite ready to meet him. But he wanted a very considerable *quid pro quo*. He proposed a close alliance between the two states, and this alliance was to take the form of "commendation".

Commendation in feudal law meant the voluntary acceptance by one party of the suzerainty of the other party. It is important that the exact contractual relationship between Paris and Normandy should be defined, for we depend much on this for the interpretation of the future relations between France and Normandy. Dudo, while glorying in Richard's independence, admits the shadowy precedence of the King. We may take what he says as substantially true; for it is obvious that when the settlement on the Epte prior to Richard's restoration was concluded, the Norman diplomatists would never have agreed to any real control by the King over Richard. As for the commendation, we have the evidence of a contemporary charter for its existence. It is true that this charter is of later date—it was done in 968—but it is none the less conclusive: it runs as follows: "*Cum assensu Senioris mei Hugonis Francorum Principis.*" Good evidence, also, is the close alliance between Paris and Rouen, the existence of which is confirmed by Frodoard.

Richard, therefore, commended himself to Hugh of Paris and betrothed himself to the latter's daughter, Emma, then but a little girl. She was too young to marry and the ceremony was postponed, but the betrothal was made as solemn as possible by the usual oaths and protestations.

F

The commendation of Richard to Hugh was followed by an important reorganization of the Norman military system. We have noticed the rapid development during the second quarter of the 10th century of the feudal system in France, the increase in the number of castles and the evolution of the heavy cavalry soldier. The distribution of the land of Normandy by Rollo to his adherents was no doubt of a haphazard character—the tenure was allodial; but doubtless there was some kind of military obligation, though it was all very vague. With the advent of more settled conditions it is not surprising that the tenure of land and the obligation of military service should be placed on a more settled basis. By a general rearrangement the allodial tenure which had hitherto prevailed was converted into feudal tenure, which carried with it the reorganization of the army on modern principles; at the same time, although the change to feudal tenure was general, some allodial holdings still remained.

We are told that this was carried out by Richard on his own initiation, but one must remember that in spite of Gunnor he was still very young, too young to carry out such an important reform by himself. No doubt he thought he would like to imitate his future father-in-law-to-be, who had knighted him on his betrothal, and pose as the head of a brilliant galaxy of feudal nobles and trusty vassals; but we may be pardoned for believing that the real work was carried out by Bernard the Dane, Osmund de Centeville and Ivo de Bellèsme, who are said to have been enrolled as the three premier barons of Normandy.

This is the last historical appearance of Bernard. He must have died shortly after, though the actual date of his death is uncertain. He left a son named Torf, and a grandson named Thorold, who is said to have been the ancestor of many of the noble families of Normandy and of England—especially of the important houses of Harcourt and Beaumont.

CHAPTER IX

RICHARD THE FEARLESS—PART III

Reform of Norman military system—Normandy and Paris unsuccessfully invaded by the King—Flanders and Otto of Germany—Death of Hugh of Paris—Richard becomes guardian of Hugh's children. Richard marries Emma—Her death—He marries Gunnor —Their children—Death of King Louis and succession of Lothaire—Bruno of Cologne— War between Lothaire and Richard—Harold Bluetooth again—Death of Lothaire—Hugh of Paris King of France—Richard's last years—Raoul d'Ivri—Richard's administration —The Norman Church—The Clugniacs—Condition of Normandy at the close of Richard's reign—His death.

THE alliance between Normandy and Paris was regarded with no little concern by the King and the other French powers—especially by Flanders.

Arnulf made the first move; he approached King Louis and suggested to him that they should apply to Otto for help against the new combination. At first Otto seemed apathetic, but the energy of Arnulf overcame the difficulties, and Otto agreed to come to the rescue. Not only did he come himself, but he persuaded King Conrad of Burgundy—although that worthy enjoyed the pseudonym of Conrad the Peaceful—to furnish him with a strong contingent of Burgundian troops.

There was no doubt but that this powerful alliance boded ill for Hugh and Richard. The allies besieged Lâon, Senlis and Rheims, but they were only successful in taking the last-named town. They then proceeded to invade Hugh's Duchy of Paris and Normandy. Here again we are at a loss to discover the exact course of events. Dudo, it is true, overwhelms us with detail; but the French chroniclers Frodoard and Richer are silent; Widukind, the German, is only slightly less reserved. All that we can be sure of is that the allies ravaged both the duchies. They did not apparently attempt the siege of Paris, but they tried and failed to take Rouen. Hugh himself was obliged to retreat to Orleans, but Richard remained in Rouen, and no doubt Dudo is correct when he tells us that the young Duke distinguished himself. Perhaps he then became grateful to Raoul Torta for his prudent strengthening of the Rouen fortifications.

There is no doubt that the successful defence of Rouen had an important if not a decisive effect on the war, though what actually happened is obscure. The allies began to quarrel among themselves. Dudo naturally lays the blame on Arnulf and his Flemings. Otto was much distressed by the death of his nephew in action outside the walls of Rouen. But, whatever the details were, it seems that the Normans inflicted a considerable defeat on the Germans. Arnulf retreated to Flanders, but succeeded in regaining Montreuil on the way; so his efforts were not by any means altogether in vain.

The war dragged on: Otto was obliged to return to Germany to deal with events of more importance to him than the quarrels of his brother-in-law with the other French Powers. The brunt of the fighting fell now on Hugh of Paris, but he received the hearty support of Normandy, and we learn from Frodoard that Richard's troops were perhaps the backbone of Hugh's army. Eventually, however, in 950 a peace was patched up. King Louis regained Lâon and, on the whole, came fairly well out of the war; but in the main object—namely, the defeat of the Norman and Parisian powers—he failed completely.

For the rest of his life King Louis had other things to occupy him than Normandy, which he left severely alone. One rather comic incident took place in 951, while Louis was suffering from a severe attack of illness. His mother, the elderly Ogiva, eloped with the disreputable young Herbert of Vermandois. Louis was still a young man, or comparatively so; but illness and constant worry had sapped his powers. He nominated his eldest son, Lothaire, to be King with him, but when he recovered from his illness his vigour returned and he prepared again to take the field against Hugh of Paris. It was not for long, however, for he had a bad accident out hunting, followed by a recurrence of illness which carried him off in the year 954.

During the seven years since the siege of Rouen, Richard had been leading a peaceful life. His relations with his suzerain continued excellent, but beyond supplying him with troops they were not intimate. Doubtless Hugh was content. So long as he had the soldiers he could quite well do without his prospective son-in-law to command them. But apparently he did not like all he heard from Rouen as to Richard's intentions regarding Emma. The young man showed no signs whatever of desiring to carry the alliance beyond a formal betrothal. He was, no doubt, quite happy with Gunnor. But Hugh was getting old. He had apprehensions as to the future. His son, Hugh, was but a boy, and old Hugh was anxious to make sure that the alliance would be maintained in full vigour after his death; also, he feared lest Lothaire might exercise his rights of wardship over his son.

Hugh had no one to rely on but Richard, and he was most anxious that the marriage with Emma should take place. He made careful provision for his death. He made a will, naming Richard as the guardian of his son and entrusting young Hugh's inheritances to him during the boy's minority. He confided his wife to Richard's care and commended Richard to his vassals. In 956 he died.

The death of Hugh altered Richard's position completely.   Instead of being the junior partner in the alliance he became its pivot.   With him as Duke of Normandy and guardian of the young Duke of Paris, the centre of gravity shifted to Rouen.   But still he hesitated to marry Emma, and it was not till 960 that the poor girl got her husband.   The legitimate wives of the early rulers of Normandy were not very lucky.   Gisela, if she ever really lived, got small consideration from Rollo.   William Longsword treated Liutgarda with scant kindness; and poor little Emma received no affection from her husband.   In spite of her beauty and accomplishments, on which Dudo expatiates at great length, Richard cared nothing for her. He was not actually unkind, he always treated her with courtesy and consideration, for he was a kindly man; but he had no love for her.   All his affection—or, at any rate, most of it—was for Gunnor.   Poor Emma passed her life at Rouen alone and solitary, and eventually she pined away and died about the year 962.

There had never been any difficulty about the succession in the past and no question was raised over the legitimacy of either William Long-sword or Richard, but the Normans were gettting more civilized now and they were anxious that the legitimacy of Gunnor's children should be rendered unquestionable.   Besides Richard the eldest, there were Robert, later Archbishop of Rouen; Mauger, Count of Mortain; Maud, who became Countess of Blois; Emma, afterwards Queen of England; and Avice, who married the Duke of Brittany.   Gunnor was of good old Scandinavian stock, beautiful and popular, and everyone wanted the Duke to marry her now that he was free.   Richard, we may assume, was nothing loth, and no doubt it was a wise thing to do.

One might gather from Richard's soubriquet of "the Fearless" that he gained his chief reputation as a warrior and a general.   But this is not the case.   Richard was successful in the field, and no doubt shared to the full the family courage; but it is to his success as an administrator and diplomatist that his fame is due.   After the death of Bernard the Dane his chief advisers continued to be Osmund de Centeville and Ivo de Bellèsme, and later he added Waleran de Meulan to them.

Until 959 King Lothaire was too much occupied to concern himself with the affairs of Paris and Normandy.   But he had not forgotten his captivity at Rouen, and neither he nor his mother had any love for Richard.   The latter had contented himself by paying no attention to Lothaire and, indeed, it must be admitted that he was careless of his own interests.

Lothaire and his mother, Gerberge, were not slow to take advantage. By some means or another they succeeded in enticing young Hugh and his brother, Odo, to Lâon.   Lothaire ignored Richard and claimed his feudal right to settle the inheritances of the two boys.   To Hugh, the elder of the two, he allotted the Duchy of Paris and the overlordship of Poitou.

This had been claimed by Hugh's father, but resisted by the Count of Poitou in the past.   What the latter had to say on the subject is not known, for Lothaire did not put himself to the inconvenience of consulting him. To Odo Lothaire allotted Burgundy.   Luckily for young Hugh and Richard, Odo died not long after and, with the death of his brother, Hugh reunited his father's dominions.

Richard certainly was put at considerable disadvantage by this manœuvre. It is difficult to discover how Lothaire managed to get hold of Hugh's children; but one may perhaps guess that Richard was not over-popular at Paris. He had treated Emma with scant courtesy, and he never appears to have visited Paris or to have extended much, if any, consideration to his wards. However, he made up for it now and proceeded to renew to Hugh the commendation he had offered to his father; so that young Hugh now became the suzerain of Richard instead of his ward. Perhaps this change of status may have been slightly galling to Richard's pride, but, after all, the guardianship could not have lasted for ever, and the fresh commendation cemented the alliance between Normandy and Paris and was an answer to Lothaire's blandishments.

Queen Gerberge and her son were at this time largely guided by Bruno, Archbishop of Cologne. This man was a brother of the Queen's and also, therefore, a brother of King Otto (who became Emperor of the West in 962). On the death in 954 of Archbishop Wickfried, Bruno succeeded him and in 955 his brother made him Duke of Lorraine. Bruno was, therefore, the most important potentate on the Rhine and he had, like his brother and sister, every reason to be jealous of Normandy and Paris. It is difficult to disentangle the exact course of events from Dudo's flamboyant narrative, though the facts stand out fairly clear. Directly a chance presented itself, Normandy's enemies came forward to join in the attempt to humiliate the pirates, as they still continue to be called by the French chroniclers. Arnulf of Flanders, though very old (he lived to be ninety-one and died in 954), Theobald and Liutgarda of Chartres, again appear in the combination.

Apparently Bruno pretended to attempt to negotiate with Richard, and proposed a conference at Amiens in 960. According to Dudo, Theobald of Chartres had persuaded Bruno and Lothaire to follow the example of Arnulf of Flanders and to assassinate Richard at Amiens, as William Longsword had been assassinated at Picquigny. This story may or may not be true; anyway, Richard—duly warned of his danger, according to Dudo—did not turn up at Amiens. Whatever may have been Bruno's intention on this occasion, in 961 Lothaire summoned a general assembly of the chief men of his realm at Soissons. We do not hear of this from Norman sources, because Richard did not cut a very grand figure on this occasion, but from Frodoard, who unfortunately does not say whether Richard was formally summoned or not. We learn from him, however, that the Normans turned up and endeavoured to disperse the assembly by force but were prevented.

Next year (962) Tricky Theobald seized Evreux. Richard defeated him and he took refuge with Lothaire, and the result was war between Lothaire and Richard. The French chroniclers are reticent on the campaign; Dudo, on the contrary, is prolix. One may gather both from the negative and the positive sources of information that Richard was successful. Whether he inflicted a crushing a humiliation on Lothaire as Dudo claims, is doubtful, perhaps. But the upshot is clear: Lothaire and Theobald were defeated, Theobald had to return Evreux, and Lothaire was obliged to give up his attempts against Normandy.

But now we have a difficult circumstance to account for. In spite of Richard's success, and in spite of the fact that he never seems to have been in real difficulty—for if he had we should have heard much more about it from Frodoard and Richer—Dudo tells us again he called in Harold Bluetooth from Denmark. When, however, the Danes arrived, King Lothaire had been subdued. We are again face to face with the question whether Harold Bluetooth really came. M. Prentout holds that Harold never did come to Normandy; Sir Francis Palgrave gives the fullest credit to Dudo; Professor Freeman maintains a neutral attitude, but he points out that only twenty-four years later Dudo was a canon of St. Quentin and a visitor to the Court of Richard, and, therefore, in a position to hear the truth from Richard himself. Moreover, we know that Dudo derived information from Raoul d'Ivri, Richard's brother. It seems therefore improbable, if not impossible, that Dudo should have invented the story.

The French writers do not tell it, but there is no reason why they should. William of Jumièges certainly supports Dudo. Moreover, there does not appear to be any particular reason to doubt it. Harold by this time had established himself as the chief Scandinavian power. Besides being King of Denmark, he was Over-king of Norway. He was undisputed master of the sea. There was no doubt a close connection between the Scandinavians and the Normans. It seems, accordingly, very probable that Harold Bluetooth did visit Normandy on this occasion. There was ample reason for it, quite apart from any call for military help from Richard. The Danish incursion had a twofold object. Stripped of Dudo's verbiage, we may accept the fact that the intention of a part of the expedition was destined for peaceful colonization in Normandy, while the other had equipped itself for a buccaneering expedition against the Moors of Spain.

The main facts in regard to the somewhat conflicting accounts of the events of these years stand clear. Richard consistently maintained his friendship with Paris and successfully resisted the hostility of King Lothaire. Such, then, was the state of affairs in 962. Richard of

Normandy and Hugh of Paris remained firm allies; Lothaire, on the other hand, began to drift apart from Germany. These facts were the main reason for the collapse of the Carolingian Monarchy and the substitution therefor of that of the Capets.

In 962, Gerberge's brother, King Otto I—or the Great—was crowned Emperor of the West by Pope John XII, at Rome. He died eleven years later, but his latter years were occupied more particularly with Italian affairs. Otto's preoccupation in the south may have encouraged King Lothaire to hope that he might regain in Lorraine and on the Rhine some of the advantages which he and his predecessors had lost in the north. It was unfortunate for Lothaire that in 966 his mother died. Gerberge was the guiding spirit of the family. It was due to her that the failing line of the Carolingians attained such success as fell to them during the reigns of her husband and son. She had the wisdom to see that they could only maintain their position against Paris and Normandy by the aid of powerful allies, and she was consistent in her policy of seeking support from her brothers, Otto and Bruno, when she could get it.

After her death in 966 Lothaire began to intrigue with the Lotharingians and the Rhineland nobility; but he was careful not to disclose himself until the death of Otto the Great in 973 and the accession of the latter's son, Otto II.

Important as were the results of the substitution of the Capets for the Carolingians, Richard and Normandy played but a subordinate part in their achievement. Richard, in spite of his title of "Fearless", never made war for war's sake. We need not, therefore, dwell in detail upon the events which finally led to Hugh Capet's triumph. So far as Normandy was concerned, Richard's policy was firmly to maintain his alliance with Hugh; to accord him diplomatic support and probably to lend him Norman troops as had previously been done to his father.

Friendly relations had been maintained for many years between Lothaire and Hugh, and since 960 there had been no breach between the former and Richard. In 978 Lothaire, apparently with the approval of Hugh, suddenly attacked Aix-la-Chapelle, the German capital of the Empire. Otto II and his wife, Theophano of Byzantium, were hard put to it to escape. Otto soon drove Lothaire away, invaded his dominions, and ravaged the country as far as Paris. Lothaire concluded a hasty peace and gave up his claims on Lotharingia. But the peace was but a truce. On the death of Otto II in 983, Lothaire renewed the invasion. The war, however, ended by Lothaire's sudden death. He was succeeded by his son, Louis V, who reigned only for a year.

There remained but one remaining Carolingian—Charles, Lothaire's last surviving brother. He was unpopular and of no account. It was clear now that the line of Charlemagne was extinct. They had no friends. They had quarrelled with their Eastern cousins: they could not stand up against Hugh of Paris, backed by Normandy. On the death of Louis V a council was held at Senlis. Richard, though the most powerful vassal of Hugh, did not take the lead. This was done by Aldabero, Archbishop of Rheims, who had played a prominent part in the furtherances of Hugh's interests. There was practically no discussion and no opposition. Everyone accepted Hugh as King and gave him their allegiance. He was crowned at Noyon on June 1, 987.

The elevation to the throne of France of Hugh Caput made a slight alteration in the status of Richard of Normandy. The Duke of Paris had, since Richard's commendation, been the suzerain of the Duke of Normandy. Richard had done homage to Hugh and to Hugh's father. He had always avoided doing homage to Lothaire. Now that Hugh had become King, Richard became the direct vassal of the Crown.

There is not much more to tell of Richard's political activities, except of his services as a mediator between the new King and Vermandois. His diplomatic talents in this direction had been solicited before. In 965, when old Arnulf of Flanders died, his successor refused his homage to Lothaire. The latter proceeded to invade Flanders, but Richard, who was called in to mediate, succeeded in negotiating an arrangement. In this present case Albert of Vermandois tried to make capital for himself by supporting the Pretender Charles. King Hugh was proceeding to make short work of him, when the terrified Albert implored the mediation of Richard, who succeeded in bringing about an agreement. The interest in this rather trivial event lies in the fact that Albert's envoy to Richard was Dudo, Canon of St. Quentin, and it was on this occasion that the latter made the acquaintance of the Duke of Normandy.

The last ten years of Richard's life—the years during which Dudo knew him—were spent quietly. His reign of more than fifty years was the most important epoch in early Norman history. The victory gained by Bernard the Dane and Bernard de Senlis over King Louis and Hugh of Paris decided that the Norman State was to be a permanent institution. Any hope that the pirates could ever be packed off bag and baggage to Scandinavia was gone. There they were and the French had to make the best of them. Hugh of Paris accepted the fact and allied himself with Richard, and this alliance was cemented by his son. Lothaire would not accept it. He attempted further hostilities against the Normans, and the upshot was the extinction of the Carolingians and the substitution for them of the Capet dynasty as Kings of France.

From Richard's restoration till his death the time was spent in bringing order into the Norman State. Unluckily, the records are extremely sparse. Dudo says scarcely anything of institutions, methods of Government or administration. William of Jumièges tells very little. We hear a slight degree more of religious foundations, but it is all vague. There are two charters extant of the reign of Richard I—the earliest written documents in Norman history. The first is dated 968 and the second 989. They do not tell us much, but the signatures of the witnesses to the Charter of 968, which was a grant confirming Bretteville to the Abbey of St. Denis, give us some information as to who were Richard's chief advisers. These were Raoul d'Ivri, not yet a Count, for he simply signs his name. Raoul, Richard's uterine brother, was for the last thirty years of his reign his chief minister and commander-in-chief. He seems to have been a man of versatility and ability. Not only was he a soldier and administrator, but he was a patron of literature. He it was who supplied Dudo with most of his information, and it is possible that he was himself the author of a *History of the Normans* to which Dudo had access, but which is now lost.

In addition to Raoul d'Ivri there were Osmund de Centeville, Richard's old tutor; Ivo de Bellèsme; and Thorstein, or Thurstan, the son of Oslac, who was Lord of Briquebec and of Montfort sur Risle. Thorstein's sister, Anscelene, married Turquetil, the grandson of Bernard the Dane and son of Torf of Tourville (Torfville). Turquetil was the father of Ansquetil, the progenitor of the Harcourts. Thorold, Turquetil's brother—Baron of Pontaudemer—was Richard's brother-in-law, as he married Gunnor's sister, Veva. Osbern de Bolbec was also a brother-in-law of Richard and husband of Gunnor's other sister, Adelina.

Although our written information is meagre, we can form some opinion of Richard's achievements from the settled and ordered state of affairs which we observe in the next reign. Richard II no doubt carried on his father's work and improved it; but before Richard I little had been accomplished.

We have noticed that Richard I introduced the feudal system into his Duchy and we find seventy years later that Normandy was one of the most highly feudalized states in Europe. Almost all the landowners held their lands on a feudal basis, doing homage to the Duke and rendering him Knight's service. A calculation has been made by the late Mr. Corbett as to the number of fully armed mounted knights that Richard could bring into the field, and he puts it at perhaps rather less than 800, certainly not more. Apparently the average number of Knight's services due to the Duke from each tenant-in-chief was five, but there were a couple of dozen larger estates from whom ten to twenty were due. From this we can calculate that the number of baronies in Normandy was, roughly speaking, 100 to 120.

It must be remembered, however, that in Richard I's time the doctrine that fiefs were indivisible did not obtain. In the absence of an agreement or settlement, all the sons had rights of inheritance, and in default of sons, daughters might inherit and divide up the fief. This, of course, would make the number of fiefs variable. Later the doctrine of primogeniture became accepted and younger sons, in order to inherit, had to become subtenants. But it cannot be said that any definite amount of military service was fixed in relation to specific land in Richard's time, at any rate, in regard to lay fiefs. It must be remembered that a Norman barony was much less in extent than a similar possession in England.

Normandy was a small country, a good deal smaller, for instance, than the Kingdom of Wessex. Moreover, the Duke held large personal domains in almost every part of the Duchy. The administration of these domains was entrusted to the Viscounts. In France during the 10th century the Vicomté was the usual unit for administrative purposes and was often of considerable extent. In Normandy it was much smaller. We have no direct evidence of a documentary character to the effect that Richard introduced this system into Normandy. But in his son's time it was in full vigour and nothing gives us to believe that it was an innovation of Richard II. We can be even more sure that the system was not established by Rollo or by William Longsword.

The Viscounts in Normandy were the Duke's Civil Administrative Officers and were removable at his pleasure. There were but few Counts in Normandy—the Dukes were careful how they created powerful feudatories. The Counts, however, differed but slightly in status from the Viscounts. It is true that they tended to become hereditary and that their jurisdiction was more independent of the central Government than was that of the Viscounts, but, generally speaking, a Count was but a glorified Viscount. His greater independence of the central Government was perhaps due more than anything to the fact that in the counties there were no large ducal domains.

Richard's position as regards the Church was peculiar and important. The Norman Church had for many years been isolated. The ravages of the Danes in the 9th and early 10th century, the prevalance of heathendom and the consequent laxity of morals and discipline had completely disorganized the whole ecclesiastical system. No synods had been held for many years, nor were they held in Richard's time or, indeed, for long afterwards. The whole ecclesiastical patronage was in the hands of the Duke. The Archbishop of Rouen, Hugh, had been appointed by William Longsword. He was not a strict upholder of morality, but he was an able man and one of Richard's trusted advisers. When he died in 994, Richard appointed his second son by Gunnor, Robert, to his place. Robert was no stricter in his mode of life than his predecessor; but Richard, having to provide for his numerous brood, had for long designated Robert to succeed Hugh. It is said by the continuator of William of Jumièges that one of the reasons why Richard married Gunnor was to legitimize Robert and so remove the canonical objection of his illegitimacy to Church preferment. Whether this was so or not, Richard was careful that Robert should receive a good education to fit him for episcopal office.

Robert was a married man : Sir F. Palgrave suggests that the marriage was a Danish one, but I see no reason why it should not have been a Christian marriage, for the heathen marriage of a Christian Archbishop would be a strange anomaly. It is perfectly true that efforts to suppress clerical marriages had been constant ever since the council of Ancyra in 314, but the practice continued, and in Richard's day married clergy were frequent. Even as late as the days of Henry I we read of the married Bishop of Salisbury and his son—also a bishop.

So that it is unlikely that this deviation from the strict paths of clerical virtue would have been shocking to Norman opinion. Nor even if it had would Richard have cared. Robert had three sons: Richard, Ralph Wace, who became Hereditary Great Constable of Normandy, and William, the companion of Robert Guiscard. Besides being Archbishop of Rouen, Robert was created, either by his father or perhaps by his brother Richard II, Count of Evreux, and he was consequently known as the Count Archbishop. He was succeeded in his county by his eldest son, Richard, who is said to be the ancestor of the Devereux family.

Richard's control over the Norman Church was not confined to patronage. He did not allow even the highest ecclesiastic to exercise the jurisdiction of a Count in his own See. In every bishopric the Viscount had authority.

We have seen that both Rollo and William Longsword were not un-generous to the Church, and endowed it with grants of property. Richard, in developing the feudal system, increased this policy and created ecclesiastical as well as lay baronies; it is possible that the system of fixed quotas of Knight's service was introduced in his reign in respect of some of the ecclesiastical fiefs, though this is not certain.

Richard's monastic foundations were Fécamp, Mont St. Michel and St. Ouen at Rouen. Fécamp was actually founded by William Longsword, but greatly extended by Richard. The abbey which he built is the first of the many great abbeys, churches and monasteries for which the Norman architects are so justly famous. But it is not so much for the building itself that Fécamp is renowned, as for its monks.

In 910, William of Aquitaine founded the monastery of Clugny in the diocese of Macon. Its first abbot was Berno, who died in 927 and was succeeded by Odo, who devoted himself to the vigorous reform of the Benedictine system in France. The principal of the Clugniac Order was its enfranchisement from temporal control and its subordination solely to the Pope. The influence of the Order grew rapidly during the 10th century, and a number of monasteries, both old foundations as well as new, came under its rule. The monastic revival which had so great an influence in later days owed its inception to Clugny. In 954, Mayeul became abbot, and during his rule of forty years the Clugniac influence spread rapidly throughout the west. Among the foundations touched by the reforming zeal of the Clugniacs was Fécamp. Hitherto it had been occupied by secular canons; but they, like the other ecclesiastics of Normandy, set no example of the saintly life. Richard turned them out and applied to Mayeul for monks from Clugny to take over the abbey. Thus Fécamp was the source whence the monastic revival and the reform of the Church permeated gradually from Clugny into Normandy.

Fécamp became a favourite residence of Richard, as it was of his father. At the doorway of the church he placed a large empty sarcophagus. This was "both within and without the walls". It was filled weekly with wheat and the almoner of the monastery regularly distributed *largesse* from this source to the poor of Fécamp. When he came to die, this sarcophagus was Richard's place of burial.

We have scarcely any information as to Richard's fiscal policy. It is said that there was a mint at Rouen in William Longsword's time, but more probably Richard was the first Norman sovereign to coin money. The "*Sol rouennais*" is the earliest extant example of Norman coinage.

With the Duchy's long seaboard and its commercially minded Danish population, mercantile prosperity increased. The towns grew. Fairs were established. Foreign trade was encouraged, for a luxurious court always implies imports from abroad. One may conclude that agriculture flourished and that the peasantry shared in the general prosperity that peace engenders, for we shall see from the events that took place early in the next reign that the peasants were a numerous and independent body.

We have tried from the very meagre sources at our disposal to give some sort of account of the probable condition that Normandy attained during the reign of Richard I. It is admittedly speculative, vague and perhaps inaccurate in more than one respect; but we may certainly conclude that Richard maintained the autocracy established under his father and grandfather; that he improved the administration of the country; that he kept a strict control over the Church; that he did much to encourage monasteries and to reform abuses; that he revolutionized the system of land tenure and modernized the army, but did not fall into the error of creating large fiefs or of allowing his tenants to grow too powerful; that he encouraged trade and agriculture, improved his forests, and that in commissioning Dudo to write the *History of Normandy* he may be reckoned as a patron of letters.

Personally, Richard preserved through life the striking appearance that had distinguished him in his youth. He was tall, fair, active and good-looking; in old age he had a thick thatch of white hair and a long beard. In character, he was open-handed and generous, and popular with all ranks and classes. Shortly after 990 his health began to suffer, though he was not yet an old man—he had not reached the age of sixty. He retired to Fécamp, his birthplace, but it was clear that he was failing.

Raoul d'Ivri had fears as to the succession, for Richard had many sons. Primogeniture was not yet completely established D'Ivri summoned the chief men of Normandy to Fécamp, and they begged Richard to nominate his successor. Richard was not without apprehensions on that score himself, and had no difficulty in acceding to D'Ivri's request: he nominated his eldest son as his successor and commended him to the councillors. Shortly after this he died.

Dudo concludes his work with Richard's death, and winds up with a characteristic poem entitled, "*Apostropha Clausula hujus operis.*"

It is with some regret that we part from Dudo; unreliable though the old chronicler may be, he is rather an attractive character, for through all his bombastic, fantastic flamboyance and verbiage he displays a genuine affection for his dukes and, though he was not a Norman, a true love of Normandy. We now depend mainly on William of Jumièges, who tells us that for the history of Richard II and his successors he relies partly on the evidence of men whose age and experience render them reliable witnesses, and partly on his own personal knowledge; and in addition we have the valuable history of Ordericus Vitalis, supplemented by the works of William of Malmesbury, Henry of Huntingdon and others.

CHAPTER X

RICHARD II—PART I

State of Normandy—Raoul d'Ivri, Chief Minister—Peasant revolt—Rebellion of William d'Arques—Richard marries Judith of Brittany—His children and subsequent marriages —Black Fulk—Richard II adheres to Richard I's foreign policy—Relations with Anjou, England and Scandinavia—From Swegen to Athelstane—Murder of King Edward— Ethelred the Unready marries Emma of Normandy—Normans in England—Danes invade England—Emma of England.

WHEN Richard II succeeded, things were very different from those which obtained when William Longsword was murdered. We have tried to reconstruct and to summarize the work that Richard I did for Normandy; the Normandy of which Richard II became the ruler was not a semi-heathen, semi-Christian, partly Scandinavian and partly French State. Heathenism was dead; Norse may have lingered in some of the remote villages of the Cotentin or near Bayeux. But Richard II was regarded as a French prince, a vassal and peer of France and the principal ally of the new French Kingdom with its capital at Paris; not the outcast Dux Piratorum who everyone wished should be packed back to Scandinavia. Richard's father and the King, Hugh Capet, died almost at the same time, and the cordial relations which had existed between them were continued by the new Duke and the new King, Robert.

Richard II continued to employ his uncle, Raoul d'Ivri, as his chief minister, and the first event in his reign was a formidable movement among the Norman peasantry. We may believe that they were largely of Frankish stock, while the ancestors of the townsmen were Scandinavian. During the peaceful reign of Richard I, the Norman peasants had enjoyed tranquillity and tranquillity had produced prosperity.

The communal movement in the Middle Ages flourished most extensively between the dates 1100–1400, so that the associations of the peasantry of Normandy which troubled Richard at the outset of his reign must be regarded as a very early example of its beginnings. The object of the movement was the combination of individuals for the purpose of increasing their material prosperity. William of Jumièges says that there arose throughout Normandy a number of peasant organizations whose object was self-government and independence of the regular jurisdiction, either ducal or baronial. These communes arose in the interior as well as on the sea coast, so that the movement was of a widespread character.

Apparently the organization reached a considerable development, for William of Jumièges records that each commune elected two deputies who went as representatives to a central assembly. The object of the assembly was to receive the views of the separate communes and to formulate a general policy for all.

According to Wace, the peasants were prepared to rise against the oppression of their feudal masters and calculated that they outnumbered them by twenty to one. There was, naturally, considerable alarm when this communal movement was discovered. Raoul d'Ivri was instructed to deal with it. He did so faithfully. The wretched peasants, armed only with scythes or other primitive weapons, were no match for the heavily armed Norman cavalry soldiers. A considerable force of the latter was called out and a complete defeat of the movement ensued. Raoul d'Ivri carried it out with as great cruelty as efficiency. He dissolved the assemblies, seized the deputies and, cutting off their hands and feet, sent them back to their constituents as examples of the folly of the sin of rebellion.

Rather to our disgust the monk of Jumièges recounts this incident with considerable satisfaction. But the communal movement was not altogether barren of result, as Normandy became within a short time the freest state in France. Not long after we learn from early written records that absolute servitude had become obsolete. One may infer that the state of the Norman peasantry was more prosperous than was that of the peasantry in other parts of France. To rebel and to try and obtain a better state of things argues a certain amount of prosperity, for no one is likely to try and improve his political position until his economic state is more or less satisfactory. A man must eat before he can fight, and he must be able to provide to a certain degree for his wife and family.

Rollo, William Longsword and Richard I had been, on the whole, singularly free from revolt and rebellions in their own territory. The introduction of the feudal system, though no doubt at the outset of advantage to the Government, began to show its disadvantages. Although Richard I had not created many counties and had kept the fiefs of the barons within small limits, the great curse of the feudal system—that of turbulent nobles—now began to show itself.

William the Bastard, Richard the First's son, was created by his brother Count of Hiesme. In conjunction with certain other lesser Barons he began to make extravagant demands upon his brother, and eventually, as he failed to get all he wanted, he took up arms against him. Raoul d'Ivri was again entrusted with the restoration of order. He made comparatively short work of William and shut him up as a prisoner in Rouen. His adherents, however, continued in the field and made a considerable nuisance of themselves. D'Ivri dealt with them with much more severity than he did with William; he hunted them down, hanged

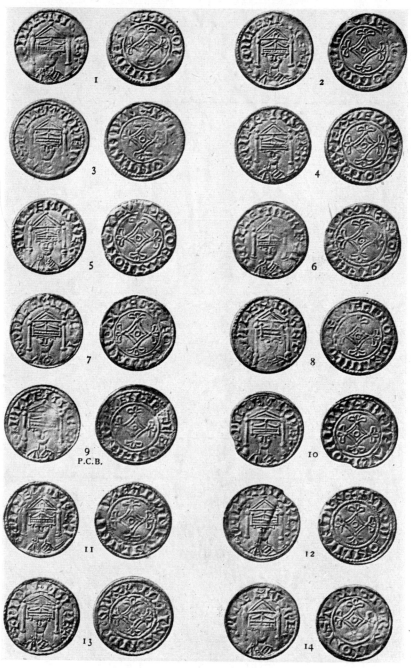

I. Coins (silver pennies) of William I's reign.

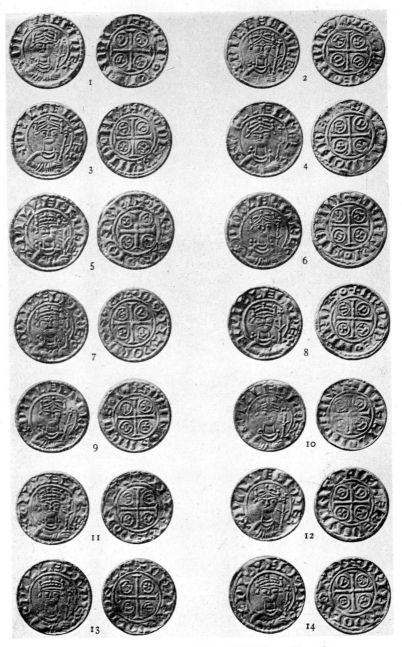

II. Coins (silver pennies) of William I's reign

those whom he could catch, and drove the others out of the country. William was five years a prisoner, but eventually he escaped. He had a love affair with Alice, the daughter of Turquetil, grandson of Bernard the Dane, who was his gaoler. She succeeded in smuggling a long rope into William's prison by which he let himself down from a window and so escaped.

However, D'Ivri was close after him, and, though he did not succeed in catching him, William found things so disagreeable that he determined to make his submission. Coming upon the Duke one day while he was out hunting in the forest of Vernon, he begged forgiveness. Richard, who was a good-natured man, forgave him and made him Count of Eu.* This fief had become vacant by the misdeeds of another relative. Richard I had made another bastard, Geoffrey by name, Count of Eu and Brionne. On this man's death his son, Gilbert, quarrelled with his uncle the Duke, and also with his cousin, Ralph Wace (Archbishop Robert's son). The latter murdered him and the Duke resumed the counties of Eu and Brionne.

It is difficult and puzzling to know how to describe adequately Richard II's relations with his neighbours and other foreign Powers. Normandy was a small but prosperous and powerful state for its size. It had a good army, but no fleet. During a long interval the country had known peace: agriculture was flourishing; commerce was increasing, as is shown by the number of fairs; and there was a considerable overseas trade.

We have seen that Brittany had from very early times, if not indeed from the days of Rollo himself, been a vassal of Normandy. But the tie had always been loose and the Breton princes not always the most loyal of vassals. Richard II sought to remedy this and to improve relations with Brittany by marriage. In the year (996) of his accession to the throne, Richard II married Judith, sister of Godfrey, Count of Rennes, whom he recognized as Duke of Brittany. Godfrey became doubly Richard's brother-in-law, for he married shortly afterwards Hadwisa, Richard's sister.

Judith's marriage with Richard was the first regular marriage of a Duke of Normandy, the fruit of which inherited the throne. She had three sons, Richard III; Robert the Magnificent—or, as he was otherwise called, Robert the Devil—both of whom became Dukes of Normandy; and William (or Nicholas, as he is variously called), who became a monk. There were also several daughters; the eldest, Alice, married Renaud, Count of Burgundy, and the youngest Baldwin, Count of Flanders.

Judith died some years later, and Richard II is said to have

---

* In the Charter William obtained the right to hold private Seignorial Courts and the Duke gave him Alice, Turquetil's daughter, in marriage, which seems as if she must have been her father's daughter and heiress.

G

married Estritha, a daughter of Swegen Forkbeard and, therefore, a sister of King Cnut; but there can be no truth in this story. If Estritha ever married a Norman Duke, it was Robert, Richard's son; but it is very doubtful. Richard II, however, did marry again after Judith's death, his wife being Popa, of whose family we have no information. This lady became the mother of William, Count of Arques, and of Mauger, Archbishop of Rouen, both of whom acquired an unenviable reputation.

Richard I maintained two cardinal principles in his foreign policy: friendship and alliance with Paris and good relations with the Scandinavian Sea Powers. Richard II followed his example, but he had a more difficult row to hoe. It is true that Flanders gave him less anxiety, perhaps, than it did to his father; but he had always to keep a sharp eye on Chartres and Blois. Tricky Theobald was dead, but his successor, Odo, had no more friendly feeling for Normandy than his predecessor. Moreover, a new power was growing up in the south-west.

In 843, when the Vikings first made their appearance on the Loire, plundering Nantes and massacring the Bishop at Mass, the legend says (and it is probably true) that one Tortulf led the resistance against their depredations. Tortulf is described as a "Woodman". This does not mean that he was a forester or charcoal-burner or anything of that sort, but a refugee in the forests who conducted thence a guerilla war against the invader; or, possibly, against others as well when there was no invader to repel. Tortulf was a sort of 9th-century Robin Hood, and for his services and those of his son, Ingelger, he received large grants of land on the Loire from Charles the Bald.

Ingelger's son, of whose historical existence there is no doubt, became Count of Anjou (or, perhaps, only Viscount) in 888 and reigned until 931. To him succeeded Fulk the Good, a prudent ruler who avoided war and built up the material prosperity of Anjou. Fulk's son and successor was Geoffrey Greygown. The latter had a brother, Burchard, who was educated at the Court of Hugh of Paris and who married Elizabeth, widow of Aymon de Centeville (Osmund's son) and was Lady of Corbeil and Melun. We mention this relationship now as the ownership of Melun is a matter in which Richard became involved. Geoffrey Greygown's son was Fulk the Black, who was the real builder of the Angevin power. Even in the days of Arnulf of Flanders, Herbert of Vermandois, Tricky Theobald of Chartres or Swegen Forkbeard, there was no greater ruffian or viler rogue than Black Fulk of Anjou, and withal there was probably no abler or more courageous ruler in Europe.

Black Fulk had great gifts in peace and in war, and he was as brave as he was wicked. Even in the rough times in which he lived, compared with all others he seemed destitute of any decent sentiment. He stole, he lied, he cheated, he tortured, he murdered, and he robbed. He burnt his wife at the stake in her wedding dress, he maltreated his son for no cause and made him crawl on all-fours, with a saddle on his back and a bit in his mouth. He betrayed his most loyal subject, Herbert of Le Mans, in order to steal his property. There were no wickednesses he shrank from and few that he did not commit. This was the ruthless ruffian who was steadily building up the Angevin power.

With England Richard I's relations had been distant but good and with Harold Bluetooth cordial. Normandy had a long coastline but no fleet, and it was essential, therefore, to keep on the best of terms with the Sea Powers. Richard II followed his father's policy of peace. He had conciliated the Bretons, always a doubtful element, by his double marriage and by his recognition of the Count of Rennes as Duke of Brittany.* This must have been a more far-reaching act than perhaps appears. Hitherto the Breton potentates appear as Counts of Rennes or Vannes, or other places in Brittany. Richard I claimed the title of Comes Bretonum. Now, however, his son conceded the title of Duke of Brittany to his brother-in-law.

Richard II's relations with England and Scandinavia were more complicated than those of his father. His object seems to have been to keep on the best terms he could with both and to avoid being mixed up in their quarrels. It must be remembered that both were Sea Powers and therefore capable of raiding the Norman coast. Richard had as much trouble as he wanted on his frontiers with his French neighbours to wish to be mixed up in the struggle between the English and the Danes across the Channel, but the cordial friendship between Scandinavia and Normandy which subsisted in the days of Harold Bluetooth and Richard I no longer existed.

Harold Bluetooth's son, Swegen Forkbeard, renounced Christianity, rebelled against his father and killed him in 988. He was the last of the old Vikings. Associated with him was Olaf Tryggvasson of Norway. We need not follow in detail the events of the new Danish invasions of England which culminated in its conquest, the acknowledgment of Swegen as King at Bath, and the subsequent subjugation of the country by his son, Cnut; but perhaps some few words are necessary in an attempt to understand the state of affairs in England—so different from those existing in the days of Athelstane. It is important to our story, for in the reign of Richard II there began that intimate connection between England and Normandy that culminated in the Conquest.

When Edward the Elder died he was undisputed King of England, and two years after his accession his son, Athelstane, was acknowledged by the princes of Strathclyde and Wales and the last semi-independent Chief, Ealdred of Bamborough, in Northumberland. But Athelstane's

---

* This recognition seems to have been disputed at a later date by Richard's successors.

kingdom had to be defended. None of the subject princes was really loyal, and they caused constant trouble. Athelstane, however, was too strong for them, and in 937 the victory of Brunanburh finally consolidated his position.

Athelstane's son, Edmund, reigned but five years and his brother, Eadred, had hard work to hold his own against Eric Bloodaxe of Norway, who succeeded in re-establishing Scandinavian dominion at York. But when Eadred died the throne seemed as firmly established as had been the case in the days of Athelstane. With Eadred's premature death in 955 the decline began. His successor, Eadwig, was a weakling. After he had reigned but a year a revolution in Mercia and Northumberland led to the election of his brother, Eadgar, as King of all England North of the Thames.

Luckily, perhaps, Eadwig died in 959 and his brother became King of the South of England as well as of the North. Eadgar was only thirty-two when he died in 975 and from his peaceful reign he was known as Rex Pacificus, but it would seem that he owed his peace to permitting the disintegration of his kingdom. The great men of the country, ecclesiastical as well as lay, ruled. At their head was Dunstan, who became in quick succession Bishop of Worcester (957), of London (959), and Archbishop of Canterbury (960).

Eadgar's son, Edward, was but thirteen when he succeeded, and immediately trouble began. What caused the dispute between the Magnates, who during the reign of Eadgar had managed to live peaceably together, is not clear. Perhaps the activity of Dunstan was resented and the unrest was due to distrust and dislike of the Archbishop.

King Edward was the only son of Eadgar's first wife, Aethelflaeda, after whose death he married Aethelfrith, the mother of Ethelred II, the Unready. In 978 Edward went to visit his stepmother at Corfe. As he was entering the gates he was surrounded by Aethelfrith's retainers and brutally murdered.

Nothing shows the weakness of the English Government of the time more clearly than the fact that this murder was apparently condoned. Dunstan seems to have made no protest, nor did Ethelwold, Bishop of Winchester. Aethelfrith seems to have quietly seized the government, for Ethelred II was but a child of ten.

The two Archbishops, Dunstan and Oswald, crowned the young King at Kingston-on-Thames, and his mother proceeded to carry on the government without let or hindrance. That she was allowed to do so seems to be the more extraordinary since besides the two Archbishops and the Bishop of Winchester there were still living Edward's Ealdermen, Aethelwine of East Anglia, Brithnoth of Essex, and Aelfhere of Mercia. The fact seems to be that England was breaking up into great principalities, in the same way that France had done in the time of the later Carolingians, and the Ealdermen and great ecclesiastics were not much concerned as to the central government so long as they were left to do as they liked.

But with the accession of Ethelred II the downfall became rapid. His name of the "Unready", or the "Redeless", seems due to the fact that he was never able to make a right decision, or to take the advice of an honest man. He was restlessly energetic at times, at others careless and slothful; but his energy was perhaps more mischievous than his sloth, for he was always active in the wrong direction. He wasted his substance on distant expeditions and failed to defend his own base. As the Anglo-Saxon Chronicler who seems to have had a good sense of humour says, "When the enemy is to the West our troops are kept in the East, and when he is to the South they go to the North," And again, "Anything that may be counselled never stands for a month."

We now come to an incident the details of which are extremely obscure, but it is important in that it deals with the relations between England and Normandy, relations which eventually led up to the Norman Conquest in 1066. According to William of Malmesbury, Richard I in 991 quarrelled with Ethelred II (the Unready). What the quarrel was over is not said. The explanation (which, however, must be accepted with the greatest caution) may be the following.

About the year 980 Viking raids upon England were renewed. At first these were mere buccaneering expeditions, but later, in 988, they took on a more serious nature. At that time Swegen Forkbeard, the son of Harold Bluetooth, and Olaf Tryggvasson of Norway were the leaders of a successful invasion of England on a considerable scale. These operations doubtless resulted in the acquisition of considerable plunder by the Vikings. Naturally, as one would suppose, the plunderers wished to realize on their booty. The prosperous condition of Normandy under Richard I may well have offered a profitable market for such ill-gotten gains and the Norman merchants of the Channel ports may perhaps have acted as receivers of stolen goods. If this were the case it would not be difficult to infer that there was considerable discontent at the matter in England and that the English Government were moved to make strong remonstrances.

Be that as it may, William of Malmesbury tells us that open war did not ensue, but that the Pope, John XV, was called in as mediator. He sent Leo, Bishop of Trier, to England and Normandy to make peace. The negotiations were successful and amicable relations between the two Powers were resumed. It is, however, difficult to tell from this meagre statement by William of Malmesbury how a subsequent and more serious quarrel between England and Normandy arose nine years later. For this event we have only the story of William of Jumièges, who does not mention the incident of 991.

William of Jumièges says that an English fleet invaded the Cotentin and landed an army which was defeated and destroyed by Nigel de Coutances. Now, we know from the A.S.C. that in the year in question the main Danish fleet suddenly left England for Normandy. Why they did this, or what they did when they got there, is unknown. But it appears that Ethelred, taking advantage of their absence, undertook an expedition to the North of England and ravaged Cumberland. Inefficient as Ethelred undoubtedly was, he could hardly have been so foolish as to leave his southern coast entirely unguarded whilst he and his main force were away on an expedition in the north. Now, according to the A.S.C., Ethelred had taken into his service about this time Earl Pallig, the husband of Gunhilda, sister of Swegen Forkbeard, and his ships. It is possible that Pallig's fleet was left to watch the Channel. Pallig was but a common pirate; he was bought by Ethelred, but in 1001 he deserted him and rejoined the Vikings, so clearly he was animated by no feelings of loyalty to the English King. It is conceivable, therefore, that the raid on the Cotentin had nothing to do with Ethelred, but was merely a private venture of Earl Pallig.

The matter is obscure and the details and explanation are not important. What, however, is important is that after this event better relations arose between England and Normandy. This was due to the marriage of Emma and Ethelred, which made the latter the brother-in-law of Richard II.

According to the Chronicle, but not according to William of Jumièges, who puts the date of Emma's marriage as previous to the Cotentin expedition, Ethelred's wife, Aethelflaeda, died in 1002 and he immediately afterwards married Emma. This would seem probable and suggests that the Anglo-Norman marriage was the tangible expression of the better relations between England and Normandy.

Emma must have been a bride of somewhat mature years, for in those days girls married very early. Richard I's connection with Gunnor began long before 960 when he married Emma of Paris. He did not marry Gunnor till after Emma died some time after 962. Most of his children were illegitimate, and it was to regularize their position that the marriage with Gunnor took place. As Emma of England subsequently married King Cnut in 1017 she was probably born after Richard I's marriage with Gunnor somewhere about 970, but, even putting her birth later, she must have been well over forty when she married Cnut, and probably more than thirty when she married Ethelred, and she had two children by each husband, but ladies in those days seem to have continued their child-bearing activities well on into middle life, since Ogiva had two sons by Herbert of Vermandois after she eloped with him in 941. King Louis was born in or about 920, so his mother must have been nearly fifty when her children by her second marriage were born.

Perhaps the Chroniclers or the scandalmongers thought Emma a lady who preserved her youth and vigour well into advanced years, for Brompton says that in 1050 (she must have been at least eighty then!) Archbishop Robert persuaded her son, King Edward the Confessor, that his mother was on too friendly terms with the Bishop of Winchester, Aelfwine. Emma indignantly denied the charge and proved her innocence by walking barefooted over nine red-hot ploughshares. Of course, the King and the Archbishop were confounded; they begged for pardon, were flogged by the Queen and the Bishop, and each gave nine manors to the See of Winchester. At this time Aelfwine was dead. The Winchester Chronicler tells the story, but in order to get over the fact that Aelfwine was no longer alive he moves the date to 1043, when, however, Robert was not Archbishop. One wonders what object there was in inventing this nonsensical story. According to William of Malmesbury, Emma was hated in England and was doubtless accused of many misdemeanours. The tale, therefore, may be a hotchpotch of stories invented to clear her character.

But to turn from legend to fact, it may be safely said that the marriage and the connection with Normandy led to the Norman Conquest. Henry of Huntingdon, indeed, states that William the Conqueror's relation to Emma gave him "*Secundum jus gentium*" (!) a claim to the English Crown.

Civilized and Gallicized as the Normans had become during the reign of Richard I, the old Adam soon arose within them when the chance of getting something for nothing presented itself. Troops of impecunious young Normans followed Emma to England and soon began to inveigle themselves into English estates and profitable posts. During the sixty-four years between the arrival of Emma and that of her great-nephew, the Conqueror, this process continued to grow, and the result contributed to the rapid conquest of a great country by a small and comparatively insignificant State.

Queen Emma obtained a rich dowry from her English husband; Rutland and even the city of Winchester fell to her; to these was added Exeter, and there she installed a Norman as Governor, named Hugh. When she became Queen of England Emma changed her name to Aelfgifu, for though the English admired her beauty and called her the "Gem of Normandy" they could not pronounce her name. She was the mother of two sons by Ethelred—Alfred and Edward the Confessor.

CHAPTER XI

RICHARD II—PART II

Swegen ravages England—Emma takes refuge in Normandy—War with Burgundy—Danish attacks renewed—Swegen conquers England—Ethelred and Emma again refugees at Rouen—Deaths of Swegen and Ethelred—Emma marries Cnut—Frontier difficulties with France and Chartres—Count Odo—Richard in the field—Scandinavian aid invoked—Norman feudalism—Richard's administration of Normandy—Peace and order—Increase of trade—Death of Richard at Fécamp.

PERHAPS one of the greatest follies of Ethelred's reign was perpetrated just after his marriage with Emma. Apparently with the consent of his Witan, he planned a general massacre of the Danes in England. Letters are said to have been sent out secretly all over the country, ordering the slaughter. Details of this event are contradictory in the various chronicles and they are unimportant. But there is no doubt that the massacre was carried out on a considerable scale and that a number of prominent Danes who were living in England on the faith of a recent treaty were killed. Among them was Gunhild, the wife of Earl Pallig, who had deserted Ethelred's cause. Pallig himself as a traitor might perhaps legitimately have been executed, but Gunhild seems to have been a hostage for the performance of the terms of the recent treaty which it was not suggested had been violated by the Danes.

Her murder was a particularly foolish act, for she was the sister of Swegen. It was not long before retribution overtook Ethelred. In 1003 Swegen arrived from Denmark. The Danes took Emma's newly acquired city of Exeter. She seems to have been badly served by her Norman commander, who apparently surrendered the place without trying to defend it. From Devonshire Swegen's army swept eastward, ravaged the country, and sacked and burnt Wilton and Salisbury, or, rather, Old Sarum.

Queen Emma took refuge in Normandy. It is not quite clear why Emma left her husband at this juncture; some say it was due to a personal quarrel with Ethelred, others that it was for political reasons. But one can hardly say, in spite of the misfortunes which beset Ethelred's cause, that she had to fly to Normandy for safety. Nor do we know exactly when she came back. It is not unlikely that Richard II found Emma's presence as a refugee in Normandy somewhat of an embarrassment. Swegen was a formidable person. Norman sympathies were perhaps, as

Freeman says, more inclined to their Scandinavian kinsmen than to their English neighbours. Tradition and sentiment bound the Normans to Norway and Denmark, and, unless Richard had put himself at the head of a kind of Crusade on behalf of the Christians of England against the Northern heathen, there was no reason for him to espouse Ethelred's cause.

This he was in no position to do, even had he wished to, for the rise of the new Angevin power on his southern frontier made it doubly necessary for him to follow a cautious policy. Also in 1003, as we shall see, he was occupied in assisting his ally, King Robert, in his campaign against Burgundy. Moreover, it is alleged that about this time Swegen made a treaty with Richard II of perpetual alliance, under which he permitted the sale of spoils taken from England in Norman ports and agreed to allow sick and wounded Danes to take refuge in his Duchy.

Whether this is true or not is uncertain, it is very doubtful if any definite agreement was concluded; but no doubt Richard was careful not to quarrel with Swegen and one can well imagine that the Normans were only too ready to act as receivers.

The Danish attacks on England were renewed in 1004 and, though Swegen went back to Denmark in the next year, he returned in 1006 with a considerable fleet. Ethelred's resistance gradually broke down and in 1007 he bought Swegen off with £36,000. But he had only a respite for a year. He tried to use it by preparing a fleet and by levying "ship money". He also made a further appeal for help to Richard II. Henry of Huntingdon tells us that a mission was sent by Ethelred to Normandy in 1009, but Richard II was no more ready to take up the cudgels for the English King than he had been when Emma first took refuge in Normandy.

For the next three years the struggle went on in England. Swegen gradually overcame the resistance of the English. In 1013 Emma fled again to Normandy, escorted by Aelfsige, Abbot of Peterborough. Her two young sons, Alfred and Edward, afterwards Edward the Confessor, went with her under the care of the Bishop of London. Ethelred took refuge on board ship in the Thames, but he soon followed his wife and in 1014 went to the Isle of Wight and thence to Normandy. It is said that he took the royal treasure from Winchester with him. This could hardly be the case, for Winchester was in Swegen's hands. But it may be that for safety Ethelred had hidden his valuables in the Isle of Wight and that he went there to recover them.

Arrived at Rouen, he joined his wife and children and Richard II gave him hospitality. Soon after his arrival the luck changed and Swegen, who had been acknowledged King of England at Bath, in 1013, died suddenly at Gainsborough. Ethelred and his wife returned to England and with the aid of his son by his first wife, Edmund Ironside, endeavoured to regain the kingdom from Swegen's son, Cnut. At first he had a slight measure of success, but his health was failing and in 1016 he died. Edmund Ironside carried on the war, but he died also a few months later. Eventually, Emma submitted to Cnut and married him in 1017.

The final conquest of England by the Danes and the marriage of Cnut to Emma must have relieved the anxieties of Richard II, so far as his maritime neighbours were concerned. So long as the war between the Danes and the English continued there was always danger to Normandy, and it was imperative, therefore, for Richard II to hold the balance and to observe a strict neutrality. It is for this reason, and also to give some description of Anglo-Norman relations at this time, that we have ventured to give a brief account of the situation in England during Richard II's reign. We must now turn back a little in order to trace the course of events on Richard II's land frontiers.

When Richard II succeeded his father Normandy was filled with a number of idle people who were on the look-out for an outlet of their energies in war. There had been little for soldiers to do for ten years. Moreover, there was always a trickle of fortune-hunting Danes and Scandinavians flowing into Normandy in the hope of employment. Richard I had kept the peace with a strong hand. On his death Richard II had had trouble with his rebellious brothers. It must have been something of a relief to the Duke, then, to find his suzerain, King Robert, seeking his aid in a war against Burgundy, in 1003.

The Norman troops apparently formed part of the French army more as mercenaries than as allies. Now, although the Burgundian war was not primarily a quarrel of Richard's it was useful to him for more and weightier reasons than for the employment and training of his idle troops. Normandy had enjoyed what for those days was peace since the restoration of Richard I, and with peace had come prosperity. But it must be remembered that the sword of Damocles always hung over the head of the Duke of Normandy. The State was surrounded by potential enemies with whom differences might arise at any moment; so that Richard welcomed an opportunity for cementing his alliance with Paris, especially as it gave occupation to his somewhat troublesome vassals. Just before the outbreak of the Burgundian war, Richard was able to render a small but significant service to King Robert. Bouchard of Anjou, son of Fulk the Good, was being educated at the Court of Paris. He was in high favour there with the King, who was anxious to provide for him by a good marriage.

It will be remembered that Osmund de Centeville accompanied Richard I as a boy to his captivity at Lâon and was the means of effecting his escape. Throughout Richard I's reign Osmund was one of his most trusted advisers. His son, Aymon, held the important fiefs of Corbeil and Melun, not under the Duke of Normandy but as a direct vassal of the Crown. Aymon de Centeville went on a pilgrimage to Rome not long after his marriage, but unfortunately died in Italy. His wife, Countess Elizabeth, was a childless widow and held her husband's fiefs of Corbeil and Melun. Young Bouchard of Anjou married the widowed lady and King Robert confirmed him in the possession of the two towns.

It was important both to France and to Normandy that an independent and trustworthy person should hold Melun. Bouchard, though an Angevin, was more likely to look to France and Normandy as the stronger powers than to Anjou, especially as he was threatened by Chartres, which was also a menace to the Kingdom and the Duchy. Tricky Theobald's descendant, Odo II, inherited his evil qualities. He was an ambitious and unscrupulous man. He had gradually pushed the frontier of Champagne (he was Count of Champagne as well as Chartres) almost up to the French frontier, and King Robert's security depended to a considerable degree upon the loyalty of the holder of Corbeil and Melun. To hold Odo of Chartres and Champagne in check was as important to Normandy as to France, for Odo had claims on the County of Dreux, a debatable land lying between Normandy and Chartres.

Odo was anxious to get hold of the frontier fortresses and he bribed Walter, the Governor of Melun, to hand over the place. Both King Robert and Richard II were equally incensed, and it was Richard who acted. He advanced on Melun, defeated Odo, took the place and hanged Walter and his wife outside the castle as an example. This close alliance with France undoubtedly contributed to the prosperity and security of Normandy, and we see in it the same skill that Richard II displayed in his dealings with England and Denmark. But in 1007 a cloud spread over the relations between the Kingdom and the Duchy.

The County of Dreux, as has been noted, lay between Normandy and Chartres. Its line of independent Counts died out in the days of Richard I and the County was quietly annexed by Normandy. In 1007 Richard II built the castle of Tillières, a strong fortress which considerably enhanced the military value of the County. Now, all this would have been indifferent to King Robert had he only had his Norman ally to deal with, but it became a very different thing when Normandy began to draw closer to Chartres—Champagne. Odo II sought better relations with Normandy, and Richard II, in pursuance of his habitual peace-seeking policy, was ready to meet him. Not only did he agree to the marriage of Odo to his sister, Maud, but he granted her as a dowry half the County of Dreux; with the condition, however, that should Maud die childless her dowry should revert to Normandy. Naturally, such an accession of strength by Chartres was regarded with misgiving by King Robert. But the old relations between France and Normandy were soon restored.

Maud died childless in 1015, but Odo declined to hand back her dowry. Richard immediately attacked Chartres. Odo was supported by

Hugh, Count of Maine, and Count Waleran de Meulan. Odo and his two allies gathered a formidable army, but Richard attacked, thoroughly defeated them and scattered their forces. This battle is the only record we have of Richard II's personal abilities as a general in the field. Judging from his success on this occasion, one may perhaps think that had he not been so successful a diplomatist he might have been equally successful as a soldier. In spite, however, of this defeat, Odo was by no means conquered. Indeed, he recovered himself completely and was later able to press Richard severely—so severely that the latter was obliged to call in Scandinavian help, and William of Jumièges tells us that King Olaf of Norway and King Lacman of Sweden arrived in the Seine with their fleets.

Apparently they had been engaged on a piratical expedition to Brittany, and Richard II must have been indeed hard-pressed to call in as allies pirates who had been plundering his vassals. The story is obscure and inaccurate as told by William of Jumièges, since there was no "Lacman", King of Sweden. He was probably a "lagman", or lawman. Olaf of Norway, however, can be identified; he appears subsequently as St. Olaf.

It is curious that King Robert did not come to the assistance of Richard II. Had he done so the two together could have made short work of Odo. Perhaps he thought that both of them were getting too powerful and a little mutual reduction of strength would do no harm to the Kingdom of France. But the appearance again of Vikings in the Seine thoroughly alarmed the French. King Robert acted promptly. He summoned a great Council of his tenants-in-chief, a rare event in France. The Duke of Normandy and Count of Chartres were called to attend, and King Robert settled the dispute by a judgment of Solomon whereby Chartres kept Dreux and Normandy Tillières. This arrangement proved satisfactory, though the dispute and the war with Chartres were the least successful of Richard II's ventures, and the least fortunate part of his policy of securing peace by marriages between the House of Normandy and its neighbours.

In other directions that policy had met with great success. His own marriage with Judith of Brittany and that of his sister, Hadwisa, with Judith's brother, Godfrey, contributed in no small degree to more satisfactory relations with Brittany and Normandy. His diplomacy with England and Denmark was doubtless assisted by Emma's marriage, first with Ethelred II, and still more by her second marriage with Cnut. The marriage between Maud and Odo of Chartres was certainly a political failure, but it was repaired by the marriage of Richard II's daughter, Alice, with Stephen of Blois, Odo of Chartres's son by Ermengarde of Auvergne. More important, however, was the marriage of his daughter, Adeliza, to Reginald, Count of Burgundy.

A campaign in support of Reginald was the last event of importance

of Richard's reign.   The disreputable and predatory Bishop of Auxerre
and Count of Chalons seized the unfortunate Reginald, put him in a
dungeon and generally maltreated him.   Richard immediately sent a
force under his son, afterwards Richard III, to liberate him.   Young
Richard, though not yet of age, seems to have conducted a most successful
campaign.   He liberated his brother-in-law, took Chalons, and forced
the wicked old Bishop to crawl out on all-fours and to offer Richard a
ride on his back—or so the story goes.   It is said that this campaign was
the origin of the quarrels between Richard and his brother, Robert.
Richard the elder was in command and Robert was so jealous that he
refused to accompany the expedition.

Any account of the life of Richard II must include some description
of the internal condition of Normandy, the growth of its institutions, its
trade, commerce and general development.   Unfortunately, the material
for such a description is very meagre indeed.   But we can glean a little
here and there.   In the first place, we may be sure that the country
enjoyed internal peace.   Normandy became rapidly feudalized under
Richard I and the feudal system of government developed under his son.
But Norman feudalism was free from many of the evils it suffered from in
other countries, and it differed in many details from the system as it
developed in other parts of France.   In the reign of Richard I the vassal
of the Baron held from his Lord a *precarium*, that is to say he was a tenant-
at-will and the tenancy could be dissolved at the Lord's pleasure.   In
the days of Richard II, or even perhaps late in the reign of Richard I, the
precarium became a *beneficium*: i.e. the tenant derived his rights from his
Lord, but they were of a more permanent character than the original
tenancy-at-will.

All through the reign of Richard II the hereditary principle was
gaining ground rapidly, and in the latter part of the reign the *beneficium*
gradually became a *feudum*, denoting that the holding descended from
father to son.   Parallel with the growth of the recognition of hereditary
descent, the feudal rights of the Lord in regard to wardship and mamage
grew up.   Women could inherit land and the Lord claimed and exercised
the right of choosing the husband of the heiress of his vassal.   Similarly,
the Lord exercised the right of wardship over a minor heir and claimed a
succession duty on his inheritance.

Throughout the history of the early Dukes we see that the sovereign
maintained his authority unimpaired.   Fiefs were small in size: the ducal
officers, the Viscounts, became more important under Richard II than
they were under Richard I.   They were the Duke's lieutenants and they
were the main factors in the government; they commanded the Duke's
troops and castles, maintained order, administered justice and collected
the revenue.   A careful check was kept on the Barons.   Private war,
though not wholly suppressed, was strictly limited.

It seems to have been impossible to abolish this custom entirely, even for strong Dukes like Richard I and Richard II. But they exercised a rigid control. The Duke's licence had to be obtained before such a war could be started. He claimed to exercise supervision over the campaign which was conducted under his rules and limitations. Licences were required to build castles. In disputes over claims for lands, ravaging was forbidden, assaults and ambushes were not allowed in the ducal forests, nor might the arms, horses or property of a prisoner captured in a blood feud be retained. It is true that all these details are not recorded until the reign of William the Conqueror, and some of the developments may only date from his time, but there is no doubt that Richard II extended his father's general scheme to maintain peace and order and to prevent feudalism from becoming a pest.

That peace and order reigned in the land we can tell from William of Jumièges. After the revolt of the peasantry which was suppressed by Raoul d'Ivri, and the rebellion of William of Arques right at the beginning of his reign, we hear no more during Richard II's time of revolts of the nobles or of serious disturbances. The fact that many Norman barons sought adventure abroad shows that in an age when the only occupation for a gentleman was fighting there was not much to do at home. The Burgundian war gave occupation to some, no doubt. Others sought their fortune in England. But the most important independent exploit of the Normans in Richard II's reign was the beginning of the conquest of Apulia and Sicily by the sons of Tancred.

Another expedition, though not so successful a one, was that of Roger Toeny in 1018. Roger was one of the few Norman nobles who did not trace their origin from the bastard children of the Duke's mistresses. According to William of Jumièges, Roger was descended from Malahule, a brother of Earl Rögnwald, or perhaps of Hilda, his wife, for he is described as the uncle of Rollo. Roger Toeny went to Spain to fight the Moors and carve out a kingdom for himself. He married the daughter of the Countess of Barcelona, but though he was a tough fighter he failed to establish himself in Spain.

From the scanty material at our disposal in Richard II's Charters we can trace the development to a certain limited extent of the ducal Court, and we hear of a chamberlain, a constable, a chancellor and a hostianus. Probably the dapifer, or seneschal, existed in Richard II's reign, for we hear of him early in the time of Robert I. But it is interesting to note that their official duties seem to have been of limited extent. The Bishops appear to have had more to do with the machinery of government than had their great officers, and the Viscounts had as before much more power in civil administration than the Bishops.

Wace tells us an exaggerated story of Richard II's fiscal system. He says that the Duke shut himself up in the tower at Rouen and went through his accounts with his Viscounts and his provosts, but though this story is untrue Richard certainly had a ducal treasury, for he gave £100 from his "camera" to redeem the lands of Saint Benigni, and he made a permanent grant of the tithes of his Camera to Fécamp. We also learn that the profits of the coinage and the "Customs", the "Census" and the tolls, were not included in the Camera. In fact, the Camera must have included the extraordinary income in contradistinction to the fixed revenues.

From very early days we hear praise of the justice of the Dukes of Normandy, but we know very little about its organization. All we can say is that the Dukes kept a very tight hand on their feudal tenants and controlled and limited the rights of Seiqhurial jurisdiction. Criminal justice certainly developed rapidly in early Normandy, and nothing is heard of the system of compurgation, though it was practised both by the Franks and the Northmen.

Trade and commerce flourished under Richard II; sometimes it was rather shady trade, as, for instance, the profits obtained from the Danes who pillaged England. But there was a regular system of legitimate commerce between Rouen and London. The intercourse grew and flourished, and in the reign of Edward the Confessor and, perhaps, during that of Richard II, the Rouen merchants owned their own wharf at Dowgate, London. Important fairs and markets grew up. We hear of the fair of Caen and of boroughs gaining commercial importance in various parts of the duchy.

Richard II has been called the Good by monkish historians, probably because of his munificence to the Church, but perhaps he deserves the title more for the general prosperity which he brought to Normandy. He was a generous patron of monasteries, especially of Fécamp, which town was always favoured by the Dukes. It was at Fécamp that he held a regular assembly each Easter and it was there that he issued his great Charter to the abbey in 1025. Richard's partiality for Fécamp is natural, perhaps, in view of the particular connection of his family with that place, and his Charter of 1006 in which he grants to Fécamp freedom of election, according to the Custom of Clugny, shows the growth of the influence of Clugny in Normandy.

Although the Normans were the descendants of Vikings, Normandy was not a naval power and had no fleet, but Richard's army was well armed and well organized, though small. The number of knights at his disposal was no greater than those available to his father; perhaps actually less, in view of the overseas adventures undertaken by so many Normans during his reign.

It is regrettable that we have so little material for a history of Richard II. It is clear that during his time the power of Normandy, its prosperity and its wealth, developed rapidly, as we learn from the emigration which took place that the population increased beyond the means of subsistence, which is proof of the development of agriculture. It is noticeable, also, that the Scandinavian element increased. Probably this may have been due in some degree to immigration from Denmark and Norway, but also to increase in the numbers of the descendants of the original Scandinavian settlers.

To us the obscurity in which the history of the reign is involved is particularly tantalizing, for it was during the reign of Richard II that the close connection between England and Normandy began which culminated in the Norman Conquest.

By Judith of Brittany Richard had two sons, Richard and Robert. The former had gained distinction, as we have seen, by his conduct of the Burgundian campaign to release his brother-in-law, Reginald. Unfortunately, there was bad blood between the two brothers, increased no doubt by the designation of the elder as heir to the duchy just before Richard II's death in 1026. The latter probably expected trouble between the brothers after his death, for he especially commended Richard to the Bishops, Counts and Barons on his deathbed, and he left the rich country of Hiesmes to Robert, an ample provision for a younger son. Richard II died at Fécamp and was buried there, like his predecessor.

CHAPTER XII

RICHARD III

Accession—Betrothal to Adela of Paris—Quarrel with his brother, Robert—Siege of Falaise
—Richard and Robert reconciled—Richard's death and Robert's accession—Possible
alternatives—Nicholas of St. Ouen.

YOUNG RICHARD succeeded peacefully enough to his father's throne. The
Barons accepted him readily and paid him their homage as vassals; he
was duly invested at Rouen, whence he proceeded to Paris to do homage
en parage to King Robert. On this occasion he became betrothed to
the King's infant daughter, Adela. Richard made a generous settlement
on his future bride—Cherbourg, Caen, Valognes, Cerisy, Oglander,
Mohun, and other places mostly situated in the Cotentin. Richard's early
death, however, prevented the marriage being carried out.

Meanwhile, Robert, the young Duke's brother, was nursing a griev-
ance. His father had made him Count of Hiesmes, but he had not included
Falaise. The town was really part of the Hiesmois and there seems to be
no particular reason why Robert should not have had it. Robert had no
love for his brother, of whom he was bitterly jealous, and his bad temper
was nourished by an individual named Ermenold, a Breton who was
suspected of black magic. Ermenold was killed in a duel, but Robert
still nursed his jealousy and he began to attract round him numbers of
idle young people ripe for any mischief. He became a kind of "Black
Michael". At last he seized Falaise. This was more than his brother
could stand. Hitherto Richard III had paid no attention to Robert's
complaints. But now that he was in open rebellion Richard besieged
Falaise; he soon brought Robert to reason, and an accommodation based
on the *status quo ante* was arranged. Robert remained Count of Hiesmes
and Richard kept Falaise.

In this settlement Richard III showed his wisdom. Robert was
popular in the duchy and had many adherents. It was obviously the
wisest thing to do to try and make a good subject of him. Whether this
would have happened or not one cannot say. After the reconciliation the
two brothers went to Rouen and rejoicings took place. During these
Richard gave a great party, after which he and a number of other guests
were taken seriously ill. Poor Richard died and so did some of his
companions. Of course, poisoning was hinted at and gossip grew about

Robert.   Indeed, he was generally suspected and the suspicion hung about him for the rest of his life.   It was not infrequent that people were assumed to be poisoned in the Middle Ages.   Doubtless many a case of appendicitis was attributed to foul play.   It is probable, however, that many people were actually poisoned.   Culinary hygiene and cleanliness were sadly to seek in those days and cooking-pots were not free from suspicion.   Ptomaine and botulism were no doubt often the cause of death, and the victim certainly died of accidental poisoning.   Very likely this was the case here and the unfortunate Robert was quite wrongly suspected.

From all accounts Robert was an open-handed, kindly natured man and it would seem foreign to his character to commit so abominable a crime as to murder his brother and, in doing so, a number of perfectly innocent people as well.   So we may well give him every benefit of the doubt.   Moreover, the very fact that he was accepted without any difficulty as his brother's successor argues that the poisoning story was but malicious gossip.   There would have been a possible alternative heir, for Richard III had a son named Nicholas.   Probably, to avoid his coming forward with a claim to the throne, Robert took advantage of the fact that young Nicholas had a bent for religion.   He placed him in the Abbey of Fécamp, and as the youth was a member of the ducal family he soon became Abbot of St. Ouen.

Nicholas shared the family ability and that taste for architecture that was beginning to show itself among the Normans, and nowhere more than among the members of the reigning house.   He rebuilt the Church of St. Ouen, including the well-known apse, and as he attended the funeral of William the Conqueror he must have lived to be an old man.

CHAPTER XIII

ROBERT I—PART I

His character—Quarrel with Archbishop of Rouen and Bishop of Bayeux—Arletta of Falaise
—Birth of William (the Conqueror)—Rebellion of William de Bellèsme and his sons
suppressed—William Talvas—War with Flanders—Death of King Robert of France
—Disputed succession—Robert takes the part of Henry—Vexin annexed to Normandy
—Peasant rising in Brittany—Bretons refuse homage—Invasion of Brittany—Duke Alan
does homage.

ROBERT I had much of the ability of his father, but little of his patience and caution. He was extravagant in his habits and spent much of the money saved by his prudent parent. His habit of spending made him popular and earned him the title of Robert the Magnificent. To this nickname he could justly lay claim, but why he should also have been called "Robert the Devil" no one has been able to explain. Robert began his reign by a violent quarrel with the Church and with his uncle and namesake, the Archbishop of Rouen. This prelate was also Count of Evreux, and Ordericus Vitalis, in order to excuse his breach of the vow of celibacy, says that ,"in his capacity as Count of Evreux" he took a wife !

The Duke besieged the Archbishop in his stronghold of Evreux, drove him out and forced him to take refuge with King Robert at Paris. From this safe abode the ecclesiastic launched the anathema of the Church against his nephew and Normandy. Probably owing to the good offices of the King, a reconciliation was effected and the Archbishop returned to Rouen, where he, a builder too, occupied himself in re-erecting the cathedral. Later, Robert and he seem to have become quite good friends, as the Duke called him into his counsels and we see his name quite frequently as a witness to Robert's Charters.

The quarrel with Archbishop Robert was not the only breach between the Duke and the Church. Hugh d'Ivri, Bishop of Bayeux and son of Raoul d'Ivri, Robert's great-uncle, provisioned his castle of Ivri and laid in a store of arms there. Then he went to France and surreptitiously raised a body of knights to garrison the castle. But Robert got to hear of the Bishop's proceedings and surrounded Ivri, so that when Hugh returned from France with his knights he found his men shut up in the castle and himself shut out ! Hugh had to make terms with the Duke to surrender the castle and to go into exile.

William of Jumièges tells us nothing about the reasons for these quarrels with the Church, but clearly they were not entirely personal and there must have been some political reason. William of Jumièges, being the Court historian, glosses the matter over and ascribes Robert's anti-clerical actions as due to evil counsellors. Richard de St. Vannes, for instance, is mentioned as such by Hugh de Florigny. Other writers, such as Gradulf, Abbot of St. Wandville, are more downright in their criticism.

It may have been at this time, or perhaps previously, before Robert succeeded to the dukedom, that his romance with Arletta of Falaise occurred. The Duke always showed a peculiar affection for this place. It was over Falaise that he and his brother, Richard III, quarrelled. Falaise is one of the most picturesquely situated towns in Normandy. It stands on a rocky height on the right bank of the Ante, a small tributary of the Dive. The castle in which Robert lived is still, though a ruin, in some kind of preservation. It stands on a promontory of rock jutting out into the valley opposite the Mont Misnt. In the keep of the castle, the room where, it is said, William the Conqueror was born is still shown, and also the window whence Robert I saw Arletta paddling in the Ante. More prosaic people say that he met the young lady at a dance and fell in love with her then. Perhaps he did both.

But there were disadvantages about Arletta, even in the easy-going society of the day. The Danish wives or mistresses of Rollo, William Longsword and Richard I were, at least, ladies; but poor Arletta was not only a plebeian but almost of outcast origin. We have had occasion to observe that Falaise was the centre of the Norman leather trade, and its suburb, Guibray, held, and still holds, a well-known and flourishing horse fair between August 10 and 25. Arletta's father, Fulbert—or Hulbert, as he is variously called—was in large business as a tanner. Now, in the Middle Ages the trade of a tanner was despised as a low trade, necessary though it was at a time when leather was used so considerably in arms and clothing. The reason for this aversion is not far to seek: tanning and skinning are dirty, messy occupations and the smell of a medieval tanyard, and probably also of a medieval tanner, was disgusting even to medieval nostrils.

Fulbert was a Walloon by origin, according to Albert of Troisfontaines, and had been born at Chaumont, near Lièges. His wife was named Doda. When they came to Falaise is unknown, but Fulbert's tannery business throve and he grew rich. But he was unpopular because of his trade and became more so when he added brewing to tanning. There was a strong prejudice against the amalgamation of the two industries. In England it was forbidden. The reason is not far to seek, for people do not like their beer to be mixed up with the refuse of the tanyard, and there were disagreeable stories that beer was improved in taste by the addition of animal matter which unscrupulous brewers put into their vats. So, either from his trade or perhaps because of jealousy from his wealth, Fulbert and his family were ostracized in Falaise.

But Robert cared nothing for this. Sexual morality was not a strong point with any of Rollo's brood, and Robert cared little for public opinion. He frequented Fulbert's house, ran after his daughter and eventually carried her off to his castle. To do them justice, Fulbert and Doda had no wish to see their child the mistress of the Duke; they would have preferred to see her properly married to a man in her own station of life. But Norman princes were powerful people in matters of this kind and Fulbert's objection weighed nothing with Robert, nor, it must be added, with Arletta, who was quite ready to accept the situation for her virtue was easy as her face was pretty. Though he never would marry her, Robert was faithful to his mistress, nor do we hear of any backsliding on her part. Fulbert, perhaps, was conciliated, since shortly after he was made Chamberlain to the Duke, and Arletta tried not wholly successfully to assume the position of Gunnor. After Robert's death she married Herluin de Centeville, a Norman of good family, by whom she had several children, the most famous of whom was Odo, Bishop of Bayeux and Earl of Kent.

To Robert and Arletta were born but two children—William the Conqueror and a daughter. Although much more disreputable love affairs of former and later Dukes of Normandy were regarded with complete tolerance by the Norman upper classes, many of whom were the descendants of such connections, the affair with the tanner's daughter caused a great scandal.

It will be remembered that when Richard I created the Norman nobility the first three of his Barons were Osmund de Centeville, Bernard the Dane and Ivo de Bellèsme. The Bellèsme family were of the highest rank, therefore, in Normandy, and they were not descendants of ducal bastards. In actual fact the fief of Bellèsme lay along the Border between Maine and Normandy and was held directly from the King of France. Unlike the Norman Barons to whose fealty the Dukes were entitled, the Lords of Bellèsme regarded themselves with some justice as sovereign princes. Their territory was greater, their jurisdiction wider and their authority more extensive than that of the other Norman nobles. William, the great-grandson of Ivo, called William Talvas, was the first to voice his annoyance.* Wace, though he may not be altogether the most trustworthy of our authorities, tells us that when young William was born Talvas chanced to come from Alençon to Falaise and was taken to see the

---

* He was the younger brother of Yver, Bishop of Seéz, who succeeded his brother, Robert, when the latter was murdered in 1033. William Talvas was never Lord of Bellèsme. Bishop Yver died in 1070 and was succeeded in most of his property by his daughter, Mabel, who married Roger Montgomery, Earl of Shrewsbury.

baby, whom he cursed, saying, "*Hunte soit, car par toi e par ta ligne iest la mienne moult abaisse.*"* It was a prophecy that came true, but Wace wrote after the event. Still, whatever the accuracy or inaccuracy of the details of the story, it shows that the Norman aristocracy were in truth scandalized and feared doubtless that the bastard brat might be foisted on them as their sovereign.

Whether old William Talvas was moved by this insult offered to the Norman peerage, whether Robert's easy-going government tempted him, or whether he was in some way mixed up with Archbishop Robert and Bishop Hugh of Bayeux, we cannot tell. But he rose in rebellion against the Duke. Lax as Robert was in some things, he was an able soldier and his forces were sufficient to deal even with such powerful vassals as the Bellèsmes. He promptly besieged Alençon, forced William Talvas to surrender, and made him come before him barefooted with a saddle on his back to make his submission. After which the easy-going Robert handed him back all his possessions.

The Bellèsmes were bad blood, surly, revengeful and cruel, not only in this generation but in later ones as well. Old Talvas bitterly and somewhat naturally resented the indignities put upon him, although no one can say that they were not deserved. William Talvas had four sons, cruel and unscrupulous young men like their father. The elder, Guerin, murdered his cousin who came to pay a friendly visit to his father, and for this crime, so William of Jumièges tells us, he was seized and strangled by Satan. It is curious that the latter should have punished the murderer, who seems to have been one of his most apt disciples! The other three sons, Fulk, Robert and William, shared their father's rage against Duke Robert, and shortly after their elder brother's demise, by diabolical or natural agency, they again took up arms against the Duke and set out on a raiding expedition in the latter's domain.

Robert does not seem to have been obliged to come against them in person, for the three young rebels were completely defeated by his local troops in an engagement in the forest of Blason. Fulk was killed, Robert wounded severely, and William de Bellèsme the younger apparently escaped to tell the tale to his wicked old father, who promptly died of rage and spite. The victories that Robert had obtained over the Bishops and the Bellèsmes appear to have put an end to the internal disorders and left him free to attend to other things.

Duke Robert's next exploit was a campaign in Flanders. It will be remembered that when Richard III visited his suzerain, King Robert, at Paris to do him homage *en parage* on his succession to the Duchy, he became engaged to the King's infant daughter, Adela. As Richard III died shortly after, Adela became free and Count Baldwin of Flanders solicited

---

* "Shame. For through thee and thy line mine will be greatly brought down."

her hand for his son, Baldwin de Lisle. Adela was sent to Flanders to be brought up, and at a very early age she was married to the younger Baldwin. This young man, apparently relying on the help of his father-in-law and very possibly thinking that the traditional Norman French *entente* would neutralize Normandy, proceeded to rebel against his father and drive him out of Flanders. The elder man took refuge at the Norman Court.

It is possible that had Richard II been still alive he would have followed the same cautious policy as he had done in the case of Ethelred II, when he fled with his wife, Emma, to take refuge from Swegen Forkbeard at Rouen. But Robert I was of rasher temper than his father. Regardless of any repercussions on his relations with Paris, Robert immediately took up the cudgels on behalf of the elder Baldwin, who, indeed, enjoyed considerable support still among the Flemings. The Norman Flemish army invaded Flanders and gained an immediate and complete success. In this campaign Robert I is said to have behaved with great cruelty towards the rebels; and it was his behaviour, so it is said by some, that gained him the name of Robert the Devil.

In any case, young Baldwin had a severe lesson and made a complete submission to his father. King Robert made no move on behalf of his new son-in-law. Perhaps the reason was his failing health, for soon after peace was restored in Flanders he died. His son, Henry, had been associated with his father in the kingdom for some time. He was not his mother's favourite and he must have known that on his father's death he might have trouble in asserting his right to the succession. Perhaps for that reason France had been cautious in the recent Flemish dispute and careful not to antagonize Robert of Normandy.

King Robert of France married in 996 the widow of Odo of Chartres, Tricky Theobald's son. Bertha was the daughter of Conrad, King of Arles and King Robert's cousin, though a cousin only in the third or fourth degree. A dispensation in the case of such a relationship was occasionally granted, but Robert did not ask for it; indeed, in spite of the thunders of the Church, marriages of this kind frequently took place. If they had not done so a great many people could never have been married at all, since in the Middle Ages practically the whole of the upper classes in Western Europe, at any rate, were distantly connected. Whilst, therefore, marriages of this kind often occurred and the consanguinity was conveniently ignored, the Church's rules provided a useful means of dissolving unions which had proved unsatisfactory.

Unluckily for Robert and Bertha, Pope Gregory V was the son of Otho, Duke of Carinthia, and was on very bad terms with the King of France. Gregory V had reinstated the Archbishop of Rheims, whom King Robert had taken prisoner. Robert refused to give him his liberty or allow him to occupy his See. Relations between Rome and Paris became very strained. At last, after long negotiations, Robert agreed to liberate the Archbishop on the understanding that the Pope would legalize the marriage by dispensation. But, having got his Archbishop, Gregory V refused to perform his part. Not only did he refuse to legalize the marriage but he summoned a Council at Rome, at which the Emperor, Otho III, was present. Robert and Bertha were excommunicated and an interdict laid on France. The French clergy were the strongest in support of the Pope. It may be thought, and probably the view is correct, that religious scruples were not the only reason for the unpopularity of the marriage, for the French nobility were equally hostile. Poor Queen Bertha had no friends. At last Robert had to give in and the Queen was repudiated.

There were no children; perhaps luckily so, as they would no doubt have been stigmatized as illegitimate; and Robert was married again to Constance, daughter of William, Count of Arles. She was an attractive, pretty woman, but she had a hasty and domineering temper. Given, as she was, to violent likes and dislikes, it is a wonder that her husband put up with her for so many years. She had three sons, Henry the eldest, whom Robert at the end of his life associated with himself in the kingdom, Robert, who became Duke of Burgundy, and Odo.

Now, Queen Constance hated her son Henry, and loved the younger Robert. When old King Robert died, Henry stepped naturally into his place, but his mother started a rebellion against him in favour of Robert. She successfully drove the unfortunate Henry out of France. Henry, like Baldwin and Ethelred before him, fled to Rouen. Duke Robert took up his suzerain's cause with as much enthusiasm, but with more caution than he had espoused the interests of Baldwin of Flanders. Chartres, as usual, was on the look-out to make a profit out of any trouble either in France or Normandy. Robert had to conciliate the younger Odo of Chartres before he could hope to make much headway on Henry's behalf against Queen Constance. Odo demanded Sens, the important outpost on the frontier between France and Chartres. Having secured the position on the French frontier, Duke Robert, assisted by the Lord of Corbeil, invaded France. They were completely successful. Constance and Robert were defeated and driven out, and the former died shortly after of disappointment. But Duke Robert's greatest success, perhaps, was that he was able to make Odo of Chartres hand back Sens, which had been so recently surrendered to him. After his efforts on his behalf, King Henry could hardly deny the Duke anything he might ask. As a matter of fact, Robert asked for nothing, for Henry knew what he wanted and forestalled any demand by an offer.

Drogo, Count of the Vexin, was an intimate friend of Robert I. He had married a daughter of Ethelred II. After his death, she married Eustace of Boulogne. His dominions geographically belonged to

Normandy, but actually Drogo was a vassal of France. The Vexin was important to Normandy; its Count wished to become the vassal of the Norman Duke, who was his personal friend, so perhaps it was not at the time a great sacrifice to Henry. With the Vexin went its appanage of Mantes. But the cession of the Vexin proved more of a trouble to Normandy than a gain. It became a constant bone of contention between Normandy and France, and perhaps in the long run Normandy would have been better without it. However, this was not apparent at the time.

Robert's next difficulty arose with Brittany. Geoffrey, the husband of Hadvisa, the sister of Richard II, came to a curious and rather inglorious end. He undertook a journey to Rome. Being fond of hawking, he took with him a number of hawks. One of these birds got loose at an inn at which the Duke was staying and began to prey upon the innkeeper's chickens. The latter's wife, furious with rage, threw a heavy pot at his head which cracked his skull and killed him. This was in 1008. Geoffrey's son, Alan, was only a child and his mother, Hadvisa, acted as regent. A couple of years after Geoffrey's death (1010) a serious insurrection of peasants took place, somewhat similar to the revolt which occurred in Normandy, and was put down by Raoul d'Ivri at the beginning of the reign of Richard II. The position was alarming, but Alan, with his mother, faced it courageously. Young as he was, he put himself at the head of his loyal troops and soon suppressed the rising.

A short time after the Duke of Brittany came to terms with the Count of Rennes. Geoffrey had unjustly seized some of the lands of Rennes during the minority of the young Count—the chief and most important being Belle Isle. Now, Alan of Brittany had fallen in love with Bertha, daughter of Odo of Chartres and Champagne, but the latter refused to consent to the marriage, for the French were apt to look down on the Bretons as inferiors, just as they did on the Norman pirates. Alan of Rennes came to the rescue. He raided Chartres and abducted the lady, whom he handed over to the hitherto disappointed Duke. A marriage immediately took place and the bridegroom restored the confiscated lands to the Count of Rennes.

Young Alan's successes in love and war seem to have turned his head, for he became jealous of his feudal superior of Normandy and refused Robert I homage *en parage*. As the Norman Dukes did homage *en parage* to the Kings of France, so the Breton Counts or Dukes did homage *en parage* to the Dukes of Normandy. This refusal, of course, Normandy could not admit. It had always been a cardinal point in Norman policy that Brittany should accept the Norman Duke as its feudal superior. Robert immediately took up arms and crossed the Coesnon with a strong force mainly drawn from the Cotentin, the population of which was always ready for a raid on their Breton neighbours. Niel de St. Sauveur, who fought Earl Pallig and his pirates, was Robert's principal subordinate.

Robert built a strong castle on the Breton frontier, named Chernel—or Casson, as William of Jumièges styles it—and put it in charge of Niel de St. Sauveur. Then he invaded Brittany and took Dol.

Alan and his Bretons were courageous enough, but they were no match for the Normans, who routed them completely and dispersed their forces. Alan was defeated and could no longer carry on the war. He asked Archbishop Mauger of Rouen, his uncle and Robert's, to mediate. A meeting between the two Dukes and the Archbishop took place at Mont St. Michel. Alan gave in and did homage *en parage* to Robert. The Duke does not seem to have owed him any grudge, for we shall see that shortly after, when Robert went to Constantinople, Alan was nominated Regent of Normandy.

CHAPTER XIV

ROBERT I—PART II

Robert espouses cause of Athelings—Cnut refuses proposals. Story of Robert's marriage to Estrithea—Preparations for invasion of England—Robert contemplates visit to Jerusalem—Obtains son's recognition as heir to Normandy—Duke of Brittany Regent of Normandy—Robert visits Rome and Constantinople—His extravagance—Reaches Jerusalem—Dies at Nicaea—William, Duke of Normandy.

HITHERTO Robert had had unbroken success both in war and internal administration. Now he was to receive a check to his ambition. Simultaneously with the Breton war Robert was conducting important diplomatic negotiations with Cnut. The two Athelings, Edward (the Confessor) and Alfred, were refugees at the Court of Rouen. Their mother, Emma, was now Cnut's wife. It is said that when she married him she bargained that her son by him, if she had one, should succeed to the English throne. She seems to have disliked her sons by Ethelred II, but more probably her intentions were less to exclude them than Cnut's son by his first wife, Harold (afterwards Harold I). We cannot now fathom Robert's ulterior object, i.e. whether he really wished to obtain the English crown for one of them, or whether he wished to anticipate his son, William (the Conqueror), and obtain the Crown for himself. In any case, he undoubtedly wished to extend Norman influence in England, and certainly the fact that the two Athelings had been brought up in Normandy and were Norman in sympathy would help him to attain this end. He approached Cnut carefully. He pointed out the mischief that proceeded from the fact that there were legitimate pretenders to Cnut's throne, and he suggested a settlement and a compromise. He had not to go far to find a precedent in the arrangement for a partition between Cnut and Edmund Ironside.

Robert's proceedings were ridiculous in their temerity. Normandy was a small State; the Normans had no war fleet. Cnut's domains, according to the Danish historian, Saxo Grammaticus, comprised six kingdoms. He was master not only of England but of Scandinavia. His fleets commanded the sea. He could bring Danish troops to reinforce him in England without hindrance from the Normans. The state of affairs, therefore, differed essentially from that at the later date when Harold II was King of England and William I Duke of Normandy. Some chroniclers state that Robert married Cnut's sister Estritha.

The marriage is not mentioned either by the English or the Norman chroniclers, which in itself is curious. Saxo Grammaticus and Adam of Bremen speak of it, but as they mixed up Richard with Robert and made out that it was the former who married Estritha, we may perhaps discount their testimony. Ralph Glaber, a Picard and very nearly a contemporary (he died in 1049), says that she married Robert and then goes on to say that they did not get on and Robert divorced her.

It must have been at this time—it could not have been much earlier —that the marriage took place—if indeed it ever did take place—between Robert and Estritha. It could not have taken place much earlier because she did not become a widow until 1025. It may have taken place later; but whether the marriage took place at all is doubtful.

Estritha was Cnut's sister. Her first husband was Earl Ulf, between whom and Cnut there was little love lost. The King and his brother-in-law quarrelled at Roskilds and Cnut had him murdered. By Ulf, Estritha had a son named Swegen Estruthson, who subsequently became King of Denmark.

If really there was truth in the story, why do not the English and Norman chroniclers mention it? There was no reason why they should not have done so. So the statement that there was a marriage between Robert and Estritha seems mythical. Nor is the story that Robert's dislike and illtreatment of Estritha had anything to do with his action on behalf of the Athelings more probable. Obviously untrue is the statement apparently accepted by Saxo Grammaticus that Cnut invaded Normandy. There seems to be no doubt, however, that Robert did open up negotiations with Cnut for a settlement with the Athelings and that Cnut curtly declined to consider the matter. It is very improbable that the statement made by William of Jumièges is correct, that he was tempted to come to a settlement on lines similar to those arranged between him and Edmund Ironside.

Judging by later events, Robert may have begun at this time to show those signs of eccentricity, if not unsoundness of mind, which characterized his last years. Success had turned his head. He thought of himself as Robert the King-maker, and not altogether without reason, for he had restored Baldwin to the throne of Flanders and placed Henry on the throne of France. Megalomania may have induced him to think that he could restore the Atheling to the throne of England. Anyway, he was prepared to go further than diplomatic action. Undeterred by the fact that he was involved in operations in Brittany, he set to work to prepare an expedition wherewith to attack Cnut. The transports made rendezvous at Fécamp, and it is said were on the point of sailing, but the wind changed. Robert used a part of the force to assist in the Breton operations. Luckily, contrary winds held and Robert had to abandon the expedition for the year. It is said that he contemplated a second attempt, but he dropped the scheme. Perhaps his advisers insisted on it, for the discreet William of Jumièges says that the change of wind which rendered the expedition impossible was due to the direct intervention of the Almighty, who decreed that the succession of King Edward should be accomplished without blood being spilt.

Robert's restless and perhaps disordered mind now seized on a new project. He wished to visit Jerusalem. But there was a considerable difficulty to be overcome. In the event of his death would Normandy accept William, then a small child, as the heir? There was a good deal of doubt about this. William was a bastard—there was no pretence about a marriage of any kind between Arletta and Robert. Fulbert and his trade were disliked and despised by the Norman nobility. William was but a child and there was no question as to his being old enough to be named Regent.

Some of Robert's advisers urged him to marry Arletta and so regularize William's position, as Richard I by his marriage with Gunnor had legitimized his bastard children. Although apparently he was living with her and they were faithful to one another, for some unexplained reason he flatly refused to marry her. He may have been getting tired of her and have thought that on his return from the East he would be able to drop her, but we know nothing.

Quite certainly Robert was determined that his son should be his successor, and he enforced his will on his people. His method of procedure was most astute. He suddenly convoked a meeting of his vassals and announced his intention of going to Jerusalem as a poor pilgrim and a repentant sinner. The superstitions of the age prevented the Normans from telling him that his duty was to his duchy, and that to go off suddenly on an expedition for the benefit of his soul, leaving the duchy to look after itself, was conduct of an outrageous character. Moreover, no one trusted another; there were too many people who could have put up some sort of claim to the throne. Former Dukes had bestowed rich fiefs on their children. Any one of these, if strong enough, might try to seize the throne. There were Archbishop Mauger, William d'Arques, the son of his sister, the Duchess of Burgundy, and numerous others. But Robert was accustomed to having his own way and accustomed to enforcing it. He insisted on his vassals doing homage to his son, whom he named Chief of the State. He then, to legalize the proceeding, took young William to Paris, surrendered the duchy in his favour, and caused the boy to do homage *en parage* to King Henry.

This was an important step, for it meant the legal recognition of William's rights. But William was too young himself to exercise any function of government. Robert bowed to public opinion by excluding Arletta from any control as guardian, following the example of William Longsword when he excluded Sprota from the guardianship of Richard I.

He must have had considerable difficulty in choosing a Regent, but he made a wise choice. Although Alan had been but recently in arms against him, he selected the Duke of Brittany. No doubt Alan through his mother, Hadvisa, was a possible claimant to the throne, but he stood out from the rest. He was not a Norman and he must have known that if he, as Duke of Brittany, were to try and claim Normandy he would meet with the most determined opposition. He was an able man and stood apart from all the other relations, whom certainly Robert could not afford to trust. With Alan, not as co-regents but as advisers, were associated Archbishop Mauger, Gilbert, Count of Brionne, who was blindly loyal to Robert and was charged with the important castle of Tillières, and Turquetil or Thorold—the last-named being the boy's personal governor.

Having made the best arrangements he could, Robert went off eastwards with his friend, Count Drogo of the Vexin. The two young men behaved more like a couple of rich young Englishmen of the 18th century making the Grand Tour than humble pilgrims seeking forgiveness for their sins. Relieved of the cares of government and bent only on amusing himself, Robert let his extravagance go. In those days the passage through Switzerland and over the Alpine passes to Aosta was a strenuous journey. In Roman times the roads and the inns *en route* had been carefully maintained, but in the Middle Ages they had deteriorated. Aymon de Centeville, indeed, had died of the hardships of the journey to Rome. Robert and Drogo, however, had no intention of dying, or even of making themselves uncomfortable. They devised an elaborate system of camps and provisions and arrived safely and comfortably in Rome, scattering money as they went. Robert's conduct became more and more eccentric as he went on. He began to make a fool of himself in Rome. He shod his mules with silver and only attached them by one nail so that they should easily fall off and be picked up. He put a cloak on the statue of Marcus Aurelius and generally comported himself as a lunatic.

From Rome the travellers went to Constantinople, where Robert's behaviour became even more vulgar and ridiculous. At that time the Emperor was Michael IV, the Paphlagonian. He had just succeeded Romanus III, whose death took place in April, 1034. The moment was a propitious one for Robert's visit to Jerusalem. At the end of the reign of Romanus III the Emperor and the Caliph had opened negotiations for peace; these negotiations were proceeding when Robert visited Constantinople and no doubt a truce existed between Greeks and Saracens. Michael IV was a courteous Greek gentleman. Constantinopolitan society was probably accustomed to the visits of these queer people from the North, and all the Emperor thought of was to get rid of Robert as soon as he could and with as little nuisance as possible. He probably regarded the Duke of Normandy as the courtiers of Queen Victoria did the visiting exotic potentates at the Jubilee of 1887, as persons to whose office respect should be paid and to whose peculiarities blindness should be extended.

Robert came swaggering into the Emperor's presence, with his suite apeing his bad manners. He was, as might be expected, richly and extravagantly dressed and over his costume he wore a magnificent cloak. It was not customary at Constantinople to provide seats at an audience of the Emperor; but Robert, before paying any mark of respect to his host, took off his cloak, bundled it up into a heap and sat himself down on it. Michael paid not the least attention to his bad manners and appeared not to be in any way shocked at his visitor's behaviour; indeed, he probably was not at all surprised. He treated him with the utmost courtesy. When the audience was over and Robert was leaving, some of the attendants attempted to straighten out the cloak he had been sitting on and put it on his shoulders. "It is not the fashion in our country to carry our seats with us," said the Duke of Normandy with offensive truculence. To avoid trouble Michael paid the expenses of his Norman guests and no doubt saw the last of them with sincere relief.

Whether it was his mind or his body that was failing, Robert's health became now a matter for concern. He could no longer ride and had to be carried in a litter by negro slaves. Asia Minor in those days was full of pilgrims and he met a Norman on the way home from Jerusalem. This man was concerned at Robert's state and asked him what news he should take back of the Duke's health. Robert was aware of his condition and feared that he would not be able to get to Jerusalem; but with all his faults he was a cheerful man and his good humour did not fail him. "Tell them," he said, "you saw me being carried to Paradise by devils."

Robert, however, arrived at Jerusalem in safety and so completed his pilgrimage and, we hope, ensured thereby his entry into Paradise. His last act was an orgy of extravagance in the Holy City, but the Mussalman Emir who represented the Caliph outdid him in the competition.

Robert tried to return, but he only got as far as Nicaea, where he died and was buried in the cathedral. His faithful adherent, Toustain, brought the news back to Normandy that Robert I was dead and William now Duke.

CHAPTER XV

WILLIAM II, DUKE OF NORMANDY

William succeeds as Duke—The Regency—Disadvantage of bastardy—Arletta's position—
Her children by Herlwin de Centeville—William's education—William Montgomery's
attempt to seize the Duke at Vandreuil—Thorold and Osborne murdered—Gilbert de
Brionne and Alan of Brittany killed—Rebellion of Ferrers, de Toesny and Montford—
Archbishop Mauger—The Truce of God.

SELDOM perhaps did a sovereign succeed to a throne under more un-
promising auspices than did the young Duke of Normandy. But there
were some redeeming features in the situation. Both the rulers of the
duchy who succeeded as children were lucky in their guardians. We have
seen how Bernard the Dane succeeded in maintaining the independence
of Normandy during the early days of Richard I, and young William's
guardians were equally successful; but their loyalty cost all three of them
their lives.

In the Middle Ages a demise of the Crown was always the cause of
trouble. When the sovereign died the centre of administration was
paralysed until another sovereign was acknowledged. Tribunals could
not sit; delegations emanating from the late Duke terminated and the
whole government was thrown into a state of chaos. Such was the condition of Normandy when the news of Duke Robert's death arrived from
Nicaea. Perhaps it was lucky that there was a regency already in being,
though, of course, the death of Duke Robert had dissolved the Duke of
Brittany's commission. Still, the machinery was in existence. Sir F.
Palgrave has commented in strong terms on Robert's failure to name
Arletta to be one of the boy's guardians and attributes this to the fact that
she was his mistress and not his wife.

It seems that modern historians have laid far too much stress on
William's bastardy; but William's uncle and father were the only Dukes
who could boast of true legitimacy. William I, Richard I and Richard
II were all born of Danish marriages, which, of course, the Church did not
recognize as marriages at all, though Richard II was legitimized by the
subsequent marriage of his parents. It is unlikely, really, that objection
to William on account of his bastardy was serious, for all the other possible
claimants were the offspring of more or less spurious ancestry.

It is not likely, then, that Robert failed to name Arletta as one of the
guardians for this reason. Much more probably he regarded a woman as

Church of St. Ouen, Rouen.
(see No. 4. *Notes on Illustrations.*)

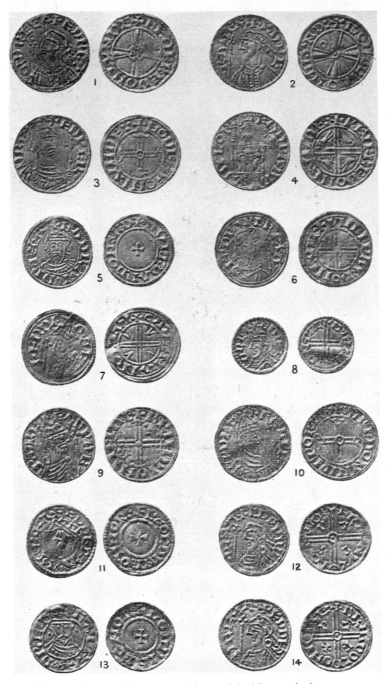

Coins (silver pennies and half-pennies)
of Edward the Confessor's reign.

unfitted to act as a guardian in the strenuous days in which he lived. He acted in the same way as his great-grandfather who left his wife or mistress, Sprota, out when he nominated the guardians of his son Richard. Moreover, Arletta married shortly after Robert's death—one Herlwin de Conteville, by whom she became mother of Odo, Bishop of Bayeux and Earl of Kent, and Robert, Count of Mortain and Earl of Cornwall, or so it is stated, but he is not so styled in Doomsday.

William's guardians were Alan of Brittany, Gilbert Count of Brionne, a member of the Ducal Family who was Constable of the Castle of Tillières, and Thorold or Turquetil, the boy's tutor or governor. Among others in his immediate surroundings were Osborne, a son of Herfast, Gunnor's brother, and his son, William FitzOsborne, who was about the Duke's own age, and Walter, Arletta's brother. For safety William was placed in the Castle of Vaudreuil, a strong fortress founded in Roman days.

It is said that, unlike his predecessors, all of whom were well educated, William could neither read nor write. This is probably an exaggeration, but the years of his early education were certainly disturbed. The hostility towards him seems hardly to have been personal. His actual recognition as Duke was not challenged and the regency continued. Pretenders to the throne might have been numerous, but none of them could obtain much support. The object of the rebels seemed to be to get control over the boy's person and so to secure the regency. The first serious attempt on Vaudreuil was made by William, son of Roger Montgomery. This Roger, besides being the father of William, had four other sons: Roger, afterwards Earl of Shrewsbury, Hugh, Robert and Gilbert. The latter three were prominent among the rebels in the early days of William the Conqueror.

William Montgomery succeeded in getting into the castle of Vaudreuil. The Duke was in bed and he tried to seize him, but he was saved by his mother's brother, Walter. Thorold, his tutor, was murdered and Osborne, who slept in the boy's room, was also killed. Thus the Duke soon lost his guardians, for Gilbert de Brionne was murdered one day while out riding, at the instigation of Raoul Wace, the son of Archbishop Robert of Rouen, and Duke Alan of Brittany was poisoned in 1040.

William's next danger came from a more serious source. Hugh de Montfort and Walcheline Ferrers rose in revolt. They were joined by Roger de Toeny. Another of the rebels was Raoul Wace, the murderer of Gilbert de Brionne. The rebellion was unsuccessful and de Toeny was killed, and a compromise was arranged by William himself appointing Wace to be his tutor instead of the murdered Thorold. But the Duke was growing up. At this time he must have been about sixteen and his stormy youth made him older than his years. He was immensely strong, a fine horseman, a good swordsman and a skilful archer.

I

William's uncle, Mauger, Archbishop of Rouen, seems to have had some control over the government of Normandy in this difficult time, but unfortunately the chronicles do not tell us much of what went on after the defeat of the rebels.   There was not much to be said in favour of Mauger, whose record is not a happy one; but he did do something to curb the anarchy which the curse of private war was causing.   In 1042 he summoned the Council of Caen and here was proclaimed the "Truce of God".

Private war had too long been recognized in Normandy.   Even strong Dukes could not stop it altogether, but the Truce of God did much to mitigate the evil.   From Thursday till the following Monday in every week peace had to be maintained; moreover, during the periods from Advent to Epiphany and from Rogation to Whitsuntide no private hostilities of any kind were allowed.   For transgression against the Truce the severest penalties were enjoined: reparation for the evil done, thirty years' penance in exile, and unless the offender repented he was denied Christian burial.   Moreover, all his followers who participated in the transgression were subject to the same penalties.

The results were perhaps more satisfactory than might have been expected, and freedom, at any rate from the intolerable nuisance of private wars, was more or less assured.

CHAPTER XVI

NORMANDY AND FRANCE

French jealousy—William surrenders Tillières to France—Guy of Burgundy—St. Sauveur's rebellion—William escapes from Valognes—Takes refuge in France—Rebellion of Guy of Burgundy—Victory of William at Val-es-Dunes—William's clemency.

IT was not long, however, before fresh trouble overtook Normandy. In spite of the traditional friendship between France and the duchy, which had lasted since the days of Richard I, there was no doubt a great feeling of jealousy in Paris. The French had never quite accepted the Norse Sea vermin or their descendants, although they were now as French as the Parisians themselves. Even in the Bessin and the Cotentin there was little left of Scandinavia. But this was not the main cause of jealousy. Paris and Rouen are both situated on the Seine and the powerful duchy lay between the kingdom and the sea. King Henry of France owed his throne to Duke Robert, and Duke William to a certain extent owed his throne to King Henry, for it was no doubt largely due to Robert having persuaded the King to recognize his bastard son as heir to the duchy that William became Duke at all.

Suddenly, and without warning, Henry invaded the Evrecin and demanded the surrender of the castle of Tillières. At first William refused and a desultory campaign took place. At last William agreed to surrender the castle provided it were dismantled and the King undertook not to fortify it again for four years. The commander, William Crispin, still held out, and it was only at William's express order that he surrendered. King Henry, instead of retiring after he had dismantled the castle, passed on to Argentan and burnt that town. Then returning to Tillières, which was now in his possession, he set to work to rebuild it again and, ignoring his agreement, to fortify it.

After the surrender of Tillières William gradually seems to have been recognized as of full age and able to govern by himself. He established his court at Valognes. One further rebellion occurred in 1042. Thurstan Goz seized Falaise, but he was soon dealt with by Wace. This event seems to have inspired the Norman Barons with the fear that William was gradually becoming their master, and in 1047 a serious rebellion occurred with the object of driving William out of Normandy and establishing Guy of Burgundy on the throne.

Guy was perhaps the most obvious heir. He was the son of Renaud of Burgundy and Alice, one of the five daughters of Richard II and Judith of Brittany—thus of legitimate birth. He had been much in Normandy as a boy and had had several baronies conferred on him. Doubtless the malcontents flattered him and induced him to join them in rebellion. The chief mover in the plot was Nigel de St. Sauveur, of whom we have heard more than once before. Grimoald du Plessis was another, and Hamo, nicknamed "Dentatus", a third.

William was living quietly at Valognes and entertaining a party. One night when he was fast asleep the Court jester, fully clad in cap and bells and armed with his bauble, rushed into his room and awoke him, urging him to save himself by flight as his enemies were upon him, all of them armed, and if he did not escape at once he would never see the dawn. William did not hesitate for a moment. Had he done so he would have been lost. He threw a few clothes on and rushed to the stables, where he saddled a horse and rode for the ford of the Vire near Isigny. He stopped for a short time at the Church of St. Sauveur to bait his horse, as he had had to ride fast from Valognes to escape his enemies. Remounting, he crossed the Vire and rode for Bayeux. But he thought it too risky to enter the city, and so rode round through the suburb of Rye and onward to the house of Hubert, near Cherbourg, where he knew he could find safety, at any rate for a time. The path he followed is still known as "*La voie du duc*." He reached Hubert's house at dawn, and there he stopped. It was not thought safe enough here, so Hubert's sons escorted him to Falaise, where the garrison of the castle were loyal and could be trusted. When he got there he found that though he could probably rely on the eastern half of the duchy the west had been seized by the rebels.

It was a bold thing, but probably the only thing for William to do. From Falaise he went to Poiny, whence he appealed to King Henry against whom he had not so long ago been in conflict over Tillières. The Duke knew, no doubt, that King Henry was jealous of him and was casting hungry eyes on Rouen and Normandy, but he calculated, and rightly so, that Henry had no desire that Normandy should fall into the hands of the Burgundians. The French King gave the fugitive shelter and promised his aid. William then turned to look around him and found the situation was not so bad as might have been thought. Nigel de St. Sauveur, Ralph de Briquessant and Grimoald du Plessis were against him, with the Vicomtes of the Bessin and Cotentin, but Rouen was strongly for the Duke; so was Caux, Eu, and the Evrecin.

William, supported by King Henry, advanced to meet the rebels at Val-es-Dunes. Here he met Ralph Tesson, one of the rebels. This man had sworn to give the first blow by striking the Duke, but when he saw the strength of the armies he made up his mind to join William. To acquit himself of his oath he gave William's helmet a slight blow and then joined his ranks. The battle was a stiff conflict. The action was the first real battle in which the young Duke had taken part and he showed himself a stout-hearted soldier. Both French and Normans were hard pressed; indeed, King Henry nearly came to serious grief and was dismounted in action with the Cotentin contingent. However, another horse was at hand, Henry remounted and continued the fight.

At last the rebels gave way. Hamo Dentatus was killed, Nigel de St. Sauveur fled to his castle of Brionne sur Rille, the others came in and surrendered. William's victory was complete, but he was wise enough to make it even more so by his magnanimous treatment of his late enemies. William was a hard man—he could be fierce and he could be cruel, but no one knew better than he did the value of concessions. The pretender, Guy, was deprived of his Norman dominions and sent back to Burgundy. The others were pardoned and in some cases even received favours. The only one harshly treated was Du Plessis. Why this was so we can only conjecture. William, for all his wisdom, was a very touchy man. Any slight or personal insult, real or imaginary, was bitterly resented by him. Perhaps Grimoald had said something to wound him, for the wretched man was thrown into a dungeon in chains. He lingered on for three years and then died, but even in death William could not forgive and caused him to be buried in his chains.

The whole of Normandy was now at last indisputably in the hands of William. Only Nigel held out at Brionne, and so strong was his castle that he was able to maintain himself for no less than three years.

Though William knew the wisdom of clemency he meant the Barons to know who was their master. Every rebel was required to make his submission; homage was exacted from all; the adulterine castles were razed to the ground and the Duke's authority firmly established throughout the duchy.

Val-es-Dunes marks the first stage in William's career. He was now master of Normandy He had conquered his Barons and gained the reputation of being not only a first-rate fighting soldier but a skilful staff officer and commander in the field.

CHAPTER XVII

ANJOU AND FURTHER REBELLIONS IN NORMANDY

War with Geoffrey of Anjou—Alençon and Domfront taken—William Warling banished—
Mortain given to William's brother, Robert—Matilda of Flanders—Bar to William's
marriage to her—Lanfranc—Tostig—William Busac's revolt—William d'Arques' rebel
lion defeated—King Henry aids d'Arques—Richard d'Huguesville—The French defeated
—William annexes Arques.

WILLIAM was not slow in paying his debt of gratitude to King Henry of
France. The latter in 1048, the year subsequent to Val-es-Dunes, became
involved in a quarrel with Geoffrey Martel, of Anjou. William had his
own quarrel with Anjou. Blois and Champagne were on good terms
with Normandy. Their rulers, Stephen and Theobald, were William's
first cousins, being the sons of his aunt Matilda and Odo of Blois. Geoffrey
made war on the Blesois brothers, drove Stephen into exile and captured
and imprisoned Theobald, who could only ransom himself by the surrender of Tours and Chinon.

This was an important victory for Anjou for, in spite of all his efforts,
Black Fulk had failed to take Tours, though he had conquered all the
rest of Touraine. But Geoffrey's offences against Normandy were more
serious still. He seized Alençon and Domfront and made friends with
the rulers of Bellèsme, always the Duke's enemies. William attacked
Alençon. Apparently the men of the town were too sure of victory.
They hung their walls with newly flayed skins, and as the Norman army
advanced beat the skins, shouting, "Plenty of work for the tanner's son!
Plenty of work for the tanner!"

Such an insult was more than the touchy William could stand. He
made a furious assault on the town and captured a number of prisoners.
These unfortunate wretches were paraded beneath the walls in full view
of their fellow citizens; their hands and feet were cut off and thrown into
the town, their eyes were put out and they were left, if they could, to
crawl home. Their friends were threatened with the same fate so soon as
they should be captured. The men of Alençon must have regretted their
joke. They were thoroughly frightened and capitulated ignominiously.
William did not carry on the feud. He accepted the surrender and then
advanced into Anjevin territory, but he pursued the war no further. He
built a border fortress at Ambières and then withdrew to Normandy
again.

Although William had defeated his enemies, both at home and abroad, he was well aware that he could not relax his vigilance. Almost immediately after his return to Normandy fresh trouble arose with the members of his family. William, nicknamed the Warling, was a son of Archbishop Mauger of Rouen and had been created Count of Mortain. This man was foolish enough to aspire to the throne of the duchy. Unfortunately for him, one of his friends, Roger Bigod by name, gave him away, and as soon as the Duke heard of the conspiracy he sent to arrest the Warling, but the latter was too quick for him and escaped to Apulia. However, Mortain was forfeited and conferred by William on his half-brother, Robert de Centeville.

Few people had any real affection for William the Conqueror, but, hard man as he was, he showed affection to his relatives and some of his friends; but he was unlucky. Most of his relatives betrayed him. Indeed, his brother, Robert, was the only one who appears to have been consistently loyal to him.

It was in the year 1048 that romance seems for the first and last time to have entered into the life of the Conqueror. Where he first met her we do not know, but he undoubtedly fell violently and genuinely in love. The objective of his affections was Matilda, daughter of Baldwin of Flanders by Adela of France. For some reason the marriage was forbidden by Pope Leo IX at the Council of Rheims in 1049. What the reason was is obscure, if not quite unknown. The general belief is that consanguinity was alleged. Adela of France had been engaged as a child to William's uncle, Duke Richard III, but certainly no marriage took place and equally certainly no consanguinity existed between Matilda and William.

That there was a legal bar of some sort is certain. Lanfranc, who was one of the first lawyers in Europe, definitely stated that such a bar existed. Naturally, every kind of guess has been put forward and theorists have been found to advocate all sorts of wild suppositions. In fact, every possible bar to a marriage has had its advocates, but no real light has been thrown on the truth. Sick of waiting, William and Matilda married at Eu, probably in 1053. The story was invented that William went to her father's home at Bruges in Flanders and seized the unfortunate Matilda by the hair of the head and kicked her, and that she then and there declared that William she would marry, and no one else! Rubbish of this sort is scarcely worth repeating, but the story has been widely spread. William the Conqueror may have been hard and he may have on occasion been ruthlessly cruel. He was, but he was a civilized man and a gentleman, and there is absolutely no ground for believing that he could have behaved like the barbarian chief of an exogamous totem. Matilda, too, was a lady and as civilized as her husband; such conduct would have been resented by her and also by her father.

Mauger, the Archbishop, and Lanfranc, the Prior of Bec, told William that the marriage was no marriage. William was furious with Lanfranc, lost his temper and in revenge ravaged the lands of Bec of which Lanfranc was Prior and banished him from the country. By chance the Duke met Lanfranc riding away to Italy. He was going very slowly on a bad horse. William rode up to him and told him to get out of the country quicker. Lanfranc was not in the least afraid of the formidable Duke and said, "If you will give me a decent horse I shall get along quicker." William, like most violent men, had a sense of humour, and like most brave men admired bravery in others. His sense of humour was touched and his admiration for courage also. He and Lanfranc made friends and they had a talk over the marriage.

Lanfranc explained to William that the law was against him, but added that he was perfectly ready to act as William's counsel at Rome and argue his case there for a dispensation. He explained that a dispensation would put the matter right, but nothing else. The upshot was that Lanfranc agreed to go to Rome on William's behalf. He was not successful immediately, but when Pope Leo died and Nicholas II succeeded him a compromise was effected, and a dispensation issued on condition that William should found an abbey for monks and Matilda one for nuns. The conditions were faithfully carried out, as the Churches of St. Stephen's and Holy Trinity at Caen bear witness. According to William of Jumièges, Matilda was a beautiful woman, and, what was better in his view, a woman of great ability. Probably he was correct, and we know that in more than one case William trusted and relied on his wife's counsel.

Matilda was the only woman in William's life. His predecessors were all of them, or nearly all, as polygamous as their Scandinavian ancestors. Legitimacy counted as little with Duke Robert as with his ancestor, Rögnwald Earl of More. Nor were William's descendants any better. His son, Henry I, had multitudes of mistresses and multitudes of children. The age was sexually amoral. Henry's I's bastard daughters were sought in marriage by sovereigns. William was a rigid moralist. Modern historians have sought to diminish his character without success. It has been suggested that the Peverels were descended from him on the left hand, but there is no atom of proof.

Some have said that William had so great a horror of his own experience of bastardy that he declined to place the same burden of shame on anyone else. This seems nonsense. There was little burden of shame on a bastard in those times. Had there been such a thing William would never have been Duke of Normandy. Moreover, William was not that sort of man. Had he wished to do a thing he would have done it, and if the result had been an addition to the numerous bastard families of the duchy he would not have distressed himself overmuch. The explanation seems plain enough. He was not a highly sexed man; perhaps, as a religious man, he tended to morality, but, above all, his centre of emotion was his love of his wife, and that sufficed him in his relations with women.

It would be interesting, however, to know what the legal bar to his marriage was. Modern lawyers have failed to find out. Contemporary lawyers had no doubt about its existence. William's marriage was a love match—it is unlikely that he would have contracted a marriage of convenience—he was too fierce and primitive a man for that, in spite of his wisdom as a statesman and skill as a diplomatist, but, all the same, the alliance with Flanders proved to be of great value to him. Baldwin of Flanders was his nearest neighbour and in the past there had been much rivalry between Normandy and Flanders. Baldwin's daughter, Judith, had married Tostig, the son of Godwin and brother of Harold, and when Tostig was banished from England and dispossessed of his earldom of Northumbria he took refuge at Bruges with his father-in-law. Furthermore, when Henry I died in 1060 Baldwin became regent of France during the minority of King Philip. All these circumstances were to enure to William's advantage.

Although the attempt of Guy of Burgundy to oust William had been successfully crushed the Duke was not free yet from attempts by his relatives. A revolt of William Busac, the son of Count Robert d'Eu, was easily suppressed, but the rebellion of William Count of Arques was more serious. This man was the brother of Mauger, Archbishop of Rouen, and so an uncle of the Duke. Both Mauger and William criticized William's marriage, doubtless in order to stir up trouble against him.

William d'Arques had received the small County of Arques, or Talon, from his nephew. As a brother of Archbishop Mauger and, therefore, the son of Popa, third wife of Richard II, he could at least claim to be legitimate, so he had a mind to become a candidate for the duchy. It is a curious thing, and one fortunate for William, that his kinsmen, who from time to time tried to oust him, could never agree among themselves and could never settle on one candidate whom they would all support. The Count d'Arques fought on William's side in the dispute over Tillières, and it would seem as though William had trusted his uncle or he would never have allowed him to occupy so strong a position as the castle of Arques.

When he began to have his suspicions of him the Duke put his own troops into the castle and occupied it. But the garrison was not trustworthy, and when the Count appeared with his men at the castle they mutinied against the Duke and joined him. The strength of the castle made the rebellion a formidable one. From so strong a base it was possible to carry on operations against the Duke with a fair prospect of success. All the robbers and malefactors among William's nobles joined the Count, hoping to revenge their defeat at Val-es-Dunes. Duke William was at Valognes in the Cotentin. As soon as he heard of this revolt he started for Arques, travelling by forced marches. At Caen he did not turn towards Rouen, for he heard that reinforcements were hurrying to join him from the capital. Instead of going to Rouen he rode on with all speed eastwards and crossed the Seine at Caudebec.

By this time he had outdistanced all his men and had only six with him when he arrived at Arques. Here he found three hundred knights and their men awaiting him, but this body was scarcely in good heart. They found Arques a more formidable place than they had imagined. Moreover, William d'Arques was gaining adherents among the local nobility. Luckily for the Duke, he caught his uncle outside the castle and, though the latter's force was the stronger, he charged straight at them and very nearly overcame them. Perhaps he would have done so had they not just succeeded in getting into the castle and shutting themselves up there. The Duke could not take the place by storm, so he was forced to blockade it. A fairly strong force under the command of Walter Giffard undertook the siege, and the Duke in the meanwhile turned to engage a more powerful force which was moving from France to the relief of Arques.

King Henry of France thought that at last he had a chance to conquer Normandy. It will be remembered that in the war with Guy of Burgundy King Henry supported the Duke. He wanted Normandy for France, not for Burgundy. But here was a different state of affairs. If he could set William d'Arques on the throne as a puppet Duke the absorption of the duchy by France might prove an easy matter.

Richard II had a daughter named Popa who married Fulbert, Advocate of Saint Valery, in Ponthieu. The second son of Fulbert and Popa was named Richard d'Huguesville and he had obtained a small fief in Talon. Richard and his son, called after his grandfather, Fulbert, stood firm for their cousin, the Duke, although practically all the other nobles of the district were in rebellion. Richard d'Huguesville, in the Duke's absence, commanded the Norman troops opposing the King of France. They ambushed the French at Richard's castle of St. Aubin near Dieppe. The enemy were advancing to relieve Arques and had with them a long train of supplies for the garrison. Near St. Aubin they halted and prepared to send these provisions to the castle.

Their intelligence service seems to have been very bad, since not only do they appear to have been ignorant of Richard d'Huguesville's force at St. Aubin, but also of the state of Giffard's besieging troops before Arques. The Normans hid in ambush and then sent a small force to attack the French. As soon as they were engaged the Normans retreated, pretending flight, and led the French right into the trap. A number were killed, including the Count of Ponthieu, and others, among them Hugh Bardolph, were captured. Ingelram, Count of Ponthieu, was the husband of the

Duke's sister. When he was killed he was succeeded in the county of Ponthieu by his brother, Guy, who seized Harold (afterwards King of England) when he was driven by bad weather into Ponthieu.

After this disastrous affair for the French, King Henry tried to raise the siege by force, but he found Giffard too strong so he retired back to France. But on his way the commander of the castle of Moulins, which lay in the county of Hiesmes, surrendered his castle to King Henry, who occupied it and placed it in charge of the Count of Gascony. What this man could have been doing in this campaign is not clear. Gascony was not involved in the war between France and Normandy, so that one may suppose he had taken service with the French as a private person. He was not the reigning sovereign of Aquitaine, but the second son of the late Duke. He succeeded later and changed his name to William, which seems to have been the generic name of the Dukes of Aquitaine, somewhat in the same manner as Heinrich is today the generic name of all Princes of Reuss.

Now that the French King was out of the way William had no more scruples about attacking his rebellious uncle. The latter was already hard pressed by hunger and the garrison were only too glad to surrender to get some food. They seemed to have bitterly repented their folly in rebelling against their Duke and in trusting King Henry. They seem also to have feared severe punishment, for many of them came crawling out of Arques with saddles on their backs, the most abject and disgraceful sign of humiliation. But William was not revengeful; he never made enemies if he could help it. He offered his uncle and his other rebellious subjects the easiest terms; in fact, the surrender of the castle of Arques was practically all he demanded. But William d'Arques did not care to remain on in Normandy, though his nephew made no objection to his doing so. He went instead to Boulogne and took refuge there with Count Eustace.

The Duke annexed Arques to the Crown and made it a ducal castle, which he placed in the charge of William Viscount d'Arques, on whose loyalty he could depend. The result of the collapse of the rebellion was that Count Guy of Gascony evacuated the castle of Moulins, which was reoccupied by Norman troops.

CHAPTER XVIII

KING HENRY'S ATTEMPT UPON NORMANDY

King Henry of France attacks Normandy—Odo—Guy of Ponthieu—Battle of Mortemer—Ralph de Toeny—Flight of Henry and his army.

THE revolt was over and the land had peace for a short space, and during this period William, in spite of the Pope, married Matilda at Eu, as we have already recorded. It was no runaway match, for her father, Baldwin, brought her to Normandy.

Quiet lasted during 1053, but in the following year trouble again broke out. The discomfited King of France naturally was more and more jealous of Normandy. Geoffrey Martel of Anjou, and, in spite of former benefits, Theobald of Champagne, had no love for William. Theobald had seized the country by revolting and attacking his nephew, Odo, whom he drove out. Odo took refuge in Normandy and was living at William's court. In remoter districts the growing power of Normandy was giving the same apprehension of William's ambition as was experienced in France, so that not only was Normandy surrounded by enemies but there were distinct signs in Aquitaine, Ponthieu, Auvergne and Burgundy that if a favourable opportunity occurred King Henry might anticipate assistance from these districts. But while these remoter Princes would doubtless have seen the defeat of William with satisfaction, none of them was anxious to take any definite action which might be costly and might merely serve to increase the power of the King of France. Even Geoffrey Martel, though one of William's most jealous neighbours, hesitated before joining the French King in open war on William.

King Henry, however, had made up his mind. He had been deeply humiliated in the Arques war. Moreover, he had conducted his operations with singular want of skill. In short, he had made a fool of himself in public. Nor was he wholly bereft of allies. Theobald, who doubtless felt very insecure on his throne so long as the rightful ruler was the *protégé* of William, and Guy of Ponthieu, who had his brother's death and his own defeat to avenge, sent troops to the aid of France.

King Henry meant to settle the Norman question for good. He raised two armies, one to be commanded by himself, the other by his brother, Odo. These troops were not just those who could be most easily raised, but they consisted of the largest power that could be got together in the

French kingdom. Even the Archbishop of Rheims, which was practically an independent principality, sent a contingent.

Odo commanded the army of the right based on Beauvais and designed to move on Caux, Fécamp and Lillebonne. As second in command Odo had Guy of Ponthieu, who was, of course, followed by his own troops. King Henry, assisted by Theobald of Champagne, had his headquarters at Nantes. His troops came from the western part of France, Berry, Bourges, and Orleans. The King's object was to advance eastwards with Rouen as his objective, where eventually he hoped to make a junction with Odo and thence to go northwards and overwhelm Lisieux and West Normandy.

The Duke of Normandy had a most efficient and active intelligence service, both in England and in France. He soon became aware of the French preparations and took immediate steps to counter them. Like King Henry, he divided his troops into two armies. He himself commanded the army of the right opposed to the French King. It was too serious a matter of have scruples of setting a bad example to his vassals by fighting his overlord. Moreover, Henry had the avowed intention of crushing Normandy, and the French army of the left, aided by the troops of Champagne, was the most formidable of the two.

The victory of Arques had taught the Normans their lesson. The Bessin, the Cotentin, Mortain and all Western Normandy came out to defend their country, and William found himself in command of a considerable army, but not equal in strength to that of the King. The Norman army of the left opposed to Odo of France was commanded by Hugh Gournay of Bray, Robert Count d'Eu, William Crispin and Walter Giffard, and they were joined by Hugh de Montfort and Roger de Mortcmer. Odo entered Normandy from France, and it is said that all along the line of advance he ravaged the country and committed every sort of atrocity.

The Normans bided their time. As soon as their intelligence service advised them that the French were in camp at Mortemer they made a night march and at dawn completely surprised Odo's army. They were billeted in houses in the town and the first they knew of the attack was to find their billets on fire. They seem to have had no sentries, no force on guard, and no organization to defend themselves. The result was their complete defeat. Many were killed, more taken prisoner and shut up in Norman prisons. Odo ran away to France. Montdidier was taken prisoner by Roger de Mortemer. The latter was Montdidier's vassal, and in view of this fact Mortcmer gave him his freedom, which shows that the feudal tie was a very real one in some cases.

In spite of William's own actions in the Arques war with King Henry and the fact that Orderic makes William say in his dying speech that De Mortemer, who was commander-in-chief of the army, rendered

Montdidier a "noble and legitimate service" for his breach of duty to himself, he banished him for a time from Normandy and confiscated the castle of Mortemer, which was given to William de Varennes, ancestor of a very famous Anglo-Norman family. De Varennes (or Warren, as the name became in English) and Mortemer were cousins, being both of them descended from Herfast, Duchess Gunnora's brother.

William was not very far away and a messenger was sent to him at once with the news. The bearer of the message was Ralph de Toeny, the grandson of the sinister Roger whose wife was a cousin of De Montfort.

Ralph, so it would appear, had a loud and penetrating voice, or it may be that something in the nature of a megaphone or speaking-trumpet had been invented even in those days. This might well be the case, for it is a very simple instrument. "Frenchmen, awake!" shouted Ralph. "You sleep too long. Go and bury your friends who lie dead at Mortemer." Naturally, this news set the whole camp talking, and it was probably confirmed by some fugitives from Odo's army. Anyway, it was enough to scare the pusillanimous King and the whole army ran away to Paris.

After the defeat at Mortemer in 1055 Normandy had peace until 1058, but the chronicles do not tell us much about these years.

CHAPTER XIX

THE RELIGIOUS HOUSES

Archbishop Mauger deposed—Maurilius succeeds him—Norman Abbeys—Clugniac influence —Bec—Herlwin de Bonneville—The Norman Church—Hildebrand—William and the Papacy—Army reorganization—The archers.

WILLIAM's marriage was still unrecognized and had been condemned by Archbishop Mauger and also by Lanfranc. It will be remembered that at first the Duke quarrelled with Lanfranc but made it up again and sent him to Rome to negotiate with the Pope for a dispensation. With Mauger, however, he never came to terms. He had plenty to say against the Archbishop. No doubt the latter had sided with his brother, William d'Arques, in that individual's rebellion. But William's main ground for his attack on Mauger was the man's bad character. It was certainly a piece of astonishing impudence for Mauger to reprove William for his un-canonical marriage when he himself was leading an openly immoral life! William had a very strong case against the Archbishop, and the latter could only plead that he was no worse than his predecessor, who, it may be remembered, was the Count Archbishop, son of Richard I, who was a married man but excused himself on the ground that he married as Count d'Evreux, not as Archbishop. Mauger, though he had children, was unmarried and was, according to Orderic, illustrious only for his birth and not for his actions. William summoned a council at Lisieux and his uncle was deposed and banished to Jersey.

We may recognize in William's action against his uncle not only gratification of his private enmity but also the beginning of his reform of the Church which was so great a characteristic of his reign. He appointed as successor to Mauger a prelate named Maurilius who was notable for his holy life and saintly character. Maurilius, unlike his predecessors in the See, was not of high birth. He was probably a native of Rheims and a student of Liège, and had been for some time resident at Fécamp. After this he became abbot of a monastery at Florence. Here his attempts to reform the monks of the abbey led them to try to poison him, so that he returned to Fécamp, and it was from that monastery that William called him to the Archiepiscopal See. Maurilius reigned as Archbishop for twelve years, and during that time he consecrated the cathedral founded by Duke Robert and brought thither the bodies of the two first rulers of Normandy, Rollo and William Longsword.

There is no doubt that until the appointment of Maurilius the Norman Church was in a deplorable condition. It is true that there had been great activity in the foundation of abbeys by the pious and the wicked for the salvation of their souls. But there were many other reasons for the multiplication of abbeys. In later years, during the civil war between Stephen and Maud, William of Malmesbury describes the abbeys in England as the "castles of God", and there is no doubt that the abbeys were the only real centres of civilization in medieval times, so that as society became more civilized, as it was doing at this time, the building of abbeys grew.

William and his wife were at the head of the abbey builders of Normandy. It is true that their great houses at Caen, the Abbaye des Hommes and the Abbaye des Dames, were built at the request of the Pope as a thankoffering for the papal dispensation for their marriage, but probably, in any case, William, who was, like all his family, a lover of building, would have left monuments of this kind to posterity; for he was certainly a religious man, and though he may have been poorly educated he was not uncultured, while his wife was a patron of the arts.

In speaking of the Norman abbeys one cannot omit further mention of the Clugniac influence on Normandy. The monastery of Clugny was founded in 910 by William the Pious, Duke of Aquitaine. Before the first abbot, Berno, a Burgundian, died in 927 the monastery was already the head of a small congregation which became the nucleus of the Clugniac Order; and offshoots from Clugny had resulted in the foundation of daughter monasteries. To Berno there succeeded Odo and Mayeul, both of whom greatly extended the Clugniac influence by new foundations and by the adherence of older monasteries under the Benedictine rule. Mayeul entrusted the Clugniac mission to Normandy to William de Volpiano in 990, and he and his successor introduced the Clugniac practices into the Norman monasteries. In one characteristic, however, their houses differed from others under the Clugniac influence; they did not own the supremacy of Clugny but maintained their local autonomy.

The number of religious houses founded at this time, in addition to those erected at Caen by the Duke and Duchess, included the restoration and rebuilding of St. Evroult, which was the monastery of Orderic Vitalis and a house renowned mainly for the copying of books and church music. Lesceline d'Eu founded the abbey of St. Peter, but the most famous of all was that of St. Stephen at Bec. The abbey of Bec played so great a part in the history of Normandy and that of its rulers that one is tempted to devote a little more attention to it than to others, and for this we must again draw on Orderic.

There was a knight named Herlwin de Bonneville who held lands of Count Gilbert of Brionne and who as he grew older became more and more drawn to piety. When he was about thirty-seven years of age he

Charter of the Reign of Edward the Confessor, 1044.

(see No. 5. *Notes on Illustrations*.)

Charter of the Reign of Edward the Confessor, 1058.

(see No. 6. *Notes on Illustrations.*)

gave up soldiering and refused to obey feudal summonses, but, of course, as he was a layman this was illegal. He asked for leave of Count Gilbert, but the latter rather naturally refused and brought him and his tenants before the feudal court. Herlwin did not say anything on his own behalf but only on that of his tenants. Gilbert saw that he was a sincere "conscientious objector" and granted his modest request to be allowed to join a monastery.

Herlwin did not want to join an existing community but to found one for himself. He was a man of means. He had property at Bonneville, near Brionne, and he began to build a church there. He also set to work to learn his letters, for he could not read. In a short time he accomplished this and in 1054 was ordained and made abbot of the new house. Herlwin spent all his money on the buildings and the community was far from rich, but his monks were in earnest and worked hard on their farm. Herlwin's mother, however, was a Fleming and a rich woman; she gave all her property to her son and his monks and attached herself as a servant to the monastery. Unfortunately, his first building was burnt down. It was not a good site; it lacked wood and water; so Herlwin moved elsewhere, but this place also was unsatisfactory—the site was too small. In this extremity his neighbours helped him and granted him the land he needed. The valley he settled in was watered by a small stream called a "beck" and from this the abbey of St. Stephen took its name.

Herlwin's foundation might have ended its days in obscurity had it not been for a lucky chance. A Lombard lawyer, Lanfranc by name, wandered northwards and set up a school at Avranches. For some reason or other he gave up his school and was travelling through Normandy when he was robbed by highwaymen near Bec. The monks befriended him and he was naturally grateful. Herlwin, as we have seen, was no scholar; he never learnt to read till he was forty, and his monks were not scholars, either, but he recognized the value of scholarship in a monastery. When, therefore, he found out how distinguished a man his visitor was he begged him to remain and set up a school, as he had done at Avranches. Lanfranc was nothing loth and the school of Bec soon became famous, and also wealthy. Lanfranc became prior under Herlwin and retained that office until he was appointed abbot of William's abbey at Caen.

After the conquest Bec received lands in England as well as in Normandy, and the possessions of the abbey in this country are commemorated in the name Tooting Bec.

It must not be thought that because there was a large number of religious houses founded in Normandy at the beginning of the 11th century that all of them were as well conducted as Bec or St. Evroul. In some—though we are not told much about it—the standard of life and behaviour was much to seek. Small wonder when we see how the Bishops

K

behaved. The chroniclers, being monks, are apt to gloss over the short-comings of monasteries and the backslidings of abbots, but they are less reticent about Bishops. William was as anxious to see good men on the episcopal bench as on the abbots' thrones, and we have seen that he dealt faithfully with his disreputable uncle, Mauger, and appointed the highly respected Maurilius in his place.

When Maurilius died John, Bishop of Avranches, was appointed to be his successor. This man was a son of Ralph, Count of Bayeux. Orderic gives no very full accounts of William's appointments to bishoprics in Normandy, but there is no doubt that the Duke's object was to gain for the service of the Church men of high character and capacity. Only once did he indulge in a family "job". He appointed his half-brother, Odo, when a boy of twelve, or even less, to be Bishop of Bayeux. Odo was as ambitious a man as his brother, William. He was more of a soldier than a churchman, and though he wore his armour over his clerical dress he disregarded the papal decree of 1049 which forbade the clergy to carry arms, though he carried a mace and not a sword.

Although William worked for the improvement of the Norman Church both in the dioceses and in the abbeys, he adhered even closer than his predecessor to his superiority over bishops and abbots. William was the contemporary of that remarkable man Hildebrand, who, first as Cardinal Hildebrand, Archdeacon of the Roman Church, and later as Pope Gregory VII, was the chief mover in the reform of the Church in the 11th century. Hildebrand was the exponent of the extreme Petrine doctrine. For Hildebrand the Universal Church was supreme over all states and all rulers. The Pope was the representative of St. Peter on earth. As an individual the Pope was nothing; as St. Peter's delegate he was everything. The Pope as the representative of St. Peter had un-limited powers of excommunication or absolution. He claimed the right to the obedience of all secular sovereigns. Hildebrand when he became Pope wrote to William, "As I have to answer for you at the awful judg-ment, in the interests of your own salvation, ought you, can you, deny obedience to me?"

Although the papacy, if the theory is carried to its logical conclusion, claimed the complete obedience of all mankind, in practice much tact and discretion were used. Although the Pope protested against the lay owner-ship of churches and denied the right of kings to control appointments, no questions were asked if the sovereigns' nominations were in themselves good. The reforming Popes were well aware of the unsatisfactory charac-ter of many bishops and abbots both in Normandy and in England, and when they knew that William was a religious man only too anxious to fill Sees and abbacies with suitable bishops and abbots in practice great latitude was allowed. It was William's policy to be on the friendliest terms with the papacy, and, although he never gave way to the extreme claims put forward, after the dispute as to his marriage with Matilda had been settled by Lanfranc he always remained on the best of terms with the Roman See.

Although we have but little evidence of it we may confidently say that William gave considerable attention in the years 1055–8 to army reorganization, reform and rearmament. Ever since the days of Richard I and the first reorganization of the Norman forces the chief weapon on which the Dukes relied was their heavy cavalry. We hear little of the light-armed troops. But during the reign of William we hear of the development of the missile weapon on a large scale. The victory of Varville was largely due to the skill and training of the archers, and as we hear nothing of them before in William's campaigns we may perhaps accept the view that between Mortemer and Varville the raising and training of the archer forces took place.

William was himself a highly skilled archer. "None but Duke William could bend Duke William's bow," it was said. He therefore knew the great value of the missile weapon. Furthermore, a large body of archers to be of value had to be kept in constant training and practice. As we understand that at Varbille William did not have time to summon a considerable army from his tenants and relied largely on his own personal troops and a *levée en masse* of the peasantry, it looks as though the archers of the Norman army were not feudal levies but the Duke's own men, whom he kept constantly mobilized and always in training. Such an arrangement seems obvious in view of the great advantage that it gave the Duke in case of rebellion.

CHAPTER XX

THE ADMINISTRATION OF NORMANDY

Military service—Ecclesiastical baronies—Feudal jurisdictions—Herfast, the Chancellor—The Curia—Castles—The Viscounts—The Great Council.

AFTER the defeat of his enemies, both internal and external, and the establishment of his authority in the duchy, William had time to attend to internal affairs. To us in England the organization of Norman government by the Duke is particularly interesting and important, since it had a considerable effect, not only to the home policy pursued by William in England after the Conquest, but also on the constitutional developments of both countries during the reigns of his sons and, indeed, during the whole period of the connection of Normandy with England.

In former chapters we have endeavoured to sketch from the very scanty materials at our disposal the work of the Dukes—notably Richard I and II—in creating the machinery of internal administration in Normandy. The result of their work was that Normandy in the 10th and 11th centuries was perhaps as highly civilized a state as any in Europe, but its weakness was that it was too much centralized. So long as a strong Duke reigned all went well, but directly the firm hand was removed from the helm disintegration commenced. We have seen this happen during the reign of Robert I, who in spite of his great abilities as a general and a diplomatist lacked administrative powers. The misfortune of his being succeeded by a minor increased the disintegration, and it needed all the ability and energy of William to restore order.

The records during the reign of William became more considerable, but they are far from voluminous. One may, however, hazard the view that in Normandy William was no reckless innovator. He sought to restore and to improve the systems of his predecessors. Normandy was a highly feudalized state. Flack, in Les Origines de l'Ancienne France, calls it the cradle of feudalism in France.

There is no doubt that the tenants-in-chief held their lands from William by military service, but there is a good deal of obscurity as to detail, and some doubt as to how far their service was fixed in amount. It seems clear from the scanty evidence at our disposal that some attempt had been made in the days of Robert I, if not earlier, to establish monastic baronies with definite quotas, and from this it has been argued that a system of knights' fees had been introduced, but how far this extended it is impossible to say. The fact, however, that stress is laid on the early development of feudalism in Normandy makes it probable that some progress had been made.

That it was extended by William seems evident by the case of St. Evroul. At some time between the years 1050 and 1057, William made the abbey a barony and the abbot's military service was fixed at two knights' fees, which were granted to two knights with the Duke's consent. There is also good reason to believe that Grimoald du Plessis, who was imprisoned by William for rebellion after Val-es-Dunes, owed the service of ten knights for his fief. We may deduce, therefore, that while the principle of a fixed rate of knight service was nothing new William regularized and developed it.

Feudal jurisdictions followed on feudal service, but we have certain knowledge that each vassal received his rights of jurisdiction not by right but by grant from the Duke. Thus we find a grant of jurisdiction in cases of arson, rape, etc., to the abbot of Préaux, but in other places the jurisdiction over these offences pertained to the Duke. The theory seems to be that all justice was in the hands of the Duke, but he could and did grant the right of administration to his vassals, ecclesiastical or lay.

The most interesting institution in Normandy to us today was the Curia. William certainly did not invent the Curia, but he developed it. It is the parent of the Curia Regis in England from which our parliamentary institutions are descended. The Duke's Curia consisted of the Bishops, the Counts and others of high rank like Roger, Montgomery and William FitzOsbern, the Viscounts, the household officers and others of the Duke's entourage.

The Curia dealt with all kinds of business. Judicial business, such as the trial of barons for criminal actions, tithes to land, disputes as to jurisdiction, civil actions between tenants-in-chief. It was also an institution for the record of agreements, and it dealt with all kinds of other matters, such as the transfer of relics, and acted as a Council of War for the arrangements connected with the invasion of England.

The Curia was a judicial court and a council. The executive, although we know very little about it, was the Duke's Chancery. But that developed as a separate entity later in William's reign. In the earlier days the Chancery and the Chapel were much confused. At first the Clerks of the Duke's Chapel seem to have performed the necessary duties of a civil service, but even this was not regularized. Later William seems to have divided Chapel and Chancery, but not before the Conquest of England, for Herfast, who was the Duke's Chaplain in Normandy, does not appear as Chancellor (in England) until 1069. But the Chancellorship and the Chancery seem to have been attached to the sovereign and not to any part of his dominions, and Herfast appears to have acted as William's Chancellor for all his dominions on both sides of the Channel.

William's system of government was simple and the organization bore the traces of his own masterful mind. At the head of the Government was the Duke. The system was feudal. Tenure of land, private jurisdiction and military organization were all based on feudal lines, but the Duke held ultimate control. In Church matters and appointments in spite of the claims of the papacy, the Duke retained control over appointments and at the same time kept on good terms with Rome. Private jurisdiction was restrained by the Duke's reserved superior jurisdiction and the powers of his Viscounts who were ducal officers. Private war was controlled by the Truce of God and also by the Duke's restriction. Castles could not be built without licence and the Duke strictly maintained the right of castle guard.

The Curia was the Duke's Council and the Duke's Superior Court. The Chancery was the Duke's Chancery; its officers were really no more than his private secretaries. The Viscounts as the Duke's officers acted as agents for his estates and also as his public administrative officers. They collected the public revenue which was the Duke's and they exercised a strict financial control. Only the Duke could coin money. The Duke was the feudal superior of his vassals and commander-in-chief of the feudal army, but he also had a considerable body of troops under his own direct command and always at hand, like the archers.

We are unable to trace distinctly any regular system for the assembly of what William of Malmesbury described as the *Concilium magnatum*; but it is clear that the Duke occasionally met his barons, though probably more for the purpose of making his will known to them than for consultation purposes, as was the case at the earlier courts sometimes held at Fécamp. The only record we have of a council that resembled the English Witan in its procedure was the Council of Lillebonne which debated the proposal to invade England, an account of which will be given in its proper place.

CHAPTER XXI

FINAL DEFEAT OF THE FRENCH

King Henry again attacks Normandy—Invades Hiesmes with Geoffrey of Anjou—Conquers Western Normandy—Defeated at Varaville—King Henry's death—Succeeded by Philip—Baldwin of Flanders, Regent of France—William's conciliatory policy towards France.

IN 1058, after the three years of peace, King Henry and Geoffrey Martel of Anjou made a joint attack on Normandy and invaded the county of Hiesmes. William was in no hurry. In the last war, when opposed by the left French army under Henry, he remained strictly on the defensive, and he now remained inactive, at Falaise. The allies struck north after taking Hiesmes, plundering and robbing the wretched Norman peasantry and townspeople. They sacked St. Pierre on the Dives, ravaged the Bessin, but kept respectfully away from Bayeux and then occupied Caen. They were full of triumph; Western Normandy had fallen into their hands without a blow. They now proposed to cross the Dive and to continue their course of plundering and devastation on the other side of that river. They seem to have become quite careless, even contemptuous, of William and his army. The crossing of the Dive is effected from Varaville, a small place a little to the north-east of Caen. The land between Varaville and the river is a flat marsh traversed then and now by a causeway leading to the river which is now crossed by a bridge. In William's day, however, there were no bridges and the stream had to be forded.

The French seem to have learnt nothing from experience. Their intelligence service was no better than it had been before, while William's had, if possible, improved. The Duke was fully aware of all the movements of the King, while the latter was in complete ignorance of the movements of the Duke. Henry seemed to think that William was still at Falaise. The Duke had not many troops with him, he seems to have been taken rather by surprise. The Western barons remained to garrison and hold their castles (which they did successfully) and the Easterners perhaps had not yet had time to mobilize. William, however, had supplemented the troops he had by summoning a *levée en masse* of the exasperated peasantry.

This somewhat heterogeneous army was held quietly in reserve until the Duke knew the intention of the enemy to cross at Varaville. Then he rapidly advanced up the valley. He got to the other side of the Dives just before the French began to cross, and hid his troops. King Henry led the army and crossed the ford, but when he and half the army had crossed on the ebb the tide began to flow, and the rearguard and the baggage with all the loot was cut off. Still quite unsuspicious, the King began to climb the hills on the left of the river. Then William attacked the rear-guard and the baggage which were all spread out on the causeway. They could not deploy—they were hampered by their loot; if they tried to fight they fell into the marsh, where they were utterly helpless. The King, who was on the other side of the river, could do nothing but see his army and that of his ally cut to pieces. The French did not know the ground, but the Norman peasants, ill-armed as they were, did, and they cut the French army to pieces, while King Henry could do nothing but gibber on the other side of the river.

The defeat of the French at Varaville was the climax of the rivalry between France and Normandy during William's reign—Henry gave in. Peace was made. Tillières was surrendered, but that was all that William claimed. All he wanted was to neutralize France until he could settle far more important matters, and his success was complete.

Orderic made William say in his last speech: "King Henry lost not a moment in putting his troops in motion and, having made a precipitate retreat, he has never reposed for a single night in my territories." The defeat of the French took place in 1058 and the invasion of England happened eight years later. It was, of course, essential to make sure of France before William undertook the conquest of England, or he would have left Normandy open to attack from Paris. He gives one to under-stand that owing to his defeat at Varaville Henry was prevented from giving any further trouble to Normandy. In this William has exag-gerated. No doubt King Henry had had enough in his unsuccessful campaigns of trying to subdue his powerful vassal. But the jealousy of France continued. Had the French been able to conquer Normandy they would have welcomed the chance.

King Henry died in 1060. He had been twice married and was childless; further, the legality of both his marriages had been questioned on the grounds of consanguinity. To be quite sure that there should be no question of this kind in regard to his third venture he chose his last bride from Russia. She presented him with an heir, Philip, who was only a child of tender years when he succeeded his father. As guardian, Henry named his brother-in-law, William's friend and father-in-law, Baldwin of Flanders. So the influence of the guardian of the King of France was all in William's favour. Moreover, William was studiously careful to cultivate the favour of France. When his plans for the invasion of England were matured he invited French co-operation and promised, if successful in his conquest, to do homage to the King of France for

England! That this was but a polite gesture must be certain and, in any case, Baldwin, on behalf of the French King, declined the proposal.

The defeat of Henry dissolved the ante-Norman alliance between France and Anjou, and this was further curtailed by the death, in 1059, of Geoffrey Martel. Luck, therefore, was with William. Geoffrey left no sons. By his will he left his dominions to the two sons of his sister, Hermengarde, Countess of Gatinois. To the elder, Geoffrey, he bequeathed Anjou and Saintogue, and to Fulk Rechin, the younger, Tours and Touraine.

William's preparations for the invasion of England by securing his base in France were now almost complete. His father-in-law and ally, Baldwin of Flanders, was Regent of France. Geoffrey Martel was dead and his dominions divided. The Norman Church was reformed or in process of reformation. The Duke's authority over his vassals was secured. The army had been modernized and the administrative, judicial and fiscal system reorganized so as to secure the unquestioned authority of the Duke.

CHAPTER XXII

MAINE

Situation in Maine—Occupied by Geoffrey of Anjou—William ravages Maine—Conquers and takes the Capital—Short campaign in Brittany.

ONE doubtful factor remained—the frontier county of Maine. To secure his base on his south-west frontier it was necessary for William to make sure of Maine.

The Normans had always put forward some ill-defined and shadowy claims to Maine. It was said that a grant of the county was made to Rollo in 924. France and Anjou made similar and equally shadowy claims. In the early days of William's reign Herbert Wakedog, as he was called, carried on an active and, on the whole, successful war on Black Fulk of Anjou. In the end, however, that ruffian got hold of poor Herbert by treachery and imprisoned him until he agreed to buy his liberty on very hard terms. Herbert Wakedog had no sons, but one daughter, Riota, who was married to Walter de Mantes, a son of Duke Robert's friend, Drogo of the Vexin, who died in Palestine. Drogo's son, Hugh, whose mother was an Englishwoman and a niece of King Edward, succeeded Wakedog. During Hugh's youth his great-uncle, Herbert Bacco, became Regent of Maine, but he was not content with the regency. However, Bishop Gervase of Le Mans, a scion of the evil house of Bellèsme, who was the godfather of Count Hugh, drove Herbert out and reinstated the boy.

Gervase found a wife for his godson in the widow of Alan of Brittany, the Regent of Normandy who was poisoned in 1040. The marriage took place in 1044. For some reason Geoffrey Martel of Anjou objected to the marriage; he laid a trap for Bishop Gervase and imprisoned him for seven years, after which he was allowed to ransom himself. Geoffrey Martel then marched into Le Mans and seized it for himself. Hugh had recently died and his heir was his only son, named Herbert. Geoffrey occupied Maine until his death in 1060, but when that event took place young Herbert appealed to Duke William for help. The latter was nothing loth. It was the chance he wanted. Herbert commended himself to the Duke and became his man. William was to succeed to Maine on Herbert's death if he had no heir, and Herbert's youngest sister, Margaret, was betrothed to William's eldest son, Robert. Herbert died within two years of this arrangement and William thus became his heir. But the people of Maine did not want to come under Norman rule. So they put forward Walter de Mantes and Riota as candidates for the throne. The leaders of this movement were Geoffrey de Mayenne and Hubert de St. Suzanne.

They fortified themselves in the city of Le Mantes awaiting the Norman attack, but William disappointed them. Leaving the city alone, he systematically destroyed and ravaged the country. Meanwhile, the supplies in Le Mantes began to fail. The whole of Maine was in William's hands. Rather an ugly story now spread. Walter de Mantes and his wife died, very conveniently for William, who was accused of poisoning them. There are no details of the circumstances, but it is unlikely that William would have done a thing of that kind. In the Middle Ages many people came to sudden death from illnesses such as typhoid or pneumonia and, as medicine was in a very clementary state, poison was frequently attributed. As for Geoffrey de Mayenne, he refused to give in. William was forced to undertake a regular siege of his castle, and he had a good deal of trouble in taking it.

With the exception of a short and unimportant campaign in Brittany, which is only remarkable for the fact that Harold, then visiting Normandy, participated in it as a volunteer and as William's guest (or prisoner?), the Maine war was the last that William was engaged in before the invasion of England.

CHAPTER XXIII

ENGLAND

Dissolution of Cnut's Empire—Godwin—Anglo-Saxon Earls—Cnut's sons—The sons of Emma and Ethelred II—Harthacnut—Edward the Confessor acknowledged King—Godwin's sons—Swein—The Witan summoned—Godwin's fall—William in England.

BEFORE attempting to describe William's Conquest of England we must give some account of the state of the country immediately prior to that event. It will be remembered that William's father, Robert, had contemplated the invasion of England and had actually made serious preparations. Luckily for him, his attempts were frustrated or he would have received a signal defeat from Cnut, who not only had the English behind him but the whole resources of his Scandinavian empire and the command of the sea. William of Poitiers, William's courtly biographer, says that God decreed Robert's failure so that the honour should fall upon his son, and there was truth in this, since had Robert received a heavy defeat in the enterprise, perhaps William would not have attempted it.

Cnut was a strong king and a wise ruler, but his empire was a personal one, and as soon as he died in 1035 it began to crumble. Indeed, it seems that he was well aware of the weakness and intended to break up his dominions between his sons. Of these he had three—Swein and Harold by Aelgifu, daughter of Aelghelm, ealdorman Ælfhem of Deira, and Harthacnut by Emma of Normandy, widow of Ethelred II and mother of the Aethelings, Alfred and Edward.

To Swein he bequeathed Norway, to Harthacnut, Denmark, and to Harold, England. Both Swein and Harthacnut were respectively in Norway and Denmark, acting as their father's Vice-regents, when Cnut died, and Harold was in England. The former were recognized as Cnut's successors, but to Harold there was opposition in England. The kingdom at Cnut's death was divided into four great earldoms. In the north, Eadulf held sway in Bernicia; Siward the Strong, a Dane who probably came to England with Cnut, was Earl of Northumbria; Leofric, son of Leofwine, was Earl of Mercia and husband of Godgifu, the Lady Godiva of legend, and Godwin was Earl of Wessex.

Curiously enough, there is some doubt about Godwin's parentage. Some say that he was of humble birth, but these were probably his enemies. It is practically certain that he was the son of Wulfnoth, a considerable thegn in Sussex. Godwin was Cnut's chief adviser—in fact, his Prime

Minister—and when he died the Earl was the most powerful man in the kingdom. When, later on, we come to discuss the changes wrought by the Conqueror in this country, his introduction of the continental feudal system will be one of the most important points, and it is necessary now to make clear that the Anglo-Saxon Earls, or Ealderman, were like the Norse Jarls—officials; they were not in the same position as the French Counts—great vassals who held hereditary fiefs. But the result was practically the same. The four great English Earls were in much the same position, compared with continental feudatories, as the Counts of Anjou or the Dukes of Normandy.

We need not linger overlong on the fact of the sons of Cnut. Leofric of Mercia and most of the northerners supported Harold. The west and south, led by Godwin, were for Harthacnut. Queen Emma did all she could for her son. But now a third candidate appeared on the scene. Alfred, the eldest of the Acthelings, the sons of Emma by Ethcldred II, arrived at Sandwich from Rouen. He was no more acceptable to Godwin than was Harold.

Godwin acted both cruelly and treacherously. He seems to have been running with the hare and hunting with the hounds for some time. His opposition to Harold was weakening, for Harthacnut delayed in Denmark. At any rate, the Aetheling was in arms against either Harold or Harthacnut, whomever Godwin chose to recognize. Godwin met Alfred at Guildford, proclaimed himself his man, dined with him, and then in the middle of the night arrested him with the aid of Harold's men and handed him over to Harold. The latter murdered the Aetheling's men or sold them as slaves, tore out Alfred's eyes and threw him into a dungeon at Ely, where he shortly afterwards died.

Harthacnut, it appears, did not dare to come to dispute the throne with his half-brother, but when the latter died in 1040 he came to England accompanied by his mother, Emma. His reign, a record of crime and cruelty, lasted only two years and hc died in 1042. Neither of the sons of Cnut had an heir, so the way was clear for the younger Aetheling, and Edward came over from Normandy and was accepted as King by practically all, but that there were dissentients is shown by Florence of Worcester, who says that his acceptance was mainly due to Godwin.

Edward the Confessor was the last of the line of Cerdic to rule in England, and that fact has made him something of a legendary hero and a legendary saint. Edward had been brought up in Normandy almost entirely. He was far more of a Frenchman than an Englishman, and French was his language. Worse still, he had had no experience of affairs, having been brought up by monks. Doubtless he was pious, but his intelligence was meagre. He thought of only two things: sport and religion—both admirable tastes; but, in practice, the government devolved on other and more energetic persons.

One of the worst results of Edward's Norman upbringing was the fact that more and more hungry adventurers came to England. Rolf, the son of Drogo, Count of the Vexin, who married the sister of Ethelred II and died in Palestine with Duke Robert, Robert (Champare) whom he made Bishop of London, and a host of others, all of whom were on the lookout for profit and succeeded in getting it.

Still, they did not have it all their own way. Godwin remained the most influential man in England and virtually ruled the country. His eldest son, Swein, had been made an Earl by Cnut and ruled over Oxfordshire, Berkshire, Gloucestershire, Herefordshire and Somerset. Harold (afterwards King) became Earl of East Anglia, and Godwin himself retained the Earldom of Wessex. His nephew, Beorn, was also provided with an Earldom and, most important fact of all, Godwin married his daughter, Edith, to the King. She was as able as her father and brother and, fortunately for herself, politically minded, since Edward, probably necessarily, proclaimed his complete chastity, even after marriage!

But Godwin's reputation suffered from his son's indiscretion. Swein carried off the abbess of Leominster and, worse still, tried to marry her, and as a result was banished. This gave the King a chance to further the Norman party's interests. Godwin's star had fallen in consequence of his son's sacrilege, and Edward used the opportunity to create his nephew, Ralph du Vexin, Earl of Hereford. But it is unnecessary to follow the tedious history of revolts, quarrels and intrigues in detail. There is no doubt that the King favoured the Normans and was bitterly jealous of his wife's family. The Danes and Norwegians still had friends in England, and Swein Estrithson, Cnut's nephew, the son of Ulf and his sister, Estritha, still claimed the throne, and Swein, the exile, was intriguing with him. The Northern Earls were profoundly jealous of Godwin and his family, and the latter was losing his influence owing to his son's misdeeds.

Suddenly Swein reappeared at Bosham with a small force. Thence he went to see his cousin, Beorn, and asked him to intercede with the King. Beorn seems to have been quite unsuspecting and rode off with Swein. The latter manœuvred him down to Bosham and there murdered him. Why, it is difficult to understand, especially as he certainly wanted to get back to England. He was publicly proclaimed "Nithing", the worst insult possible. But in spite of his crimes of rape and murder, Swein was suddenly recalled from Flanders, where he had taken refuge, and not only pardoned but actually given Beorn's Earldom, his own having been conferred on Ralph du Vexin.

The Earl of Hereford's mother was Edward's sister, Goda, and after Drogo du Vexin died in Palestine she married Eustace of Boulogne. In 1050 she and her husband visited King Edward and on their way home billeted themselves on the unfortunate people of Dover. There was a riot; several people were killed, and Eustace and his men thrown out of the town.   He complained to his brother-in-law, who forthwith ordered Godwin to punish the men of Dover in most savage fashion.   Godwin was placed in a dilemma.   His power was declining, but if he were unjustly to punish his own people in favour of a foreigner he would lose still further influence with his countrymen.   So he chose this to be the issue. He assembled his troops at Gloucester, and Swein and Harold came there, too, with their men.   They demanded the dismissal of the foreigners.   War was averted by the Earl of Mercia and all were summoned to a Witan in London.   Apparently the King had received large reinforcements from the northern Earls, as Godwin suddenly gave way and fled with his sons to Flanders.   From that moment the foreigners were in control.

It cannot be said when the idea of the Conquest of England definitely took shape in William of Normandy's mind.   It may well have been an ambition for some time, but when he got the news of Godwin's fall, and the Norman supremacy at the English Court in 1051, he determined to come to England at so propitious a juncture and see for himself how his great ambition could be realized.   King Edward was now fifty-five years of age.   His obligation of chastity rendered it extremely unlikely that he would have offspring, even if it were possible for him to do so.   The heir to the throne, Edgar the Aetheling, was an infant in Hungary.   His nearest relative was his nephew, Ralph, Earl of Hereford, who had not made himself particularly popular even with the Norman element in England.   People must have been wondering to whom the Crown would descend.   Swein Estrithson would doubtless be a willing candidate for the throne, but, in spite of the northern Earls' jealousy of Godwin and the large Danish population, no feeling for the restoration of the Danish dynasty was apparent.

Robert of Jumièges was now Archbishop of Canterbury and it seems likely that he did everything he could to assist William.   William of Poitiers says that the King, with the consent of the great men of England, made a formal offer of the succession to William and sent the Archbishop of Canterbury to him with the son and the nephew of Godwin as hostage. This, of course, is nonsense.   Certainly there was no offer of the Crown given with the consent of the Witan, as William of Poitiers suggests. But it may well have happened that Edward, egged on by the Norman Prelate, may have made an offer of the succession to William.   Of course, such an offer was quite *ultra vires*.   The Crown was only Edward's during his life.   The only authority which could legally dispose of the Crown was the Witan, and it is quite certain that the Witan were never consulted. But William got a good deal, and as it was all very vague he could make the most of it as William of Poitiers does.   So he returned to Normandy very well pleased with himself—having been careful to scatter large gifts among the Normans at Edward's Court.

CHAPTER XXIV

THE CROWN OF ENGLAND

Return of Godwin—Harold, Earl of Wessex—Aelfgar—Edward the Aetheling—Harold imprisoned in Normandy—The succession to the Crown—Tostig—Death of Edward the Confessor.

THE course of events, however, does not seem to have been popular among the English. Many people wanted Godwin back, for he was the only man who could really stand up for the English against the foreigners. Godwin and his son sailed from Flanders in 1052. They had no difficulty in returning, and the foreigners disappeared before them as they themselves had done the year before. Those of the English who had supported the King against Godwin no longer did so. Probably they saw that Godwin was the only man in England to head the national cause. Perhaps even the scheme to make the Duke of Normandy Edward's successor was suspected.

Godwin returned. The Queen, who had been banished to Wherwell Priory, rejoined her husband. Harold resumed the Earldom of East Anglia. Tostig was created Earl of Northumberland on Seward's death. Godwin's power was greater than ever. But it was not for long; he died shortly after his return. Harold immediately took his place and became Earl of Wessex; but he did not, however, assume the whole of his father's Earldom, but advised the King to create a separate Earldom for his brother, Leofwine, in Kent and the adjacent counties. Harold's other brother, Gyrth, took over the Earldom of East Anglia. Leofric, Earl of Mercia, who, we may mention, was perhaps one of the most respectable and high-minded of men and quite incapable of playing the disgusting trick on his wife which is described in the legend of Lady Godiva, died at this time full of grace and honour. He was succeeded by his son, Aelfgar.

Harold, naturally, having secured the northern Earldom, was anxious to consolidate his power by the addition of Mercia. So in 1053 he persuaded the Witan to outlaw Aelfgar. The latter submitted (as Godwin had done), but, unfortunately for Harold, Aelfgar was no fool. He crossed over to Ireland, as Harold himself had done on a similar occasion, and there bided his time, which came soon, for the Welsh King, after conquering and killing Llewellyn of South Wales, attacked Hereford.

The pusillanimous Earl Ralph sent a considerable force against him, which was heavily defeated. It is curious to note that Ralph's defeat is attributed to the use of cavalry. The horses were said to have been stampeded by a shower of javelins and to have bolted. Harold came to the help of Earl Ralph, but instead of pressing the war into Wales he made peace with Aelfgar and reinstated him in his Earldom of East Anglia. Shortly afterwards, when Leofric died, Aelfgar became Earl of Mercia, but Harold insisted on his surrendering East Anglia in favour of Harold's brother, Gyrth.

Although there seems little doubt that the King made some sort of promise to Duke William in 1051, it was either conditional or, at any rate, Edward thought himself free to change his mind. Some rumours got about of the proposed disposal of the kingdom after Edward's death, and he certainly must have found that there was the strongest national opposition to a Norman King. The Norman swarm brought to England by the Confessor had certainly failed to endear themselves with the nation, but the King was getting on in years and public opinion was getting restive as to the succession. Harold, although he had succeeded to his father's position of virtual Prime Minister, did not feel strong enough to push his own claim, if, indeed, he had the idea then to endeavour to make himself King. Possibly his position as *de facto* ruler satisfied him, and he considered that if the King died another sovereign of the same nature would suit him equally well. It was known that the Aetheling was a man of no great character; moreover, he was practically a foreigner.

The Aetheling was in Hungary. The story of his banishment is a queer one. Edward the Aetheling and his elder brother, Edmund, were the sons of Edmund Ironside, the Confessor's half-brother. It is said that Cnut sent them to the King of Sweden with a request that he would cause them to be murdered. The Swedish King had no desire to act as Cnut's bravo and sent the two brothers to the King of Hungary, who treated them well. Edmund died young, but Edward lived at the Hungarian Court and married Agatha, who was akin to—probably the niece of— Queen Gisela, the wife of St. Stephen. In 1056 Edward sent Eldred, Bishop of Worcester, on a mission to the Emperor Henry III to ask him to arrange with the Hungarians for the repatriation of the Aetheling. The negotiations were protracted and Edward did not reach England until 1057. But fate seemed against the house of Cerdic, for barely had he reached England when he died. Agatha and the children remained in England.

The boy was named Edgar and the two girls, respectively, Margaret and Christina. Margaret became the wife of Malcolm Canmore and Christina, abbess of Wilton and the stern guardian of her niece, Matilda, afterwards Queen of Henry I and mother of the Empress Maud. So the situation as to the succession continued to be obscure, and the hope may

L

now have arisen in Harold's mind that he might secure the Crown for himself.

The next seven years of Edward's reign were not eventful, except that Harold's position became more and more consolidated and a successful campaign against Wales in 1064 increased his reputation.   In 1064 Harold went to Normandy.   William of Poitiers, who, as a propagandist, would hold his own with the 20th century exponents of that art, says that the Confessor, having already solemnly declared his intention of leaving the throne to the Norman Duke, now—with the consent of the principal men of the kingdom—sent Harold to Normandy to make a formal offer of the succession!

This statement is obviously a barefaced falsehood, but there is no doubt that William was actively pursuing his claim through diplomatic channels, and the arrival of Harold in Normandy came very opportunely —especially under the circumstances in which it occurred.

What really happened seems to be this.   Harold, like his father before him, kept some ships at Bosham, close to Chichester.   The sheltered inlet of the sea near Hayling Island and farther on towards the Isle of Wight and the Solent was then, as it still is, a pleasant place for yachting and sailing.   Harold seems to have been amusing himself in this fashion when a gale of wind sprang up and blew him up-Channel.   He landed in Ponthieu.   Now, Guy of Ponthieu claimed the right to hold for ransom any unfortunate person shipwrecked on his territory, so he arrested Harold.   Guy was a vassal of Normandy and as soon as William heard that he held Harold prisoner he demanded his surrender.   William of Malmesbury says Harold appealed to William—perhaps he did; but when he got to Rouen he found himself out of the frying-pan only to fall in the fire.   William was, no doubt, perfectly well aware that Harold was his only really serious rival, either as Edward's successor as King or as Mayor of the Palace to a puppet King in the shape of the Aetheling.

Although William treated Harold with all respect and honour, he made it perfectly clear to him that he would not be allowed to return to England unless he complied with his terms.   It is quite possible that William hoped to secure Harold's friendship and conclude a bargain with him.

William of Poitiers says that Harold promised assistance and support and agreed to make Dover Castle over to the Duke, while the latter guaranteed him all his other possessions.   Like other propagandists, William of Jumièges is not quite consistent, for this latter story does not agree with the statement that Harold was sent to Normandy to offer the succession formally to William.   We are also told that Harold was offered one of the Duke's daughters in marriage and that William conferred on him the honour of knighthood.   After this, Harold made a campaign with William against Conan of Brittany.

Harold, however, was getting anxious. Prolonged absence from England was dangerous and he had to come to terms with William. He therefore agreed to swear a solemn oath to support William's claims to succeed Edward the Confessor. There seems to be no doubt whatever about this, nor of the fact that he became William's "man". All sorts of stories are current about the event. Wace says that William made Harold swear on a table covered with a cloth, letting Harold think that such an oath need not bind him. When he had sworn, it was revealed to him that under the cloth lay the relics of saints. But the true facts seem clear. Harold could not escape unless he swore. He did so, and then pleaded *force majeure* for not adhering to his pledge.

At last Harold got home to England and found things the worse for his absence. His chief difficulty was with his brother, Tostig, who had made himself thoroughly unpopular in Northumberland. The Northumbrians had no great love for a southerner; they rose in revolt against Tostig and invited Morcar, the brother of Edwin, now Earl of Mercia since his father Aelfgar's death, to become their Earl. Harold did his best for his brother, but he could not persuade the Northumbrians to stand him any longer and he had to agree to accept Morcar.

Tostig, who was the son-in-law of Baldwin of Flanders, crossed the sea to Bruges. Here again fortune favoured Duke William, who no doubt obtained full information as to Tostig's doings through his Duchess's relations.

The old King was now very near the end. He had been in failing health for some time, but he had been buoyed up with the hope of seeing the consecration of his great abbey of Westminster. But when the day came he was too ill to leave his bed and the Queen represented him. He died on January 5, 1066. Just before the end he held out his hand to Harold and commended his wife and his kingdom to his charge. He also asked Harold to treat his foreign retainers with kindness and either to accept their fealty or to let them go peaceably. The Queen, Archbishop Stigand, Harold, and Robert the Staller, a Norman who was in correspondence with William, were present at the deathbed, and we may accept the fact that Edward, actually, at the end, nominated Harold his successor. But it must be remembered that he had no right whatever to do such a thing, and his bequest to Harold was just as void in law as his alleged promise to William in 1051.

It was a bad day for Harold when he was blown across the sea to Normandy—in more ways than one. Had he remained in England he would, of course, have never sworn his unlucky oath to William; also, had he been on the spot and able to look after Tostig, the latter might have behaved himself and been the ally instead of the enemy of his brother. Tostig now was determined on revenge, which was unfair— Harold had done his best for him, so had the King and the Queen, for Tostig was her favourite brother.

When King Edward of England died on January 5, 1066, he was not an old man, but he was one of those people who had never been young. He was, or said he was, under a vow of chastity. It is doubtful if any vow was necessary. His wife, Godwin's daughter and Harold's sister, was treated by him like a daughter, not like a wife. The legend of his saintliness gradually grew up, nor was it to anyone's advantage to deny it. But he was a poor creature, the last King of a worn-out stock.

Luckily, however, for William, his life was prolonged until circumstances in Normandy made it possible for the Duke to make his attempt on the English Crown likely to succeed. Had Edward died in 1056 instead of in 1066 William's preoccupations at home would have made any attempt at foreign conquest extremely difficult, if not impossible. But Edward died just at the right moment for William.

CHAPTER XXV

THE EVE OF THE CONQUEST

Tostig—Edwin and Morcar—The succession to the English Crown—Harold King—William hears the news of Edward's death—He sends a mission to Harold—He seeks the Pope's support—The English Church—Council of Lillebonne—The Norman barons promise support—The Britons—The Anjevins—The French.

The King's funeral, in the new abbey, where he still lies, took place on the day following his death. London was crowded, as many had come there for the ceremony of the consecration of the new abbey and the precarious position of the succession had caused them to remain in the capital. Exactly who the people were who composed the Witan, which was immediately called, we cannot say. The two Archbishops were there; probably Gyrth and Leofwine and others of Harold's supporters, that is to say by the men of the south and east. Whether Edwin and Morcar were present we cannot say. If they were they would probably have supported Harold. The latter had but recently agreed to the substitution of Morcar for Tostig in the Earldom of Northumbria, and his brother, Edwin, would no doubt join with Morcar in Harold's support. The Church was also in favour of an English King. Robert the Staller was one of the few foreigners present, but no one of them had enough influence to dare to raise the question of the election of William.

The Witan was pre-eminently Nationalist and in favour of Harold. According to Malmesbury a few legally minded people raised the question of the Aetheling, but everyone knew that the contest lay between the Normans and the Nationalists and the only possible candidate to defend English interests was Harold. He was elected unanimously and immediately afterwards crowned by the Archbishop of York. Stigand was disregarded owing to his uncanonical status.

The news of Edward's death soon reached Normandy. The Duke was out hunting when the messenger arrived. He returned home immediately and we are told that for some hours he sat silent and thinking, so that no man dared approach him. It is not difficult to imagine what he was thinking about now that he was to face the great crisis of his life. Probably with the news of Edward's death he had heard that the late King had recommended Harold as his successor on his deathbed. The succession to the Crown could be settled in only one way, and that was by the Witan. The Witan could summon the Aetheling Edgar to the throne, or Harold, or William, or anyone it chose, but no one had any title to this throne, even though he were the eldest son of the late King, unless chosen by the Witan.

We shall see that the later Kings tended more and more to rely on heredity, but they always insisted that they had been duly elected even though the "election" was obviously a farce. Even today something of the old ceremony of election survives in spite of modern Acts of Parliament and the principle that the King can never die.

When a demise of the Crown takes place the heir immediately becomes King. A demise of the Crown took place when the Royal Assent—"*le roi le veult*", pronounced by the Clerk of the Parliament—was given by King Edward VIII to the Abdication Act. King George VI immediately became King, but in order that it may be known publicly who is the new King a proclamation has to be issued. It is supposed often that this proclamation is issued by the Privy Council, but this is not the case. It is true that the whole Privy Council is only summoned on the occasion of the demise of the Crown, but they meet for a different purpose and the proclamation is issued before they meet the King.

The signatories of this proclamation are no doubt most of them Privy Councillors, but they do not sign an Act of the Privy Council but a "Proclamation of the Lords Spiritual and Temporal with those of His Late Majesty's Privy Council with numbers of Other Gentlemen of Quality with the Lord Mayor Aldermen and Citizens of London". And later, when the King is crowned, the Archbishop of Canterbury proclaims him in the Abbey and the congregation accept him by crying, "God save King George".

So that even today the ancient practice of election and subsequent coronation survives in part. Harold was crowned by the Archbishop of York. Had Stigand performed the Coronation there might have been doubt expressed as to its legality. He was appointed Archbishop when the Norman Robert had been chased away by the English party in 1051. He had, indeed, received the Pallium, but only from the anti-Pope, Benedict X, so Harold was well advised in avoiding any possibility that the validity of his Coronation could be questioned. The Coronation of the King was the right of the Archbishop of Canterbury, but could be legally performed by another Bishop, as was the case on this occasion. Ealdred of York again officiated at the Coronation of William himself, and King Henry I was crowned by the Bishop of London in 1100.

The question of Harold's oath to William is another matter. It is very improbable that the Witan when they elected Harold knew of it. It would not be likely that Harold would publish the fact abroad. Indeed, he would do his best to keep it quiet.

Now that Edward was dead and Harold King, William had to plan his course and act swiftly. Probably he had not quite realized how unpopular the Normans were in England and how little likely it was that any pro-Norman party would be favoured in England. It would not, therefore, be with a rival to the throne that William had to contend but with a properly elected and crowned legal King.

Harold's position was a strong one. William's, on the other hand, was weak; he had no legal claim of any kind. The English had made it perfectly clear that they had had as much of the Normans as they had any wish for. Harold, except in Northumbria, had the full support of the country. He was a first-rate commander in the field, as he had proved in the Welsh war. He had an efficient army whose morale was certainly high; but it was not up to the modern standards of William's army. It was without cavalry and unprovided with archers. It consisted of heavy infantry supported by the light-armed troops of the fyrd.

We have seen how deftly William and Lanfranc handled the papacy in their reform of the Norman Church. William might have antagonized Hildebrand had he been unskilful, but he succeeded not only in getting his own way but also in making an ally of the powerful Cardinal. His diplomacy in the past was to bear fruit now. His first move was to try to put Harold in the wrong.

Mr. Freeman and others have discussed at some length the precise nature of the oath or promise or engagement undertaken by Harold in 1064, but the result is entirely inconclusive. As we have observed before, it would be highly unlikely that Harold himself would give information on the subject. Probably little or nothing was known of it in England. The English chroniclers, except Eadmer, are curiously reticent on the subject; the Normans are vociferous but vague. It seems probable, therefore, that William got very little out of Harold—if he had had the definite promise that some Norman writers allege he would probably have taken steps to let his claim be far more widely known in England; also one cannot help thinking he would have tried to get the promise of the succession again confirmed by Edward. But he did none of these things.

He sent a mission to Harold and claimed from him what it suited William and Lanfranc to say he had promised. Again we are in the dark as to what actually occurred; but it was plain that Harold gave a categorical refusal to concede anything to William. No doubt this was all that William and Lanfranc expected, and it gave them the opportunity to say that Harold had refused to fulfil his solemn oath. This is really the very utmost, taking things at their worst, that can be said against Harold. The Pope and the Cardinal, in spite of all the special pleading of Lanfranc and William, cannot have believed in William's right to the Crown of England unless they put some faith in the story of King Edward's bequest of the Crown to William—though this can have scarcely influenced them much since, although King Edward had no right of any kind to leave the Crown to anyone at all, he actually did nominate Harold as his successor on his deathbed, and not William.

But Alexander II and Hildebrand thought, no doubt, that Harold's title was no better than that of William's. Probably the English Constitution was unknown, or little known, at Rome. They gave small heed to the fact that, notwithstanding that the Aetheling was alive and in England, the due and formal election of Harold as King by the Witan and his subsequent Coronation constituted him the undoubted legal King of England.

Not only did the Pope regard Harold as an impudent usurper seizing what did not belong to him without any jot or tittle of legal right, but he was also a perjured villain who had sworn faith to William by the most solemn of oaths. He was William's man, his vassal, and he owed homage to William. It is true that the oath of homage was constantly broken. William had not been overstrict in its observance to his own feudal lord, the King of France, and his own Norman vassals broke their homage constantly. But to Rome and the Pope, Harold's breach of his particular oath was nothing better than rank blasphemy. In addition to blasphemy, Harold had been guilty of chasing God's Bishops from their Sees, for had not Harold ousted the Norman Robert from the See of Canterbury and placed the uncanonically appointed Stigand on his throne?

All this nonsense, when worked up with all the religious fervour of the age, impressed foreign countries as constantly repeated propaganda always does. The case for William is eloquently put by William of Poitiers, but if one reads it carefully one cannot help feeling that he must have written with his tongue in his cheek. One may perhaps say that Harold was foresworn and that he broke a solemn oath, although that oath was obtained by deceit, and we do not really know what the oath was. Certainly it was not an oath in any way binding on the Witan.

But although moral indignation against the perjurer may have been raised at Rome and in Normandy, in both places it was increased by the hope of solid profit. To the Normans the conquest of England promised endless wealth. They had already filled their pockets at the expense of the English in the days of Emma, and again at the time of the restoration of King Edward. Normans had been even more successful in Apulia. Loot loomed large in their eyes, and the promise of loot does much to improve a bad case. With the Pope and Hildebrand there was another, but an equally tempting, cause for their support of William.

England was, in those days, much isolated from Europe. There was no desire to submit to the supremacy of Rome, and it must be confessed that the English Bishops were scarcely up to the standard that Hildebrand may have considered desirable. In fact, the English Church flouted

Rome politically and, at the same time, its officers were far from setting a good example. So really the main reason that influenced Hildebrand in favour of William was the idea that he would bring the English Church into closer touch with Rome. William never accepted the full Petrine claims. He made this perfectly clear in his dealings over the Norman Church; but while jealously safeguarding his own authority he worked loyally with Rome in the choice of prelates for appointments and did not, except in the case of his brother, Odo, regard Church appointment as a suitable means for providing for his relations.

William received a banner from the Pope, the papal blessing and the name of a crusader and a missionary, instead of being called what he really was—a bandit.

The Norman Conquest undoubtedly in the long run was of the utmost benefit to England; William was one of the greatest of her Kings whom she should surely honour at the present day, but his motives in conquering England were sordid and his methods tortuous and dishonest. But all this may be forgiven William for his real greatness of character. Having secured the active support of the papacy and the sympathy of the Emperor and of his father-in-law, Baldwin of Flanders, who was then Regent of France in the minority of his nephew, Philip, he proceeded to take council with his own people, the most important among whom no doubt he had already carefully sounded, individually, long before.

It seems, if we accept Wace, that he first called a small body of his closest advisers and they recommended the gathering of a large general council. Such procedure was almost obvious. The smaller council was summoned at Lillebonne. Why Mr. Freeman thinks that William's brother, Odo, Bishop of Bayeux, was the only ecclesiastic present is obscure. One must believe that other Bishops were summoned though they are not mentioned by name. In the list of those who contributed ships for the enterprise we read the names of many other ecclesiastics besides Odo—the Bishop of le Mans, Abbot Nicolas of St. Ouen, William's uncle, Remigius, who subsequently was rewarded by becoming the first Bishop of Lincoln; so that one can hardly think that William, in summoning those from whom he expected help, can have ignored the ecclesiastics, especially as we know he wanted all the help he could get, for he called to his aid those he had banished, such as Hugh de Grantmesnil and Ralph de Toeny.

His chief support was to be found among his nearest friends as is, of course, natural. These were men like Walter Giffard, Mortemer (recalled now from banishment), De Montfort, William de Warrenne, Roger Beaumont, Roger Montgomery, afterwards Earl of Shrewsbury and husband of the wicked Countess Mabel, and members of the Duke's family, like Robert Count of Mortain, his brother-in-law Ivun al Chapel, Richard d'Evreux, the Count d'Eu. To these William made a careful statement of his plans. They all approved and advised the summons of a greater council. This was a formal affair and entailed the summons of all the barons of Normandy, which, of course, took time, and William had to wait impatiently as he was anxious to get his army ready to enable him to start his campaign while the weather was good. When they got to Lillebonne there was no semblance of any rules of procedure.

In England the debates of the Witan were, perhaps, governed by primitive rules, but their proceedings were orderly and not unduly prolonged. The debates of the Lillebonne Council resembled the proceedings of the crowds listening to the stump orators of Hyde Park. The barons asked leave of William to consult among themselves. They said they would give him their decisions later. William had to give in; he knew that he must carry his Normans with him at every stage. He had no power over them as their feudal obligations committed them to no foreign service. Nor could he afford to leave any quantity behind in Normandy while he denuded the country of every available man loyal to him, as he must do for so formidable an undertaking as the conquest of England. The Council separated into groups and listened to stump orators for and against the scheme.

It must be remembered that these people were mostly small men. "Cock Lairds" they would be called in Scotland. They were ignorant, they were unambitious and they had had a good deal of experience of warfare and its unpleasant results, but they were Normans; they were the Vikings' descendants and they loved loot—loot was bred in their bones and a good number said they would join in the enterprise and follow the Duke, but there was also strong opposition. Some said it was a harebrained enterprise, sure of disaster. Normandy, now flourishing and prosperous, would be overwhelmed by the vengeful English. Some urged their personal difficulties—they could not afford the cost of their outfit. Others urged the difficulties of transport. England was a sea power; Normandy was not.

It seemed, indeed, as if the small men of Normandy would raise so many difficulties that William's scheme would fall to the ground. Then William FitzOsbern stepped in. He persuaded the barons to let him be their spokesman with the Duke. They had not told him what to say and he was very careful that they should not do so. The assembly met the Duke in the great hall. FitzOsbern began with a long harangue, expressing their love and loyalty to their Duke. No one could object very much to this. Then he said that out of their love and loyalty they would be prepared to do anything for their sovereign. They began to look a bit askance at this, but said nothing. Then he began all sorts of promises. The barons would all go with their Duke, they would double their feudal obligations and they would do anything and everything to serve the Duke's ambition.

Gradually, as the rather thickwitted squires began to understand to what they were being committed, their apprehensions rose. Shouts of dissension were heard, but FitzOsbern was undaunted. He had been commissioned by the barons to represent them, but they had not told him what to say. Some might agree with what he said—others might not, but no one knew, for no one had tried to ascertain what the real feeling of the Assembly was, so that any sort of cohesive opinion was lacking. Some dissentients to FitzOsbern's words might have shouted —others, and the majority, perhaps, might have been with him. It was a bold and cunning scheme, and the upshot was that the barons felt that on the whole they were, whether they liked it or not, committed. Also, the feeling for fighting and plunder was always in their blood, so, having got them into this satisfactory frame of mind, William took over the running of affairs from FitzOsbern.

He took immense pains. He saw each man personally and listened to his doubts and grievances. He gave each one a fair reply. He could afford to. If he won the battle in England he could afford to pay his supporters—if he lost, both he and they would be ruined. Cajolery and promises were his weapons. He was going to win—would they not share the glorious future with him? He did not threaten; he had left that to FitzOsbern, who had painted a gloomy picture of the disagreeable fate of the stay-at-homes when the victorious Duke returned from England.

By degrees, William's tact and persuasion won them all. Instead of feudal tenants following the Duke to war, the whole Norman baronage became a company of joint adventurers joined together in a common cause for the conquest of England. To his Normans, who were the backbone of his army, he added any stout-hearted bandit he could find. The Bretons came in force under their Duke; then there were the French, who had good reason to know of William's capacity as a general; the Anjevins and, of course, the Manxeaux; a stout contingent of Flemings; adventurers from Apulia and even a few from Hungary. Scandinavians there were, too, and Germans—all the race of Dugald Dalgetty from the north to the south of Europe, and all of them first-class fighting men, well armed and well trained, for the Duke would not cumber himself with rubbish. Every man in his army was a good soldier, and his archers and his cross-bowmen were his own picked men trained under his own eye.

There is no evidence that ecclesiastics attended this Council although in the preparations it seems they must have been present. There was close liaison between the papacy and the Norman clergy. The clergy of Normandy were the Duke's men, so the Bishops and abbots hardly needed persuasion. To harangue them would be to preach to the converted.

Having persuaded his Normans to join him in his adventure, William lost no time in binding them. His clerks and officials were with him and each man was made to state his engagement and these were all carefully recorded in writing and, before he knew where he was, every vassal in Normandy found himself tied by a black-and-white agreement not only to follow the Duke to England but to bring with him such aid as he could to strengthen the Norman army. Mr. Freeman states that there is not a shadow of evidence that William had a single native partisan within the four seas of Britain. If by this it is meant that there was no one in England powerful enough to raise armed resistance against Harold in favour of William, there is truth in the statement; but it depends what is meant by "native". If Anglo-Saxon is meant, then no doubt Mr. Freeman is right; but if Anglo-Norman be not excluded then he is wrong.

William was always well served in his intelligence department, and for this we have reason to believe he was largely indebted to Robert, Edward the Confessor's Staller. This man was some kind of cousin to Edward. He is said to have been of Norman or, perhaps, Breton origin and, as Staller, to have been very near the King. He was not turned out when Godwin came into power and returned from banishment, and he stood with Harold by the deathbed of the King. Probably he sent the news of Edward's death to William. Harold did not retain him in the office of Staller, but appointed Esgar in his place. Robert, when William landed in England, sent him news of Harold's victory at Stamford Bridge and his return south to oppose William's landing. It appears that in addition to being Staller he was Sheriff of Essex under Edward, retained the Sheriffdom under William, and was succeeded in the office by his son, Swegen.

Again we read of Osbern FitzOsbern, the brother of William Fitz-Osbern, Chaplain to the King and Rector of Bosham, Harold's own particular residence. Osbern was certainly a partisan of William and later became Bishop of Exeter. Another Osbern, though driven out by Godwin in 1052, seems to have been the leading man in the colony of Normans planted at Hereford by King Edward and tolerated by King Harold. There was certainly, therefore, a number of Anglo-Normans living in England, holding office there and sympathizing with William. Some of these men may have come to England with Edward the Confessor; others may have descended from immigrants of the days of Ethelred; others, again, may have been London Normans, for we know that a colony of such existed.

Harold's brother, Tostig, had, as we have seen, been obliged to leave England on account of his maladministration of his Earldom. Tostig was an impossible person. Time after time he had been given a chance and he had invariably shown his incompetence and violence. But Harold seems always to have had some affection for him, though he never showed any for Harold, whom he seems to have thought, perhaps with some truth, was responsible for the fact that he had had to leave England, although Harold had no choice.

King Edward had a great affection for Tostig and would certainly have showed him any favour if he could. In spite of this, Tostig seems to have thought that, when Harold became King, he should have recalled him to his Earldom. This Harold could not do. No one could, or would, stand Tostig—nor was it possible for Harold to turn Morcar out. Obviously, so insubordinate a mischief-maker could not be allowed to come to England at all, and Harold had to refuse to allow him to return. Tostig, when banished, went to live in Flanders with his father-in-law, Baldwin, and, no doubt, soon got into touch with his relative by marriage. He visited Rouen immediately the news of King Edward's death reached him and begged William, with whom he had always been on friendly terms, to invade England. William had already made up his mind to do that and so shrewd a man as he was never likely to give too much of his confidence to so useless a creature as Tostig, but naturally he was ready to avail himself of his nuisance value, which, in the end, proved considerable. The only help William ever gave to Tostig was to allow him to use Barfleur for a base for a raid on England. William had no hand in Tostig's invasion of England from Norway.

And now the stage was set. The curtain was about to rise on the next act in the momentous drama of the Norman Dukes. It was the eve of the Conquest, that epoch-marking event which was to change the fortunes of England and to hail a new dynasty on her throne.

Appendix A

ORIGINAL WORKS CONSULTED

Anglo-Saxon Chronicle
William of Malmesbury
Ordericus Vitalis
Florence of Worcester
Henry of Huntingdon
Duchesne Scriptores Normani
Saxo Grammaticus
Adam of Bremen
William of Jumièges
Dudo of St. Quentin
Orkneyinga Saga

Heimskringla Saga
Frodoard of Rheims
Richer of Rheims
Landmann's Book of Iceland
Ralph Glaber
Chronicles of Rouen
Chronicles of St. Vaast
Widukind the German
Winchester Chronicle
Albert de Troisfontaines
Wace

WORKS OF REFERENCE

Complete Peerage
Official Baronage of England
D.N.B.

Blair's Chronological Tables
Deutsche Allgemeine Biographie
Encyclopaedia Britannica

APPENDIX B

DESCENT OF REGINALD, EARL OF MOERE

FORNJOT, King of Finland

—

His great-great grandson,

—

GORR, settled in the Lofoten Islands

—

Heiti

—

SVEITHI, the Sea King

—

HALFDAN, the Old

—

IVAR, Earl of the Uplands

—

EYSTEIN Glumra

—

REGINALD or RÖGNWALD, Earl of MOERE, married HILDA, daughter of ROLF NEFIA

—

ROLF or ROLLO

THE RULERS OF NORMANDY

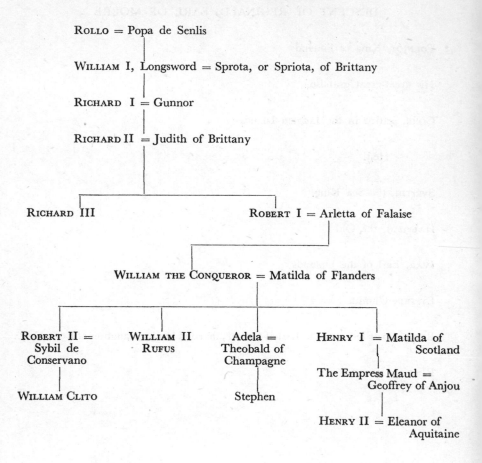

ROLLO = Popa de Senlis

WILLIAM I, Longsword = Sprota, or Spriota, of Brittany

RICHARD I = Gunnor

RICHARD II = Judith of Brittany

RICHARD III   ROBERT I = Arletta of Falaise

WILLIAM THE CONQUEROR = Matilda of Flanders

ROBERT II = Sybil de Conservano   WILLIAM II RUFUS   Adela = Theobald of Champagne   HENRY I = Matilda of Scotland

WILLIAM CLITO   Stephen   The Empress Maud = Geoffrey of Anjou

HENRY II = Eleanor of Aquitaine